# FOR MAYTENANCE OF ARCHERS

A Medieval and Tudor Sourcebook

EDITED BY E.T. FOX

This book is respectfully dedicated to all my archer-friends.

# For Maytenance of Archers
## A Medieval and Tudor Source Book

*Edited and with an introduction by E.T. Fox*

© E.T. Fox, 2020
All Rights Reserved

ISBN - 978-1-716-44410-4

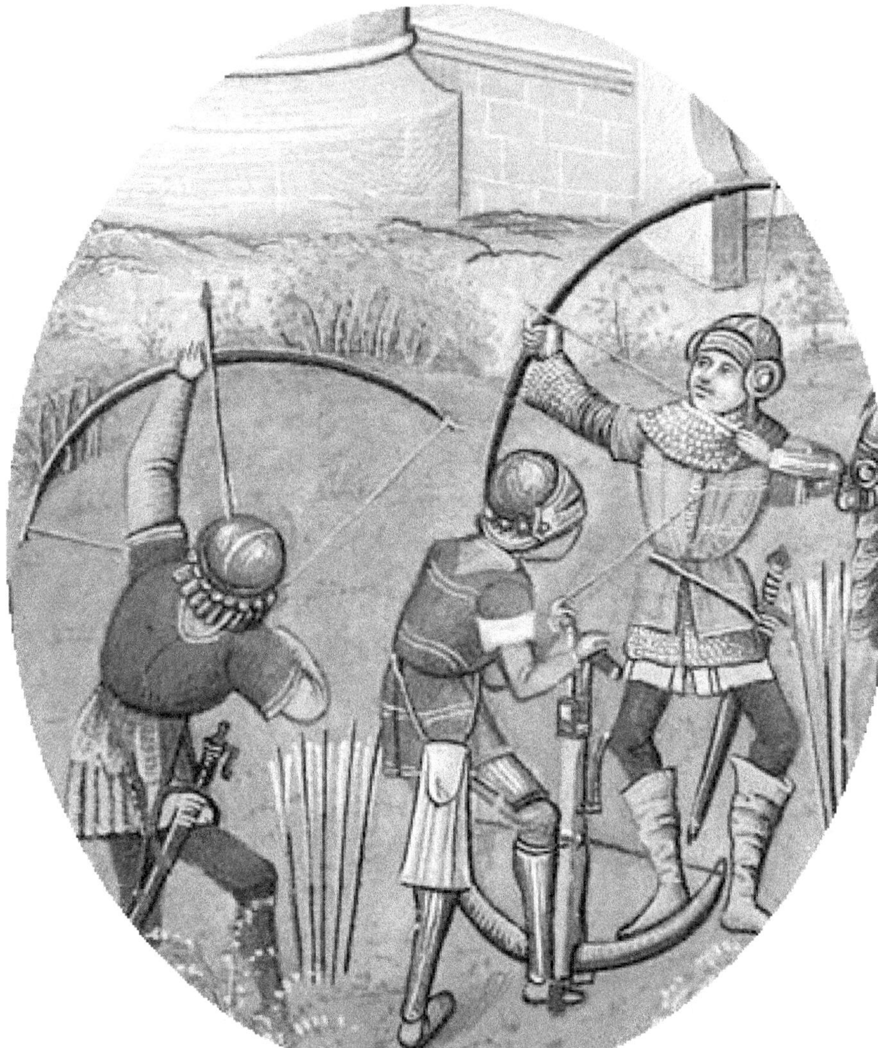

# Contents

| | | |
|---|---|---|
| | **Introduction** | 9 |
| | **Part 1. The Statutes, 1285-1571** | 15 |
| | *Table of Statutes* | 17 |
| 1 | That View of Arms be made. Hue and Cry shall be followed. Fairs or Markets shall not be kept in Church-yards. (1285) | 23 |
| 2 | The Statute of Winchester confirmed, and every sheriff shall proclaim it. (1383) | 25 |
| 3 | No servants in husbandry, or labourer, shall wear any sword, buckler, or dagger. Unlawful games prohibited (1388) | 26 |
| 4 | Arrow-heads shall be well boiled, brased, and hard (1405) | 27 |
| 5 | The Statue of 12 R.II, c.6 against unlawful games recited (1409) | 28 |
| 6 | No man shall make pattens of aspe, upon pain of an hundred shillings (1416) | 29 |
| 7 | An Act that every Englishman and Irishman that dwelleth with Englishmen, and speaketh English, betwixt sixty and sixteen in years, shall have and English bow and arrows (1465) | 30 |
| 8 | An Act for having a constable in every town, and a pair of butts for shooting, and that every man between sixty and sixteen shall shoot every holyday at the same butts. (1465) | 32 |
| 9 | Four bowstaves shall be brought into this realm for every tun of merchandise (1472) | 33 |
| 10 | An Act for bringing bowes into this realm from the realm of England, by merchants and others. (1472) | 35 |
| 11 | Against unlawful games (1477) | 37 |
| 12 | An act for the price of bows. (1482) | 39 |
| 13 | An Act touchinge Bowyers (1483) | 41 |
| 14 | An Acte agaynst the Excessyve price of Longe bowes (1487) | 43 |
| 15 | An Act that the subjects of this realm shall have bowes and other armour. (1495) | 44 |

| | | |
|---|---|---|
| 16 | The custom of bows pardoned for a time (1503) | 46 |
| 17 | An Act concerning shooting in Long Bowes (1511) | 47 |
| 18 | Acte for Maytenance of Archers. (1514) | 52 |
| 19 | Act concernyng the brynging in of Bowestaves in to this Realme. (1514) | 57 |
| 20 | An Acte concerninge Crosbowes and Handguns. (1541) | 59 |
| 21 | An Acte for Mayntenance of Artyllarie and debarringe of unlauful Games. (1541) | 70 |
| 22 | An Acte for the having of Horse Armour and Weapon. (1557) | 82 |
| 23 | An Acte for Bowyers and the pryces of Bowes. (1566) | 95 |
| 24 | An Acte for the bringing of Bowestaves into this Realme. (1571) | 100 |
| | **Part 2. Miscellaneous Sources** | **103** |
| 25 | The Welsh Longbow? 1194 | 105 |
| 26 | Recalcitrant Archers, 1326 | 107 |
| 27 | The Battle of Crecy, 1346 | 108 |
| 28 | Recruitment and clothing, 1346 | 113 |
| 29 | Provision of Equipment for Archers, 1355 | 115 |
| 30 | Provision of Bows, Arrows, and Strings, 1359 | 116 |
| 31 | Threat of Invasion, 1361 | 117 |
| 32 | Edward III to the Lord Lieutenant of Kent, 1363 | 118 |
| 33 | London Archers, 1369 | 120 |
| 34 | Recruitment of Archers, 1386 | 124 |
| 35 | The Battle of Agincourt, 1415 (1) | 126 |
| 36 | The Battle of Agincourt, 1415 (2) | 135 |
| 37 | Fletchings, 1417 | 140 |
| 38 | Inventory of arrows, 1422 | 142 |
| 39 | English Archers in Foreign Service, 1434 | 144 |
| 40 | Bows in Close Defence of a House, 1449 | 145 |

| 41 | Bridport Muster Roll, 1457 | 148 |
| 42 | An Indenture to Serve in France, 1474 | 159 |
| 43 | Lord Howard's retinue, 1481 | 163 |
| 44 | Howard Household Books, 1481-1490 | 188 |
| 45 | The Guild of St. George, 1537 | 190 |
| 46 | Bridport Muster Roll, 1539 | 196 |
| 47 | The Decline of Archery, 1549 | 201 |

**Part 3. L'Art D'Archerie** — **203**

| 48 | L'Art D'Archerie | 205 |

**Part 4. Bows and Guns** — **217**

| 49 | In support of the bow, 1589 | 219 |
| 50 | The Case Against Archery (1), 1590 | 234 |
| 51 | The Case Against Archery (2), 1592 | 237 |

**Epitaph** — **245**

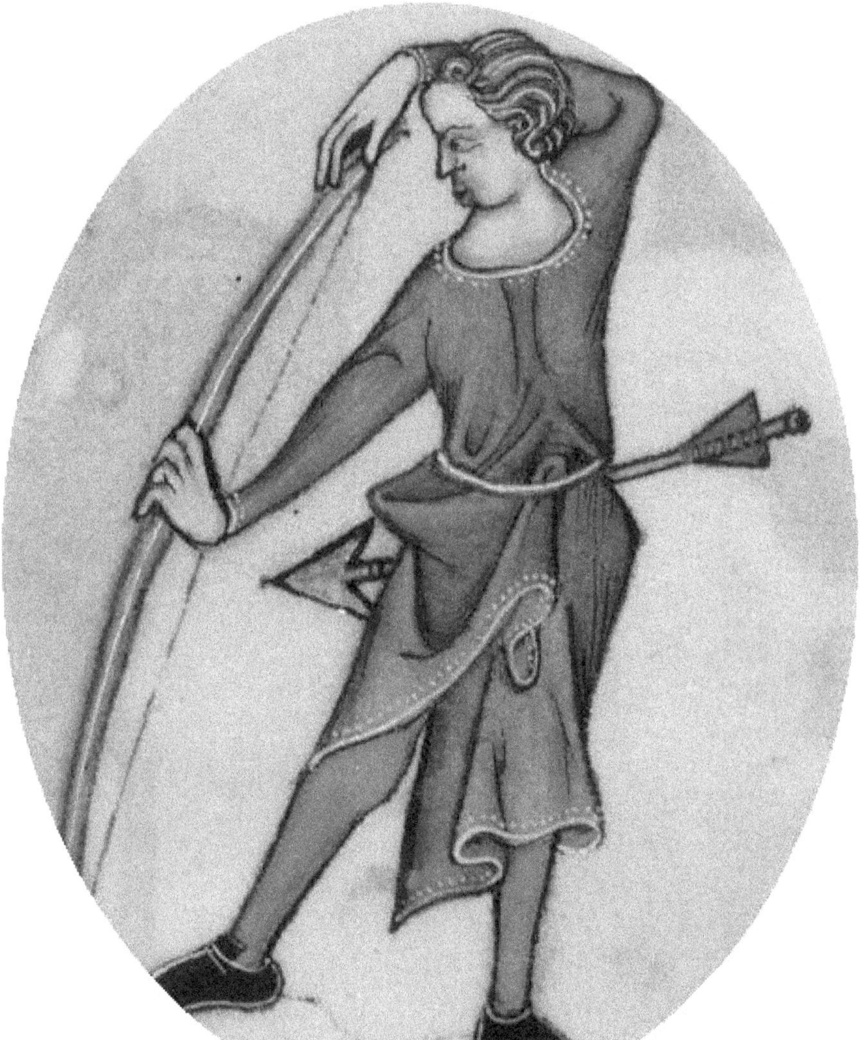

# Introduction

*'Not that I am not fully aware that there are many who know more about it than I do, and that it is unnecessary that I should speak Latin before monks, but solely because I wish that every one should become a good archer, begging that if there are faults they may be corrected, and that whatever may be found useful, may be taken in good part.'*

*L'Art D'Archerie*

The medieval archer, hero of Crecy and Agincourt, is one of the staple characters of English popular history. And why not? The idea of a small band of ragged brothers armed with sticks and string taking on the armoured might of French chivalry and emerging victorious is appealing to our modern sensibilities and plays into the narrative of the plucky underdog achieving greatness against all odds that is so beloved of both story-tellers and audience. Shakespeare understood the appeal when he made lowly soldiers like Falstaff and Fluellen heroes, and if the St. Crispin's Day speech was spoken by a king it was *to*, and *for*, and *about* the humble rank and file.

Over the last half-century or so historians have turned their attention to the men and the bows that won (and lost) medieval battles, and much ink has been expended telling their stories. How did they train? How were they equipped? How were they viewed by their friends, their enemies, and their commanders? This book is not an attempt to answer those questions: it is an attempt to give the reader the material to answer them for themselves. What follows is a collection of fifty-one primary source documents and extracts, including all of the English and Irish statutes relating to archery from the medieval and Tudor periods, beginning in 1285 with the rise of the bow as an English weapon of war and following it through to its twilight years in the sixteenth century.

There are, of course, many hundreds of primary source documents relating to archers and archery which are not included here. It would be impossible to reprint them all in a single volume, so what follows is a selection of documents chosen for the light that they shed on the historical practice of archery. I have tried to include only documents which contribute something tangible to our understanding of the men who took up the bow. There are surviving, for example, dozens and dozens of indentures made between the monarch and a knight or military commander, detailing the number of archers to be provided for a campaign or specified period, but unless one is researching that particular campaign or archers from a particular area they offer little of general interest. The one such indenture that I have included in this selection (**Doc. 42**) was chosen partly as an exemplar of all the others, and partly because it includes a little more detail about the terms of the soldiers' service than most similar indentures.

Some of the documents printed here will, I hope, go some way towards dispelling a few of the myths that surround the history of archery. How can we believe that English archers really shot 10-12 arrows a minute when even the most passionate supporter of archery, Sir John Smythe (**Doc. 49**) only credited them with being able to shoot four or five arrows in the time it took to load and fire a gun? Other documents may shed some light on the origins of some of the myths: Giraldus Cambrensis related a tale of arrows penetrated an oak door four *fingers* thick (**Doc. 25**), which is surely the origin of the idea that archers could shoot through four inches of oak. A few sacred cows of archery lore may be slain in the process. It is widely 'known' that military archers were required to shoot at butts at a distance of 220 yards with heavy 'livery' or 'war' arrows, but the 1541 statute 33 Hen.8 c.9 (**Doc. 21**) - the only statute that mentions the distance of 220 yards - does not say that butts were required to be that long, only that men over 24 years of age should not shoot *flight* arrows at lesser distances. It is important, though, to recognise that no single source can provide a definitive answer to any question. While debate rages about whether the archers at Agincourt shot arrows high into the air to drop on their enemy at long distance, or shot at a low trajectory at shorter range, Jean de Wavrin's comment (**Doc. 36**) that French knight dared not look *up* for fear of the arrows is a useful piece of evidence in favour of long-range high-trajectory shooting, but does not rule out the possibility that the archers *also* shot 'flat' against closer enemies.

The book is divided into four parts. The first section includes all of the archery statutes from 1285-1571. Some statutes mention archery in passing, such as the

1285 Statute of Winchester, 13 Ed.1 c.6 (**Doc. 1**) which is not really *about* archery *per se*, but does include the first statutory requirement for Englishmen to own bows and arrows for defence. Others deal with the manufacture and supply of bows or other archery equipment such as arrow shafts or heads, limiting the maximum price bowyers could charge for their wares and ensuring a ready supply of foreign yew bowstaves. Towards the end of the fifteenth century and into the sixteenth century both the number of archers available to the monarch and the quality of their archery were believed to be in decline, and this is reflected in both the quantity of statutes passed and the detail found in the legislation. In 200 years between 1285 and 1485 the English and Irish parliaments passed thirteen statutes regulating military archery, bows, arrows, and archer practice: in the 86 years between 1485 and 1571 ten statutes were passed relating directly to archery, and a further five limiting the use of crossbows and guns the encourage archery instead. For the sake of brevity the first four of these crossbow statutes have been omitted from this collection as they refer to archery only obliquely and are all essentially similar in their provisions. The fifth and fullest, 33 Hen. 8 c.6 (**Doc. 20**) is included to give a flavour of the others. A number of statutes regulating the hunting of games were also passed during the medieval and Tudor periods, and although some of them mention bows they have not been included here because, like the crossbow acts, they are not really about the practice of archery. Various collections of statutes have been collated and published over the centuries: the texts of the statutes printed here have been drawn from the nineteenth-century *Statutes of the Realm* series commissioned by the government in 1803, Danby Pickering's *Statutes at Large* series published between 1762 and 1806, and the *Statutes at Large Passed in the Parliaments Held in Ireland* series edited by James Goddard Butler and published in the 1780s.

Part 2 contains 23 miscellaneous primary source documents, 1194-1549. Three of them (**Docs 27**, **35**, and **36**) are chronicle accounts of the battles of Crecy and Agincourt: the Agincourt accounts written by people who were eyewitnesses, one on the English side and one on the French, the Crecy account was written by an Italian chronicler but appears to be the earliest published account of the battle and was probably based on current news and first-hand accounts. The rest of the documents are mostly drawn from royal and government documents, private household accounts, or private sources, and give insight into various aspects of English archery of the period in terms of logistics and costs, recruitment and equipping of archers, and the use of the bow in practice. When compiling and editing primary source documents such as those presented in this section the editor must walk a fine tight-rope between retaining focus on the subject at hand and not omitting anything which might be of interest to researchers whose particular scope is not the same as their own. My own inclination is to publish the documents in the fullest version possible rather than excerpt only those sections specific to the topic being explored. So, for example, the letter from Margaret Paston to her husband (**Doc. 40**) begins with a description of the difficulties of using bows to defend a house, but ends with a shopping list of items she wants her husband to buy in London while he's there. The shopping list is probably of little use to anyone whose specific interest is purely in archery, but printing only half the letter would be disappointing to anyone with a more general interest in medieval life. Similarly, the majority of the entries in Lord Howard's accounts for his 1481 retinue (**Doc. 43**) do not relate to archers, but the whole section has been printed here to give context to those parts that do mention archers. Some documents (**Docs 25, 27, 35, 36, 44**, and **47**) have been excerpted from much larger works, but the rest have been printed here in full and I ask the reader's forgiveness if they sometimes overflow into areas not specifically related to archery.

Part 3 contains the complete text of the late fifteenth- or early sixteenth-century book, *L'Art D'Archerie*. Roger Ascham's 1545 publication, *Toxophilus*, is widely hailed as the first book written specifically about archery, but in fact was only the first *English* book on the subject. At least thirty years before *Toxophilus* rolled off the presses *L'Art D'Archerie* was published in Paris. It was never as popular as Ascham's book, and was probably unknown in England until the twentieth century. It is much less substantial than Ascham's book, and despite a few references in the text to English practices there must be some doubt about its relevance to the study of English archery. Nevertheless, its importance as the earliest-known text on archery should not be overlooked. It has not, so far as I can tell, been reprinted since 1903 and so is included here out of a sense of completeness. Readers interested in early archery texts are encouraged to read *Toxophilus*, which is widely available in several editions, and is a superior and more detailed book in almost every way.

Finally, Part 4 explores the age old argument of whether guns are better than bows. Although it had been in decline for decades the real death knell of English military archery came in 1589 when the bow was no longer seen as a weapon fit for the trained bands. The early 1590s saw a flurry of publications arguing the point, for and against, of which Sir John Smythe's *Discourses* is probably the most familiar. Smythe was a passionate advocate of the bow, and his defence of archery is a well-written tract that makes a very good case and, incidentally, provides us with a huge amount of information about the practice of archery in the Tudor period. It is sadly impossible to reprint his whole book here, but one of the most important sections has been excerpted at length (**Doc. 49**). Within weeks of Smythe's book being printed Sir Roger Williams published his own *Brief Discourse* (**Doc. 50**) which had been written over a long period but which contained as hastily-inserted rebuttal of Smythe's defence of the bow. Smythe and Williams were two sides of a coin, each of them an experienced soldier with decades of military service in English and foreign armies behind them, but opposed in their views on most military matters. They were probably acquainted with one another, moving in the same small circle of English professional soldiers, and may have been rivals in life as well as in print. Williams' case was expanded by Humfrey Barwick, a less-lofty soldier than either Smythe or Williams, in his *Breefe Discourse* (**Doc. 51**) which included a point-by-point critique of Smythe's work. Together these three, particularly Smythe and Barwick, provide an admirable summary of the arguments for and against the bow. Military archery was revived briefly in the seventeenth century - English archers were last sent to fight on the Continent in 1627, and several companies of archers fought in the early years of the civil war in the 1640s - but it never recovered to its pre-1590 status.

# Part 1

## THE STATUTES, 1285-1571

## A Table of English and Irish archery statutes, 1285-1571

| Year | Statute | Title | Main Provisions |
|---|---|---|---|
| 1285 | 13 Ed.1 c.6 | That View of Arms be Made. Hue and Cry shall be followed. Fairs and Markets shall not be kept in Church-yards. ('Statute of Winchester') | Includes list of arms all men aged 15-60 were required to own depending on wealth and status. Appears to be the earliest requiring bows. |
| 1383 | 7 Ric.2 c.6 | The Statute of Winchester confirmed and every sheriff shall proclaim it. | Reissue of **13 Ed.1 c.6**, orders for it to be proclaimed in public so 'that no man shall excuse himself by ignorance' |
| 1388 | 12 Ric.2 c.6 | No Servants in husbandry, or labourer, shall wear any sword, buckler, or dagger. Unlawful games prohibited | Servants, labourers, husbandmen, victuallers, and artificers to have bows and practice on Sundays and holy days. |
| 1405 | 7 Hen.4 c.7 | Arrow-heads shall be well boiled, brased, and hardened | Arrowheads must be hardened steel at the tip, and marked with the maker's mark |
| 1409 | 11 Hen.4 c.4 | The Statute 12 R.II, c.6, against unlawful games recited | Reissue of **12 Ric.2 c.6** |
| 1416 | 4 Hen.5 c.3 | No man shall make any pattens of aspe, upon pain of an hundred shillings | Patten makers prohibited from using aspen (poplar) in order to reduce the cost of arrows. |

| 1465 | 5 Ed.4 c.4 (Ireland) | *An Act that every Englishman and Irishman that dwelleth with Englishmen, and speaketh English, betwixt sixty and sixteen in years, shall have an English bow and arrows* | Enforced bow ownership. Bows to be the archer's 'own length, and one fistmele' at least. 12 arrows ¾ 'standard' in length. Wood types mentioned. |
|---|---|---|---|
| 1465 | 5 Ed.4 c.5 (Ireland) | *An Act for having a constable in every town, and a pair of butts for shooting, and that every man between sixty and sixteen shall shoot every holyday at the same butts* | Every town in the English Pale to have a pair of butts (unspecified length), and every man 16-60 to shoot 'up and down three times' every feast day March-July |
| 1472 | 12 Ed. 4 c.2 | *Four bowstaves shall be brought into this realm for every tun of merchandise* | Every ship importing goods from Venice or other ports to bring four bow staves for every ton weight of goods |
| 1472 | 12 Ed. 4 c.2 (Ireland) | *An Act for bringing bowes into thie realm from the realm of England by merchants and others* | Every ship carrying £100+ of goods from England to Ireland to bring bows worth 100 shillings, or more proportional to the value of the cargo. |
| 1477 | 17 Ed.4 c.3 | *Against unlawful games* | Certain games detrimental to archery practice banned |
| 1482 | 22 Ed.4 c.4 | *An Act for the price of bows* | Set maximum price of 3s 4d for yew bows. |
| 1483 | 1 Ric.3 c.11 | *An Act touchinge Bowyers* | 10 bowstaves to be imported with every butt of Malmsey or Tyre wine. Bowstaves to be sold |

| | | | only to native Englishmen. |
|---|---|---|---|
| 1487 | 3 Hen.7 c.13 | An Acte agaynst the excessyve price of Longe bowes | Set maximum price of 3s 4d for bows |
| 1495 | 10 Hen.7 c.9 (Ireland) | An Act that the subjects of this realm shall have bows and other armour | Subjects to own bow and sheaf of arrows. Every parish to have butts. Every parishioner to shoot 2 or 3 times every holy day. |
| 1503 | 19 Hen.7 c.2 | Good Bow-staves may be imported without paying any Custom, until next Parliament | Bowstaves 6'6" or more in length exempt from customs duties. |
| 1503 | 19 Hen.7 c. 4 | Crossbows not to be used | Limitations of wealth and land placed on private ownership of crossbows. (*Not reprinted here*) |
| 1511 | 3 Hen.8 c.3 | An Act concerning shooting in Long bows | Compulsory ownership of bow and 4 arrows over age of 17. Children and servants 7-17 to have a bow and 2 arrows. Every bowyer to make 2 mean wood bows for every yew bow. Butts to be made in every city, town, and parish. All men to practice on holy days. Justices of the Peace required to appoint bowyers in shire towns and boroughs to make mean wood bows. |
| 1511 | 3 Hen.8 c.13 | An Acte against shooting in Crosbowes | Reissue and extension of **19 Hen.7 c. 4** (*Not reprinted here*) |
| 1514 | 6 Hen.8 c.2 | Acte for Maytenance of Archers | Essentially a reissue of **3 Hen.8 c.3** |
| 1514 | 6 Hen.8 c.11 | Acte concernyng the bryinging in of Bowestaves in | Reissue of **1 Ric.3 c.11** with the clarification that it applies only to foreign merchants |

| | | | to this Realme | |
|---|---|---|---|---|
| 1514 | 6 Hen.8 c.13 | | *Acte avoidyng shoting in Crosbowes* | New criteria for crossbow and handgun ownership. (*Not reprinted here*) |
| 1523 | 14 Hen.8 c.7 | | *Thacte for shotying in Crosbowes and Handgonnes* | Further criteria and exceptions to **6 Hen.8 c.13** (*Not reprinted here*) |
| 1533 | 25 Hen.8 c.17 | | *(untitled)* | Reissue of **14 Hen.8 c.7** |
| 1541 | 33 Hen.8 c.6 | | *An Acte concerninge Crosbowes and Handguns* | Reissue and expansion of **25 Hen.8 c.17** |
| 1541 | 33 Hen.8 c.9 | | *The bill for the maintaining artillery, and the debarring of unlawful games* | Compulsory ownership of bow and 4 arrows over age of 17. Children and servants 7-17 to have a bow and 2 arrows. Every bowyer outside London to make 4 mean wood bows for every yew bow. London bowyers to make 2 mean bows for every yew Butts to be made in every city, town, and parish. All men to practice on holy days. 220 yards established as the minimum range at which to practice with prick- or flight-arrows. Wealth restrictions placed on yew bows for under-17s Price of yew bows set at 3s 4d for adult bows, 12d for yew bows for under-14s Bowyers, stringers, fletchers, and arrowsmiths residing in London or its suburbs but not Freemen of the city could be ordered to other towns in need of them. 'Aliens' not to shoot bows or sell bows or arrows overseas. Strictures against unlawful games |
| 1557 | 4 Philip | | *An Acte for the* | Sets out in detail the arms and |

|  |  | and Mary, c.2 | *having of Horse Armour and Weapon* | armour required of citizens depending on their level of wealth or income. |
|---|---|---|---|---|
| 1566 | 8 Eliz.1 c.10 | *An act for bowyers* | Bowyers in London, Westminster, Southwark, and Surrey exempted from earlier acts. Bowyers in those regions required to keep a stock of fifty mean wood bows. Maximum prices of bows set: imported yew, best bows – 6s8d; imported yew, second bows – 3s 4d; imported yew 'of the coarse sort, called livery-bows' – 2s; English yew – 2s | |
| 1571 | 13 Eliz.1 c.14 | *An act for the bringing of bow-staves into this realm* | Reissue and clarification of **12 Ed. 4 c. 2** | |

## 1. That View of Arms be made. Hue and Cry shall be followed. Fairs or Markets shall not be kept in Church-yards. (1285)

*Since the days of the Anglo-Saxon fyrd Englishmen had been required to own arms and armour so that they might turn out to fight when called upon. In 1181 the system was codified by Henry II's proclamation known as the Assize of Arms, which stipulated specific arms and armour required of all men, depending on their social status and wealth. The Assize of Arms also restricted the possession of arms and armour by Jews. In 1252 the Assize of Arms was reissued and expanded by Henry III, and for the first time required some men to own bows and arrows. The Assizes of Arms were proclamations rather than statutes, instructions rather than laws. In 1285 this act, often referred to as the Statute of Winchester, was passed codifying the earlier proclamations into statute law and making the ownership of bows and arrows by those within the stipulated wealth-bracket a legal requirement, thus paving the way for the rise of English archery in the later medieval period.*

### 13 Edward 1. c.6

And further it is commanded, That every Man have in his House Harness for to keep the Peace after the antient Assise;[1] that is to say, Every Man between Fifteen Years of Age, and Sixty Years, shall be assessed and sworn to Armor according to the Quantity of their Lands and Goods; that is to wit, from Fifteen Pounds Lands, and Goods Forty Marks, an Hauberke,[2] a helmet[3] of Iron, a Sword, a Knife, and an Horse; and from Ten Pounds of Lands, and Twenty Marks Goods, an Hauberke, a helmet of Iron, a Sword, and a Knife; and from Five Pound Lands, a Doublet, a helmet of Iron, a Sword, and a Knife; and from Forty Shillings Land and more, unto One Hundred Shillings of Land, a Sword, a Bow and arrows, and a Knife; and he that hath less than Forty Shillings yearly, shall be sworn to keep Gisarmes, Knives, and other less Weapons; and he that hath less than Twenty Marks

---

[1] Reference to the Assize of Arms, 1181, reissued in 1252. Neither of the earlier statutes mentioned bows.

[2] 'Haubergeon' in the original French text. Despite modern differentiation between a hauberk and haubergeon the terms appear to have been interchangeable in the thirteenth century.

[3] 'Chapel de Fer' in the original French text. Pickering mis-translated this as 'breast-plate of iron.'

in Goods shall have Swords, Knives, and other less weapons; and all other that may shall have Bows and Arrows out of the Forest, and in the Forest Bows and Boults.[4] And that View of Armor be made every Year Two Times. And in every Hundred and Franchise Two Constables shall be chosen to make the View of Armor: And the Constables aforesaid shall present before Justices assigned such Defaults as they do see in the Country about Armor, and of the Suits of Towns, and of Highways, and also shall present all such as do lodge Strangers in uplandish Towns for whom they will not answer; and the Justices assigned shall present at every Parliament unto the King such Defaults as they shall find, and the King shall provide Remedy therein. And from henceforth let Sheriffs take good Heed, and Bailiffs, within their Franchises and without, be they higher or lower, that have any Bailiwick or Forestry in Fee or otherwise that they shall follow the Cry with the Country, and after, as they are bounden, to keep Horses and Armor, or so to do; and if there be any that do not, the Defaults shall be presented by the Constables to the Justices assigned, and after, by them to the King, and the King will provide Remedy as afore is said. And the King commandeth and forbiddeth, that henceforth neither Fairs nor Markets be kept in Church-yards for the honour of the Church. Given at Winchester, the Eighth of October, in the Thirteenth Year of the Reign of the King.

---

[4] 'Piles' in the original French text, probably better translated as 'stake' or 'spear.'

## 2. The Statute of Winchester[5] confirmed, and every sheriff shall proclaim it. (1383)

*This statute, enacted nearly a century after the Statute of Winchester, illustrates how difficult it was to enforce the population to adhere to the earlier act's provisions. Throughout the medieval and Tudor periods several similar acts were reissued from time to time, suggesting that they were widely ignored. Later militia muster rolls[6] certainly bear out the impression that large sections of the populace failed to produce all, or even any, of the equipment required of them.*

### 7 Richard 2. c.6

*Item, for the grievous mischiefs and complaints that do daily happen of robberies, thefts, manslaughters, burning of houses and ridings in routs and great companies in every part of the realm; it is ordained and assented, That the statute of Winchester (the tenour whereof is sent by our lord the King this year last past into every county of England, to be proclaimed) be holden and kept in all points, and put in good and hasty execution, at the complaint and pursuit of every man that feeleth himself grieved against the tenour of the same. And to the intent that no man shall excuse himself by ignorance of the same statute, it is also assented, That every sheriff of England shall be bound from henceforth in proper person to make proclamation of the same statute four times a year in every hundred of his bailiwick, and by his bailiffs in every market-town, as well within liberties as without.*

---

[5] The Statue of Winchester refers to all of the legislation passed at Winchester in 1285, including 13 Ed. 1 c.6. See **Doc. 1**
[6] See **Docs 41** and **46**

## 3. No servants in husbandry, or labourer, shall wear any sword, buckler, or dagger. Unlawful games prohibited (1388)

*In 1363 Edward III wrote to the Lord Lieutenant of Kent[7] instructing him to ensure that men conducted regular archery practice, but it was not until 1388 that the oft-cited rule requiring shooting at the butts on Sundays and holy days entered into law. Archery requires regular practice to maintain both skill and fitness, but swords and daggers were more likely to be used in domestic brawls than battles.*

### 12 Richard 2. c.6

Item, it is accorded and assented, that no servant of husbandry, or labourer, nor servant, or artificer, nor of victualler, shall from henceforth bear any buckler, sword nor dagger, upon forfeiture of the same, but in the time of war for defence of the realm of England, and that by the surveying of the arrears for the time being, or travailing by the country with their master, or in their master's message, but such servants and labourers shall have bows and arrows, and use the same the Sundays and holydays, and leave all playing at tennis or football, and other games called coits, dice, casting of the stone, kails,[8] and other such importune games. And that the sheriffs, mayors, bailiffs, and constables, shall have power to arrest, and shall arrest all doers against this statute, and seise the said bucklers, swords, and daggers, and keep them til the sessions of the Justices of Peace, and the same present before the same justices in their sessions, together with the names of them that did bear the same.

And it is not the King's mind that any prejudice be done to the franchises of lords, touching the forfeitures due to them.

---

[7] See **Doc. 32**
[8] A form of skittles played by throwing a stick instead of a ball at the pins.

## 4. Arrow-heads shall be well boiled, brased, and hard (1405)

*There is little to add to this simple and straightforward act except to note that it is one of many 'quality control' legislative acts passed in the later medieval period, covering diverse items from cloth to arrow heads. It may be that substandard arrow heads had found their way into the supplies destined for royal armies and a set of basic standards was required. Of particular interest is the stipulation for 'brased' heads. The word 'brased' in this context almost certainly has the same origin as 'brass,' and may means 'brazed' in the modern sense of joining pieces of metal with molten brass - there is some evidence of the technique being used to fix barbs onto Type 16[9] style heads - but the OED suggests that the word 'brased' could also be used to mean fire-hardened, and this seems a more likely interpretation under the circumstances.*

**7 Henry 4. c.7**

Item, because the arrow-smiths do make many faulty heads for arrows and quarels, defective, not well, nor lawful, nor defensible, to the great jeopardy and deceit of the people, and of the whole realm; it is ordained and established, That all the heads for arrows and quarels after this time to be made, shall be well boiled or brased and hardened at the points with steel; and if any of the said smiths do make the contrary, they shall forfeit all such heads and quarels to the King, and shall also be imprisoned, and make a fine at the King's will; and that every arrowhead and quarel be marked with the mark of him that made the same. And the justice of peace in every county of England, and also the mayor and sheriffs, and bailiffs of cities and boroughs, shall have power to enquire of all such deceitful makers of heads and quarels, and to punish them as afore is said.

---

[9] Museum of London typology

## 5. The Statue of 12 R.II, c.6 against unlawful games recited (1409)

*This act adds very little to our understanding of medieval archery, except to illustrate that men shirking their practice to play football or skittles instead was evidently still a problem in 1409. Earlier instructions and statutes mandating archery practice had still not produced the hoped-for nation of archers.*

**11 Henry 4. c.4**

Whereas in the statute made at Cambridge the xii Year of the Reign of King Richard,[10] amongst other Things it was accorded and assented, That the Servants and Labourers of Husbandry, and Labourers and Servants of Artificers, and of Victuallers, should have Bows and Arrows, and use the same the Sundays and other festival Days, and utterly leave playing at the Balls, as well Hand-ball as Foot-ball, and other games called Coits, Dice, casting of the stone, and Kails, and other such unthrifty Games, and that the Sheriffs, Mayors, Bailiffs, and Constables, shall have Power to arrest all that do contrary; as in the said Statute is more fully contained: Our Sovereign Lord the King will, That the said Statute be firmly holden and kept; joined to the same, that every such Labourer or Servant that doth contrary to the same Statute, shall have Imprisonment by Six Days. And the Mayors and Sheriffs, or the Mayors and Bailiffs of Cities and Boroughs, and the Constables in other Towns, shall have Power to put this Statute into execution from Time to Time; and if they do not thereof Execution, the same Mayors and Sheriffs, or Mayors and Bailiffs aforesaid, shall pay to the King for every Default xx s; and the Constables or Constable of every Town that doth not like Execution of this Statute, shall pay for every their or his Default vi s. And that the Justices of Assises shall have Power to enquire in this Case in their Sessions from Time to Time, of them that do contrary to this Statute, and thereof to certify in the chancery.

---

[10] See **Doc. 3**

# 6. No man shall make pattens of aspe, upon pain of an hundred shillings (1416)

*Aspen, a type of poplar, is a tought, straight-grained, relatively light, and fairly rot-resistant wood, and these characteristics would make it ideal for pattens as well as arrows. Aspen, of course, was not the only wood used for arrows. Roger Ascham listed fifteen different woods that might be used: 'brasell,[11]' 'Turkie-wood,[12]' fustic, alder, hornbeam, birch, ash, oak, servis (pear), holly, blackthorn, beech, elder, willow, and aspen.[13] L'Art D'Archerie suggested arrows of birch, ash, or cherry.[14]*

*It is interesting that aspen was so highly valued for arrows, for Ascham held it in rather low esteem. 'Yet as concerning sheaf-arrowes for the Warres (as I suppose) it were better to make them of good Ashe, as they were in former times, and not of Aspe, as they be now, for of all the woods that ever I prooved, Ashe being big is the swiftest, and giveth the fairest blow, by reason of its heavinesse; both which qualities the Aspe wanteth.' It is worth noting that 77% of the analysed arrows recovered from the* Mary Rose *were made of poplar.*

### 4 Henry 5. c.3

Item, That the patenmakers in the realm of England, from henceforth shall make no patens[15] nor clogs of timber called aspe,[16] upon pain to pay the King a hundred shillings, at every time that the said patenmakers make any patens or clogs of the said timber. And that every man that will sue for the King, shall have the one half of the pain so forfeit, so that the fletchers through the realm shall sell their arrows at a more easy and reasonable price from henceforth than they were wont.

---

[11] Probably sappan
[12] Unknown, poss. Turkish walnut
[13] Roger Ascham, *Toxophilus* (London, 1545), 2, p.12
[14] See **Doc. 48**
[15] Thick wooden soles strapped over shoes to protect them from mud and water outdoors.
[16] Aspen, *Populus tremula*

**7. An Act that every Englishman and Irishman that dwelleth with Englishmen, and speaketh English, betwixt sixty and sixteen in years, shall have and English bow and arrows (1465)**

*This Act of the Irish parliament is significant because it gives us one of the crucial details about medieval bows - the length. The archer's height plus a fistmele would, naturally, produce bows of varying length depending on the size of the archer, but it should also be noted that that was considered the* minimum length required for a bow, not a standard length.

*More confusing is the instruction that arrow shafts should be 'three quarters of the standard' in length. Presumably this refers to three quarters of either a yard (27") or an ell (33¾"). Though it does not say so, it may be that the act was intended to provide a minimum length for arrow shafts, as it did bows, in which case 27" is the more likely measurement, possibly-hyperbolic references elsewhere to 'clothyard' arrows notwithstanding. Furthermore, in purely legal terms, the ell was not standardised until the sixteenth century but the yard had been a 'standard' legal length since around 1300. There are too few historic English arrows to draw any firm conclusions about their typical length, but 98% of the complete arrows recovered from the Mary Rose were between 27" and 32.5", just under 1% were longer and just over 1% were shorter. The famous Westminster Abbey arrow has a shaft of slightly less than 29" in length. This data would suggest that a minimum length of 27" is a much more likely interpretation than a standard or minimum length of 33¾".*

### 5 Edward 4. c.4 (Ireland)

Item, at the request of the commons, that consideration had to the great number of Irishmen, that exceed greatly the English people that in force and augmentation of the Kings lieges, it is ordeyned by authority of the said Parliament. That every Englishman and Irishman that dwell with Englishmen and speak English, that be betwixt sixty and sixteen in age, shall have an English bow of his own length, and one fistmele[17] at the least between the necks, with, twelve shafts of the lengths of three quarters of

---

[17] A 'fistmele' is sometimes interpreted as the width of a closed fist, but most early writers agree that it was the width of a fist with the thumb extended

the standard, the bows of ewe, wych-hassell, ashe, awburne,[18] or any other reasonable tree acording to their power, and the shafts in the same maner, within two moneths next after the publication of this estatute, on pain of two mence a man from moneth to other, til that he shall have and continue the bow and shafts, and in lue of the bow and shafts broken and lost to have new, under pain of two pence every moneth till it be done. And yet not prohibiting gentlemen on horseback to ride according their best disposition to ride with spear, so that they have bowes with their men for time of necessitie.

---

[18] This may refer to 'alburn,' the sapwood of a tree, rather than to a specific wood

## 8. An Act for having a constable in every town, and a pair of butts for shooting, and that every man between sixty and sixteen shall shoot every holyday at the same butts. (1465)

*Despite the first instructions demanding regular archery practice appearing more than a century before this statute[19] this is the first statute to mandate the provision of butts at which to shoot in every town. As late as the mid-sixteenth century some towns and villages were still being order to build butts because they had none.*

### 5 Edward 4. c.5 (Ireland)

At the request of the commons, it is ordeyned and established by authority of the said Parliament, That in every English town of this land, that pass three houses holden by tenants, where no other president is, be chosen by his neighbours, or by the lord of the same town, one constable to be president and governour of the same town, in all things that partaineth to the common rule of the same town, as is in ordinance of night watch, from Michaelmas to Easter yearly, under pain of three pence every night, and also to ordeyn one paier of butts for shooting, within the town or well neere, upon the costs and labour of the said town, under pain of two shillings from one moneth to other, after the publication hereof, till the constable be made and the butts also, and that every man of the same town, in such hour as the constable or his deputy of his neighbours will assign that is betwixt lx and xvi muster before the constable or his deputie at the said butts, and shoot up and down three times every feast day, betwixt the first day of March and the last day of July, under pain of one halfepeny for every day, and that all these paines be levied of their goods or wages, from moneth to moneth, by the constable, to be spent in strengthning of the same town, or otherwise in his default, to be levied by the wardein of the peace, and that the paines lost, be spent upon the towns where the said pained riseth.

---

[19] See **Doc. 32**

## 9. Four bowstaves shall be brought into this realm for every tun of merchandise (1472)

*Earlier in the century shortage of wood for arrows had apparently been a problem in England.[20] English yew may also have been in short supply by 1472 after two centuries of intense bow-making but foreign yew, particularly Italian yew, had a reputation for superior quality and closer grain due to the more temperate climate. The English wool trade had grown exponentially in the fifteenth century, and the market for English wool in continental Europe meant that England now had a certain amount of strength in international trade, enough that the king and parliament could afford to place demands on foreign merchants visiting England.*

### 12 Edward 4. c.2

Item, because that our sovereign lord the King, by a petition delivered to him in the said parliament, by the commons of the same, hath perceived, That great scarcity of bowstaves is now in this realm, and the bowstaves that be in the realm be sold at an excessive price, whereby the exercise of archery is greatly discontinued, and almost lost; our said lord the King considering the premisses by the advice, assent, and authority afresaid, hath ordained and established, That every merchant stranger, and every, or any of their factors, attornies, or servants, which at any time after the feast of St. Michael the archangel[21] next coming, shall bring, send, or convey into this land any merchandise in carrack, galley or ship, of the city or country of Venice, or of other city, town, or country from whence any such bowstaves have been before this time brought, sent, or conveyed into this land, at every time of their bringing, sending, or conveying of any such merchandises into this realm, shall bring, send, or convey into this realm, with the said merchandises, in the same carrack, galley, or ship, whereing any such merchandises shall be hereafter brought, sent, or conveyed, for every tun weight of such merchandises which here-after shall be contained in every carrack, galley, or ship, four bowstaves, upon pain of forfeiture to

---
[20] See **Doc. 6**
[21] 29 September

the King for every Default of bringing of every such bowstaff vi.s viii.d,[22] and also the said bowstaves so brought, sent or conveyed by the said merchants, or servants into this realm, shall be searched and surveyed by the mayor, sheriffs, bailiffs, or chief governors of such cities or towns within this realm, where any such carrack, galley, or ship shall hereafter come to safe port; and the said mayors, sheriffs, bailiffs, or chief governors shall assigntwo men most expert, to search the said staves, and the said two men to be sword by the said mayor, sheriffs, bailiffs, or chief governors, that they shall truly and indifferently mark the staves that be not good and sufficient, according to the manner as such staves in times past were wont to be marked to the intent that all the King's liege people may have knowledge of them without fraud.

---

[22] 6 shillings and 8 pence.

## 10. An Act for bringing bowes into this realm from the realm of England, by merchants and others. (1472)

*The following statute was passed by the Irish parliament shortly after* **Doc. 9** *was passed in the English parliament. Ireland had very little direct trade with mainland Europe at this time, most foreign trade passing through England instead. The onus to provide bows for Englishmen in Ireland therefore fell on English merchants. It is interesting to note that while the English statute required merchants to import bow staves the Irish statute called for manufactured bows, which may suggest a shortage of skilled bowyers in Ireland.*

### 12 Edward 4. c.2 (Ireland)

At the request of the commons, whereas the land of Ireland is desolated of bowes, to the suportation of the said land, and defence of the said commons against the Irish enemies of the King, and English rebels of the same, whereupon the premisses considered, it is ordained and enacted by the authority of the said Parliament, and proclaimed in the same, That every merchant and passenger that bring merchandises into this land of Ireland, out of England, to the sum of an hundred pound, that he shall buy and bring with him into the said land in bows, to the value of an hundred shillings, and so following after the rate under or over, to the sum of twenty pounds. And if any merchant or passenger bring any merchandise in the said land, and bring with him no bows as is afore rehearsed, that the said merchant shall loose and pay the value of the said bowes, the one moyety thereof to the King, and a moyety to the searchers of the same for the time being. And that the said searchers may have an action of debt against the said persons therefore, in any court that the King have, as well for the King as for the said searcher: and that by the said authority it is ordained, That the bayliffs of the city of Dublin for the time being, be searchers of the same, within the franchise of the said city, and that the sheriffs of the town of Drogheda in like manner upon the same, within the franchise of the said town, and so in like manner the officers of the same in every city and town within this land of Ireland. And if the said searchers in any city and town within this said land, be negligent in exercising of the said search, that they shall loose to the King, for every default, fourty shillings. And the penalty of this act shall not be against any person until the first day of June next coming, and that the clerk of the Parliament make writs of proclamation to Dublin, Drogheda, and every other town, necessary upon the premisses, and that the searchers for the time being, present in the Kings bench, or in the exchequer of the King in Ireland, upon the pain of fourty shillings, the names of all the merchants or passengers which bring no bows, as before is rehearsed, and thereupon proclamation was made in plain parliament accordingly.

## 11. Against unlawful games (1477)

*Yet again the earlier statutes outlawing certain games in an effort to promote regular archery practice were found to be observed mostly in the breach. A few new games were added to the list of outlawed pastimes*

### 17 Edward 4. c.3

Item, whereas by the laws of this land no person should use any unlawful games, as dice, coits, tennis, and such like games, but that every person strong and able of body should use his bow, because that the defence of this land was much by archers, contrary to which laws the games aforesaid and many new imagined games, called closh,[23] kailes, half-bowl,[24] hand in and hand out,[25] and queckboard[26] be daily used in divers parts of this land, as well by persons of good reputation, as of small having: and such evil disposed persons that doubt not to offend God in not observing their holy days, nor breaking the laws of the land to their own impoverishment, and by their ungracious procurement and encouraging, do bring other to such games, till they be utterly undone and impoverished of their goods, to the pernicious example of divers of the King's liege people, it such unprofitable games should be suffered long to continue, because that by the mean thereof divers and many murders, robberies, and other heinous felonies be oftentimes committed and done in divers parts of this realm to the great inquieting and trouble of many good and well-disposed persons, and the importune loss of their goods, which plays in their said offences be daily supported and favoured by the governors and occupiers of divers houses, tenements, gardens, and other places, where they use and occupy their said ungracious and incommendable games: Our sovereign lord the King in considerationof the premisses, by the advice of the lords spiritual and temporal, and the commons of the said parliament assembled, and by the authority of the same hath ordained, that after the feast of Easter next

---

[23] Probably an early form of croquet
[24] An intricate form of skittles in which the ball must travel around the skittles before returning to hit them
[25] Believed to be a ball-catching game, rules unknown
[26] A gambling game involving casting dice through a funnel onto a chess-board

coming, no person, governor nor occupier of any house, tenements, garden, or other place within this realm, shall willingly suffer and person to occupy or play any of the said games called closh, kailes, half-bowl, hand in and hand out, or queckboard, or any of them within and of their said houses, tenements, gardens, or any other place, upon pain to have the imprisonment of three years, and to forfeit or lose for every offence xx li.[27] The one half thereof our sovereign lord the King, to be applied to the use of his house, in all such places where such forfeiture shall happen to fall, other than where any person ought to have the forfeiture of the goods of felons and fugitives, by any lawful grant, authority of parliament, or otherwise. And it is ordained by the said authority, That all such persons, their heirs and successors, which ought to have any such forfeitures in any such places, shall have all such half as shall hereafter forfeit by any of the premisses: and the other half to him or them that in this behalf will pursue by action of debt at the common law: In which action, like process, trial, judgement, costs, damage, and execution, shall be had as is used in other actions there pursued. And that no person from the said feast of Easter, shall use any of the said games called closh, half bowl, kailes, hand in or hand out, or queckboard, upon pain of two years imprisonment, and to forfeit for every default, ten pounds. The one half thereof to our sovereign lord the King, to be applied to the use of his house, in all such places where such forfeiture shall happen to fall, other than where any person ought to have the forfeiture of the goods of felons and fugitives, by any lawful grant, authority of parliament, or otherwise. And it is ordained by the said authority, That all such persons, their heirs and successors, which ought to have any such forfeitures in any such places, shall have all such half as shall hereafter forfeit by any of the premisses: and the other half to him or them that in this behalf will sue by action of debt in like manner and form to be had, tried, ruled, and ordered as is aforesaid.

---

[27] £20

## 12. An act for the price of bows. (1482)

*The flurry of new laws requiring every man in England and Ireland to own a bow may well have encouraged unscrupulous bowyers to artificially inflate their prices to take advantage of the ready market. In Henry VIII's reign the price of bows was seen as one of the reasons that many men failed to fulfil their legal obligations, but it can be seen by this statute that efforts by the crown to ensure a supply of affordable bows for the populace began at an earlier date.*

### 22 Edward 4. c.4

Item, whereas in the time of the noble progenitors of our sovereign lord the King that now is, and also in the time of the victorious reign of our said sovereign lord the King that now is, his subjects within every part of this realm have virtuously occupied and used shooting with their bows, whereby and under the protection of Almighty God, victorious acts have been done in defence of this realm: now so it is, that the bowyers in every part of this realm do sell their bows at such a great and excessive price, that the King's subjects disposed to shoot, be not of the power to buy to them bows, whereby shooting is greatly diminished and left, and unlawful games be used, contrary to statutes and ordinances thereupon made: our said sovereign lord the King, considering the premisses, by the advice, assent, and authority aforesaid, hath ordained, established, and enacted, That from the feast of Easter next coming, no bowyer nor other person using to sell or put to sale, or which hereafter shall use to sell or put to sale any long bow or bows of yew, shall sell anyof the same bows to any of the King's liege people about the price of Three Shillings four pence a bow. And long bows of yew under the value of the same price as the seller and buyer thereof may reasonably agree and accord, upon pain to forfeit for every long bow of yew otherwise sold above the said price of Three shillings and four pence, Twenty Shillings. The one half thereof to our sovereign lord the King, and the other half to any of his liege people that will therefore pursue and prove the said forfeiture by action or actions of debt, wherein like process judgement and execution shall be had as is commonly used in actions of debt sued at the common law. And that no defendant in any such action or actions shall be admitted to wage his law.

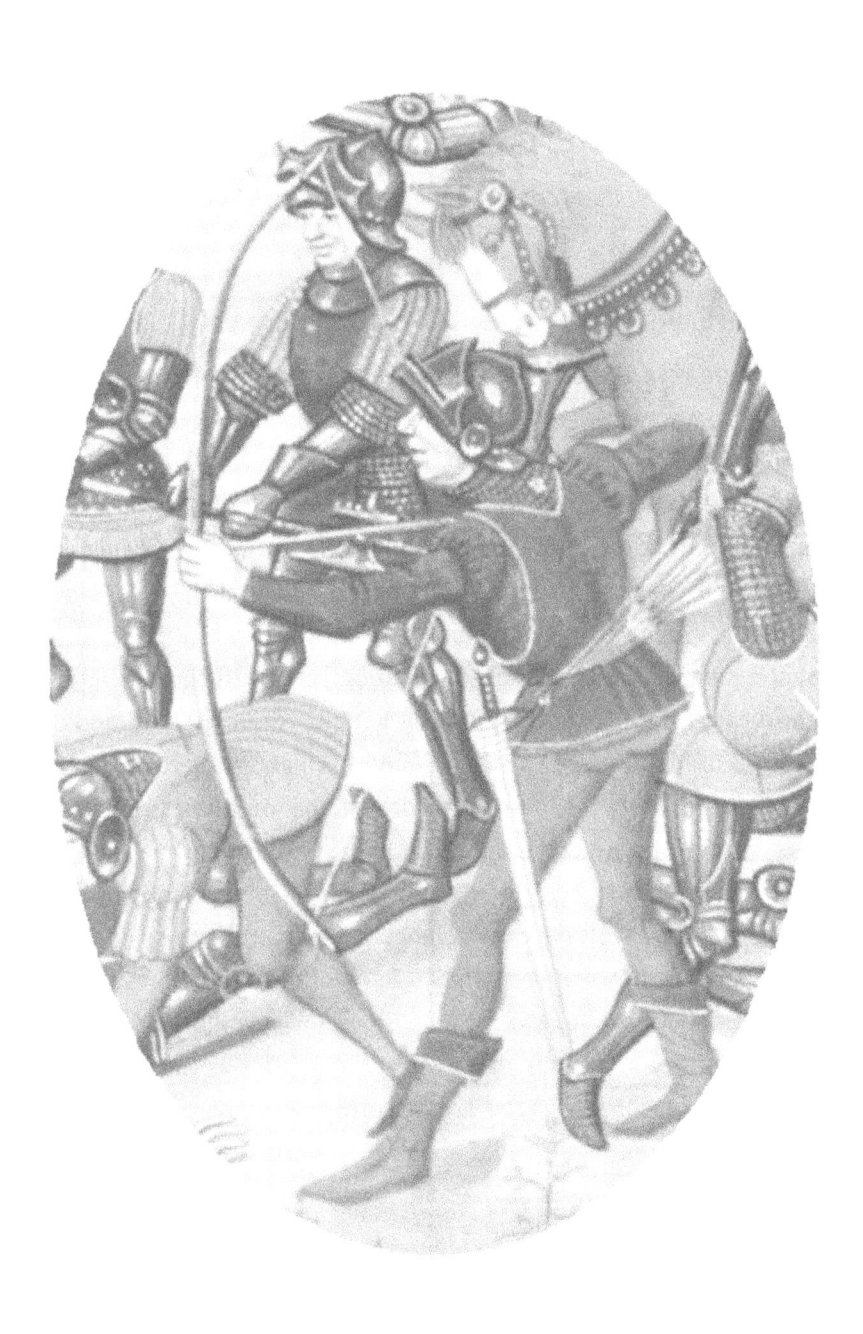

## 13. An Act touchinge Bowyers (1483)

*Legislation limiting the price of bows[28] could only reasonably be enforced if the bowyers of England were able to acquire the raw materials of their trade at a reasonable cost. It was not profiteering by the bowyers, they claimed, that led to inflated prices, but profiteering by the merchants who supplied them with good imported yew staves. The limitation on the price of bows only solved part of the problem - if the bowyers' profit margins were too slim then they could not make bows. The solution was to limit also the price of imported staves*

### 1 Richard 3. c.11

To the full honorable and discrete Commons in this present parliament assembled; Mekely showen unto youre discrete wisdoms your beseechers, the Bowyers Inhabitants within Citeez Burghes and Villages of this noble Realme of Englond, occupying Artillery to theym belonging for the sure tuicion and defence of the seid Realme, that where in tymes paste good and hable stuffe of Bowestaves aswell by Englisshe merchants as by Straungiers hath been brought into this said Reame, by the whiche the said inhabitaunts Artillers myght competently lyve upon such stuff as they than bought of Bowestaves at xl s. the C., or xlvj s. viij d. atte mooste,[29] It is so nowe, that by the subtile meanes of Lumbards usynge to diverse portes in this Realme the Crafte of Bowiers aforesaid is sore mynusshed and likly to be uttirly undone, And therby the londe greatly enfebled, to the greate Jeopardie of the same and greate comfrote to the Enemyes and adversariez therof: For by the seducious confederacy of the said Lumbards bowestaves ben nowe at so outrageous price, that is to wit at viij li. the C.[30] where they wer wont to be sold at xl s. and also they will not suffre any garbelyng[31] of them to be made, but selle good and bad at so excessyf price togedyr ungarbeled, that by lyklyhode within shorte tyme this Realme is like to lacke bothe stuff of Artillery and of Artificers of the same, without

---

[28] See **Doc. 12**
[29] 60 shillings per hundred [bowstaves], or 66 shillings 8 pence at most
[30] £8 per hundred
[31] Garbling: the act of sifting through a commodity in order to separate the quality from the refuse.

a provision of due remedy in this behalf be the more spedely found and hadde: It may therefore please your discrete Wysdoms to pray the Kinge oure soveraigne Lorde that he of his grace especiall with thassent[32] of his lords spirituel and temporel and Comens in this his present parliament assembled and by auctorite of the same to ordeigne establisse and enacte that noon of those merchants of Venice, nor other that use to repeyre into this youre Reame with merchandizes of those parts, brynge nor convey into this said Realme any merchandizes, but yf the same merchaunt and merchaunts bryng with every Butte of Malvesy[33] and with every But of Tyre x bowestaves good and hable stuff, upon peyn of forfeyture of xiij s. iiij d.[34] for every But of the said Wynz so brought and conveid, And not the said nombre of Bowestaves with the same Butt; the oon half of the said forfaiture to you soveraigne Lorde and the other moite to the partie that will sue therfore. And that no suche bowstaves be sol ungarbelled, and but to such persone or personez as be borne and shall be borne under the Kings obeysaunce; this Act to begyn to take effect at the fest of Seint Michell next comynge.

---

[32] The assent
[33] Malmsey wine
[34] 13 shillings 4 pence

## 14. An Acte agaynst the Excessyve price of Longe bowes (1487)

*The accession of Henry VII to the throne following his victory over Richard III presented a few legal problems. Richard was declared a usurper to the throne which cast doubt on the legality of statutes passed during his reign. For the most part both Henry and parliament were content to let earlier legislation stand, but the fact that Henry had to issue a new statute saying more or less the same thing as a statute passed only five years earlier may indicate that bowyers had taken advantage of the situation and once again inflated their prices.*

### 3 Henry 7. c.13

For as moche as the greate and aunciente defense of this realme hath stande by the archers and shoter in long bowes, which ys now gretly lefte and fallen in decaye, for the derth and excessyf price of long bowes; be yt therfor ordyned and establisshed by the Kyng our Soverygn lorde by thadvyce of his Lordes Spirituell and Temporell and the Comens in this present parliament assembled, and by auctorite of the same, that yf eny persone or persones, after the fest of the Puryfication of oure Lady[35] next comyng, sell eny long boe over the price of iij s. iiij d.[36] that then the seller or sellers of such bowe forfeit for evry bowe so sold over the seid price xl s.[37] to the Kyng; he that will sure for the same have an accion of detter therfor ayenst such Seller, or make informacion in the Kyngs Eschequer thereof the Kyng to have the execucion of the moyte thereof and he that sueth the other moyte, and that in such accion of dette the defendaunt have non essoyne nor proteccion for hym alowed, and be not admytted to wage his Lawe.

---

[35] Candlemas, 2 February
[36] 3 shillings 4 pence
[37] 60 shillings

## 15. An Act that the subjects of this realm shall have bowes and other armour. (1495)

*One of Henry VII's most far-reaching policy decision was to limit the power of the nobles. After 35 years of bloody and disruptive civil war Henry recognised that the existence of private armies controlled by powerful nobles had enabled factionalism to flourish. However, the nobles had also been the source of soldiers for both the defence of the realm and overseas campaigns against foreign enemies, and the dismantling of the traditional retinue system meant that an alternative method of training, equipping, and recruiting soldiers was required, and Henry sought to strengthen the militia system which had been in place since the Assize of Arms of 1182 but rarely used in the fourteenth and fifteenth centuries. In England the success of the militia system relied on the revival of the Statute of Winchester,[38] but that statute had not been applied in Ireland where the English and Anglo-Irish nobility were instrumental in managing and policing the Irish population. A new, Irish, equivalent to the Statute of Winchester was therefore required.*

### 10 Henry 7. c.9 (Ireland)

Item prayen the commons, that in consideration that the subjects of Ireland have none English bowes and arrowes for the resistence of the malice of their enemies and rebels, like as they have had in times passed; by reason whereof they be not so able to defend them from destruction, as they were at other seasons heretofore: therefore it be odeyned, enacted, and established by authority of this present Parliament, That every subject having goods and cattels to the value of x li[39]. have an English bow and a sheaf of arrowes according; every subject having doos to the value of xx li.[40] have a jack, salett,[41] an English bow and a sheafe of arrows; every freeholder, having land to the value yearly of four pounds, have his horse, jack sallet, bow and sheaf of arrowes; every lord, knight, and esquire,

---

[38] See **Doc. 1**
[39] £10
[40] £20
[41] 'Sallet' in this context is unlikely to refer to a specific type of helmet, but is used in a more general sense to mean 'helmet.'

within the said land have for every yeoman daily in their household, jack salett, bow, and arrowes, to the intent that all the commons of the said land may be able to doe the King or his lieutenant service for their owne defence and surety.

II. And by the same authority it be ordeyned, That if the foresaid persons, or any of them, doe not observe and perform the premisses as it is before specified, that then they and every of them doe forfeit to the King vi s. viii d.[42] as often times as they and every of them shall offend the foresaid ordinance.

III. And by the same authority if be ordeyned, That there be henceforward in every barony within every shire of the said land two wardens of peace, having authority as it hath bin used of old time, and in every parish constables of able persons inhabitants within the said parished, and a payre of butts to be had within every of the foresaid parishes, at the cost of the said parishioners, that the commons of the said land may the sooner attain the practise and experience of archers; and that the foresaid constables in every parish, upon pain of forfeiture of xii d.[43] at every default, doe call before them or one of them every holy day all and every of the foresaid persons, having bowes and arrowes, as afore is rehearsed, to shoot, and cause them to shoot, at the least, two or three games at the said butts.

IV. And by the same authority it be ordeyned, that is any of the said persons make default any haly day, without a reasonable cause shewed, that then the said constables have full power and authority to record their defaults, and amerce them and every of them at every such default in iiii d.[44] and the saide constables to present the said amerciaments in writing to the barons of the Kings Exchequer in the said land, to be levied and perceived in like manner and forme as the Kings revenues been levied there.

---

[42] 6 shillings 8 pence
[43] 12 pence
[44] 4 pence

## 16. The custom of bows pardoned for a time (1503)

*Yet again the price of bows was seen as a problem in need of a solution in 1503. The most interesting point in this statute is the specification that customs duties would be waived only on bowstaves 6' 6" or longer. This might imply that some foreign merchants were fulfilling their legal requirement by bringing bowstaves to England, but doing so with staves too short to be of use. It certainly tells us that 6' 6" was considered to be the shortest useful length of stave for making bows.*

### 19 Henry 7. c.2

To the Kyng our Soveraigne Lorde;

Pleas it your Highnesse for as moche as by longe tyme paste fewe sufficient Bowestaffes have ben brought into the your Realme, for skarcenesse wherof aswell the Artilery of the same is almoste decayed as the facultie of Bowyers almoste distroyed, notwithstanding many good statutes herebefore made for bringyng of Bowestaffes in to this your Realme, that to geve corage to Marchaunts to bryng into this your Realme in tyme commying good bowestaffes, more plentiously to thencrece[45] of Archers & of the Artilery of the same then they have been accustomed to bryng in tymes paste, that it maye please your seid Highnesses of your moste speciall & habundaunt Grace by thadvyse[46] and assent of your Lordes Spirituell & temporell & all of the Comens in this present parlement assembled and by auctoritie of the same, that it may be ordined enacted & establisshed, that no Custome be payd after the makyng of this Acte for eny sufficient Bowestaffe or Bowestaffes conteynyng the length of syx fote & a halfe or above, that shalbe brought into this your realme by any merchaunte straunger or other betwene this & the nexte parlement; but that all maner merchaunts for bryngyng into this your realme of eny sufficiaunt Bowestaffes of the length of syx fote & a halfe or above be discharged of all Customs for the same Bowestaffes duryng the seid tyme.

---

[45] The increase
[46] The advice

## 17. An Act concerning shooting in Long Bowes (1511)

Henry VIII was a keen archer himself, renowned for his skill with the bow. His predilection for glorious military campaigns against France meant that he needed, more than his father had done, an efficient functioning militia system that could provide him with adequate troops both for foreign campaigns and defence of the realm against French or Scottish enemies. The statutes of his reign were consequently the most detailed and far-reaching of all the statutes relating to archery. On the whole they followed the same patterns as earlier statutes: restricting gaming, mandating ownership of bows and regular practice, limiting the price of bows etc.

Among the new legislative innovations that were introduced were further measures to ensure a supply of affordable bows throughout the country. Bowyers now had to make two cheaper 'mean wood' bows for every yew bow they produced, and Justices of the Peace had the power to appoint bowyers in provincial towns to make mean wood bows. The crown continued to purchase large numbers of yew bows which were issued to ships and castles, as well as stored in royal arsenals, but among the militias who defended the country against invasion and insurrection the majority of bows were probably made of elm, ash, hazel, and other woods. The 1511 act also extended the Irish requirement for towns to build butts into England for the first time.

### 3 Henry 8. c.3

The Kyng our sovereign Lord callyng to his most noble and gracious remembraunce that by the feate and exercise of the Subgiettes of this his Realme in shotyng in long bowes that hath contynually growen and ben within the same grete nombre and multitude of good Archers which hath not oonly defended this Realme and the Subgiettes therof ayenst the cruell malice and daunger of theire owte ward enmys in tyme heretofore passed, but also with litell nombre and puyssaunce in regarde have done many notable actes and discomfetures of warre ayenst the infidelis and other. And furthermore subdued and reduced dyverse and many regyons and Countrees to theire due obeysaunce to the grete honour fame and suertie of this Realme and Subjects and to the terrible drede and fere ot all straunge nacions any thyng to attempte or do to the hurte or damage of theym or any of them; and albeit that diverse gode and profitable statutes in the tyme of his noble progenitours and predecessours kynges of this land for the mayntenaunce of Archery and longbowes heretofore have ben made, amongest wich the right famose Kyng of noble memory Henry the vij[th] Father to our said Sovereign Lord by auctoritie of diverse parliamentis caused good and notable actis and statutes to be establisshed and made, And that shotyng in Crossebowes sholde be set on parte and not used and also that grete nomber of Bowstaves of Ewe shuld be brought and conveied by Marchaunts reparyng into this Realme from those parties where these grow uppon cereyne paynes in the same statutes lymyted and conteyned; yet never the lesse Archerie and shotyng in longbowes is right litell used by dayly mynessheth decayth and abateth more and more for that much partey of the commialte and parell of the Realme wherby of old tyme the grete nombre and substaunce of Archers hath growen and multiplied, be not of power nor abilite to bye theym longbowes of ewe to excersise shotyng in the same, and to susteyne the contynuall charge therof; And also by meanes and occasion of custumable usaige of Teynes Play Bowles Classhe and other unlawfull games prohibett many good and beneficiall estatutes by auctorite of parliament in that behalf provided and made grete impoverisshement hath ensued; And many heynous Murdurs Roberes and Felonnes be committed and done, And also the devyne by such missedoers on holy and festivall dayes not herd or solempnised to the high displeasure of Almyghty God; Wherefor the Kings Highnes of his most blessed disposicion greate wisdome and providence And also for zele to the Publique weale suertie and defence of this his Realme and Subgiettis and the auncient fame in this behalf to be revived and repared by the assent of his Lords spirituell and temperall and his Comons in thys present parliament assembled and by auctoritie of the same hath ordeyned enacted and establisshed that the Statute of Wynchester for archers to be putt in due execucion. And over that every man beyng the Kyngs subgiett not lame decrepute or maymed nor havyng any other lawfull or resonable cause of impediment beyng withyn the Age of lx. yeres, except to tho men, spirituall men, Justice of the one benche and of the other Justices of Assise and Barons of the Escequere, do use and exercyse shotying in longbowes, and also to have a bowe and arrowes redy contynually in his house to use hymself and do use hymself in shotyng; And also that the father governours and rulers of such as be of tendre age do teche and bring upp theum in the knowledge of the same shotyng; And that every man havyng a man child or men children in his house shall provide ordeyne and have in his house for every man childe beyng of the aige of vij yeres and above tyll he shall comme to the age of vxij yeres a bowe and ij shafts to enduse and lern theym and bryng them upp in shotyng and shall delyver all the same bowe and arrowes to the same yongman to use and occupie: And yf the same yongmen be servaunts that then theyre Masters shall abate the money that they shall paye for the same bowes and arrowes of theyre wagis: And after all suche yongmen shall comme to the age of xvij yeres every of theym shall provyde and have a bowe and iiij arrowes contynually for hymself at his propre costis and charges, or ells of the gyft ot provision of his frends and use and occupie the same in shotyng as is afore rehersed. And that the Justices of Assise of Gayle delyverey Justices of Peas and Stuardes of Fraunceses Lets and Laudays have power to enquire of all the premisses in theire Sessions Lets and Lawe days and here and determyne the same; And also by their discrecions examen all personnes lakkyng and not havyng bowes shaftes and arrowes accordyng to the fourme afore rehersed, And every persone that shalbe founden by such inquire or examynacion in defaute or nott providyng and havyng bowes arowes and shaftes redy by the space of one moneth shall forfett and paye for every such defate xij d.[47] And where and such forfeyture shall happen to be founden within the precynt of eny Fraunches Lete or Lawday then the Lord of the same Fraunches Lete or Lawday shall have the forfeiture therof, And in all other places all such forfeitures to be the Kynges soveriegn Lords his heires and successours; And that all Statutes heretofore made ayanest them that use unlaufull games be duely putt in execucion and punysshement had accordyng to the penalties of the same aswell ayenst the offenders and occupiers of such unlaufull games as agaynst them that be owners or kepers of houses or other such placis whare any such unlaufull games be used accordyng to the perport tenore and intent of the

---

[47] 12 pence

same statutes; And furthermore that all Justices of the Pece Mairs Baillifes Shreffes Constables and all other hed officers and every of theym fyndyng or knowyng and maner of person or persones usyng or exercisyng any unlawfull games contary to the said estatute have full power and auctorite to commytt every such offencer to ward ther to remayne without bail or mayne prise to suche tyme he or they so offendyng be bounden by obligacion to the kynges use in suche summe of money as by the discrecion of the said Jusctices Maires Bailliffes or other hedofficers shalbe thought reasonable that they nor eny of them shall not from thens forth use any unlawfull games, And that every Bower within this Realme alwey make for every oon bowe of ewe that he maketh to sell at the lest ij Bowes of Elme, Wiche[48] or other Wode of mean price; And if they or eny of theym refuse soo to doo, and it founden byfore the Justices of pese in the Shire or Maires Bailliffes or other Hedofficers of Cities or Borowes within theire Cities or Borowes by presentment of xij men or by due examinacion byfore the said Justice of Pease or ij of theym or byfore the said Maires or Bailliffes that then the same Justices Maires or Bailliffes have full actoritie and power to committ theym to warde there to remayn without baile or maymeprice by the space of viij days or more by the discrecion of the said Justices Maires or Bailliffes. And also that Buttes be made in every Citie Towne and Place accordyng to the lawe of aunciant tyme used; And that the inhabitaunts and dweller in every of theym be compelled to make and conynewe such buttes and to exercise theymself with long Bowes in shotyng at the same and else where in Holidays and other tymes convenient. And over that it is enacted by the said auctoritie that every Justice of Peace within this Realme or ij of theym within theire severall Jurisdiccion have full power and auctoritie to take assigne and appoynt Bowers in iij, ij or moo places by their discrecion withyn every Shire Citie or Borowe where the most comen repare and resort is of his subgiettes and there to inhabite and make long bowes of Elme Wiche or other Wood of lytell price and value to save the commynaltie for the due exercise of shotyng; And to take and compell as meany of theym as they shall thynke necessarie by their discrecions to inhabit at suche place for the same, and

---

[48] Presumably wychelm, *Ulmus glambra*

so in like wise as often as the case shall require and thought behovefull; And that all Bowstaves of Ewe herafter to be brought into this Realme to be sold by open and not solde in bundelled nor clos to thentent[49] the byers of theym may have perfite knowledge of the goodnes of them and geve the better price for them if they be so worth. And be it also enacted by the auctoritie aforsaid that all Maires Bailiffes Shreffes and all other Hedofficers shall make open proclamacion of these presentes in every market and feire to be holden within their severall Jurisdiccions and Auctorities. And also that the Justice of gaole delyverie Assises and Justices of Peace doo cause the same to be proclaymed in theire severall cercuittes and cessions before theym to be holden. This Acte concernyng the makyng of Bowes of elme wiche or other then of Ewe to begyn to take effect at the fest of Lammas[50] next commyng, And the residue of all this acte to take effecte and put in execucion immediatly and to endure to the next parliament. Item that no Straunger borne out of the Kynges obeysans not being denyson shall not conveye no do to be conveied into any parties out of the Kynges obeissaunce and Longboews Arrowes or Shaftes without the Kynges speciall licence uppon payne of forfeture of the same wher soever thei shalbe takyn withyn this the Kynges power and uppon payn of enprisonament without baile or mayneprise unto suche tyme he or they so beyng in ward have made a resonable fyne to the Kyng for his or theire offences afore the Justices of peas of ij of theym in theyre Sessions in the same Countie where he or they shalbe committed to warde or fynd sufficient suertie for the payment of the same fyne. Item that no maner persone not beyng borne withyn the Kynges obeisaunce not made denyson use withyn the Kyngs obeisaunce shotyng with Longbowes without the Kynges licence upon payn of forfeture such bowed arrowes and shaftes as they shalbe fonden so shotyng with and every of the Kynges subjectes may have auctoritie to take and sease the same forfaitures to his own use.

---

[49] The intent
[50] 1 August

## 18. Acte for Maytenance of Archers. (1514)

*This act is, to all intents and purposes, the same as the act of 1511. Its importance lies not in the content but in the fact that it was passed in 1514. In 1511 England joined the Holy League in alliance with Spain and the Holy Roman Empire against France and Scotland, and in 1513 Henry VIII himself led an expedition to France. The expedition captured the towns of Therouanne and Tournai, and defeated a French army at the Battle of the Spurs, but none of these achievements were particularly glorious and Henry failed in his great ambition to emulate his forbear and namesake, Henry V. Meanwhile, a Scottish army crossed the border into England at the request of their French allies and was defeated at Flodden Field by a scratch army hastily assembled by the aged Earl of Surrey and his sons under the auspices of the queen, Katherine of Aragon, who had been appointed Regent while Henry was fighting in France.*

*Archers were present both in France and at Flodden, but had not made any significant contribution to the overall victories in either place. The effects of nearly thirty years of peace on the quality of English archery was thrown into stark relief, but Henry had new possessions in France which had been captured and needed defending, as well as an agreement with the Emperor to continue the war against France. It was essential to Henry that English archery should not be allowed to slip further into decay.*

### 6 Henry 8. c.2

Prayn the Comons in thys present parliament assemblyd that where in the parliament holden att Westmynster the fourth day of Februarj the iij$^d$ yere of the reygne of oure Soveraigne Lord the Kyng that now ys our seid Soveraigne Lord than callyng to hys most noble & gracyous remembraunce that by the fete & exercyse of the subjettys of thys hys Realme in shotyng in long bowes ther hath contynually growen & bene wythin the same grete noumber & multytude of good Archars whych hath not only defendyd this realme & the subjectys thereof agaynst the cruell malyce and daunger of their outward enmyes in tyme heretofore passed, but also wyth lytell noumbre and puyssaunce in regard have done many noble actys & dyscomfytures of Warre agaynst the infydeles & other, And furthermore subdued and reducyd dyvers & many regyons & countrees to their due obeysaunce, to the grete honour fame & surety of thys Realme & subjectys & to the terryble drede & fere of all straunge nacyons any thyng to attempt or doo to the hurt or damage of them or ony of them: And albe ytt that dyverse good & profytabull Statutys in the tyme of hys noble progenytours & predecessours Kyngs of thys land for the mayntenance of Archery & long bowes heretofore have bene made; amongest whyche the ryght famous Kyng of noble memorye Henry the vij[th] fader to our seyd Sovaygne Lorde by the auctoryte of dyverse parliaments causyd good & noble actys & statutys to be establysshed and made, & that shotyng in Crossebous shuld be sett on parte & nott used; And also that grete noumbre of bowestaves of Ewe shuld be brought & conveyed by marchauntes reparyng into thys realme from thos partyes where they growe uppon certen paynes in the same statute lymytted & conteyned: yet neverthelesse Archery and shotyng in long bowes ys right lytell used butt dayly mynysshyth & decayth & abateth more & more, for that moche party of the Comonalte & poore people of the Realme, wherby of oold tyme the grett nombre & substaunce of Archers hath growen & multyplyed, be not of power nor abilite to by them long bowes of Ewe to exercyse Shotynge in the same and to susteyne the contynuall charge therof; and also by meanes and occasyon of custumable usage of tenys playe bowles closshe & other unlaufull games prohybet by many good & benefycyall estatutys by auctoryte of parliament in that behalf provyded & made; grette Impoverysshment hath ensued and many heynous murderes robies & felonys be comytted and done, And also the devyne Servyce by suche mysdoers on holy & festivall dayes nott herd or solemnysed to the hygh dyspleasure of Almyghty God: Wherfore the Kynges Hyghnes of hys most blessyd dysposicyon greate Wysedome & provydence and also zele to the publyke wele suertye & defence of this hys realme & subjecte & their auncyent fame in this behalf to be revyved & repared; by the assent of hys lordes spyrytuall & temporall and hys Commons in this seyd parliament assembled & by the auctorite of the same had ordenyd enactyd & establysshed that the Stateute of Wynchestre for Archers to be putt in due execucion. And over that that every man beyng the Kynges Subjecte nott lame decrepitt nor maymed, nor havyng ony other laufull or resonable cause or impediment beyng wythin the age of lx yeres, except men spirituall Justices of the oon benche and of the other, Justyces of Assyce & barones of the Eschequer, shuld use & exercyse shotyng in long bowes: And also to have a bowe and arrowes redy contynually in hys house to use hym selfe and doo use hym selfe in shoting And also the father governours & rewlers of suche as be of tender age doo teche and bryng up; them in the knoolege of the same shotyng; And that every Man havyng a Man chyld or men chyldern in hys house shall provyde ordeigne & have in hys house for every man chyld beyng of the age of vij yerys and above, tyll he come to the Age of xvij yeres, a bowe & ij shaftys to enduse and lerne them & bryng them uppe in shotyng ; and shall delyver all the same bowe & arowes to the same yongman to use & occupye; And yf the same yong men be servauntes that then theyr Masters shall abate the Mony that they shall paye for the same bowes & arowes of their Wages; And after all suche yong men shall comme to the Age of xvij yerys every of them shall provyde and have a bowe & iiij arowes contynually for hym selfe, at hys proper costes & chargys, or elles of the gyfte or provisyon of his frendys, & use & occupye the same in shotyng as ys afore rehersyd. And that the Justyces of Assyses of gaole delyvery Justyces of Peas and Stewardys of Fraunchyses letys & lawe dayes have power to inquere of all the premysses in their Sessyons letes and lawe dayes and here & detmyne the same; And also by theyr dyscrecyons examyne all persons lakkyng & nott havyng bowes shaftys & arowes accordyng to the fourme afore seyd, And every person that shall be founde by suche inquere or examinacion in defaut & nott provydyng & havyng bowes arowes & shaftys redy by the space of oon moneth shall forfayte & paye for every suche defaut xijd.[51] And where any such forfayture shall happen to be founden wythyn the precynte of any Fraunchyse lete or lawe daye then the Lord of the Fraunchyse lete & lawe day shall have the forfayture therof; and in all other placys all suche forfaytures to be the Kyng our Soveraygn Lorde hys heyres & successours. And that all Statutes heretofore made agenst them that use unlaufull games be duely putt in execucion, & punysshment had accordyng to the penaltes of the same, aswell agenst the offenders & occupyers of suche unlaufull games as agaynst them that be owners or Kepers of houses

---

[51] 12 pence

or other placys where ony suche unlaufull games be used accordyng to the purport tenour & intent of the same statutys. And furthermore that all Justices of the peas Mayers baylyffes shreffs constables & all other hed Offycers & every of them fyndyng or knowyng ony maner person or persons usyng or exersysyng any unlaufull games contary to the seyd estatutys, have full power & auctoryte to comytt every suche offender to Warde, there to remayne wythout bayle or maympryse to such tyme he or they so offendyng be bound by obligacyon to the Kyngys use in suche some of Mony as by dyscrecyon of the seyd Justices Mayres baylyffes or other hed offycers shalbe thought resonable that they nor any of them shall nott from hens forth use any unlaufull games. And that every Bower wythin thys realme alway make for every oon bowe of Ewe that he makyth to selle att the leest ij bowes of Elme Wyche or other woode of meane pryce: And yf they or any of them refuse so to do & ytt founden before the Justyces of peas in the Shyre or Mayres bayles or other hed offycers of Cytees or boroughes by presentment of xij men or by due examinacyon before the seyd Justyces of peas or ij of them, or before the seyd Mayres or baylyffe, that then the same Justices Mayers or baylyffe have full auctoryte & power to comytte them to Warde there to remayne wythout bayle or maympryse by the space of viij dayes or more by the discrecion of the seyd Mayres & baylyffe. And also that Buttys be made in every Cyte Townes & places accordyng to the lawe of auncyent tyme usyd. And that the Inhabytantes & dwellers in every of them be compelled to make & contynewe suche buttes & to exercyse them selfe wyth long bowes in shotyng att the same & elleswhere on holy dayes & other tymes convenyent. And over that ytt ys enactyd by the seyd auctoryte that every Justyces of Peas wythyn thys reame or ij of them wythyn theyr severall Jurisdicions have full power & auctoryte to take assigne & appoynt Bowers in iij ij or more places by their dyscrecion, wythin every Shyre Cytye or borowes where the most comon repayre & resort ys of hys Subjette, & therto inhabite & make longe bowes of Elme whyche or other wode of lytell pryce & value to serve the comynalte for the due exercyse of shotyng; And to take & compell as many of them as they shall thynk necessarye by theyr dyscrecyons to inhabyte at suche places for the same; And so in lyke wyse as often as the Case shall requyre & thought behovefull. And that all bowestaves of Ewe hereafter to be brought in to thys realme to be sold be open & nott sold in bundelles nor close, to thentent[52] the byers of them may have perfyte knowlege of the goodnesse of them and gyve the better pryce for them if they be so worth. And be ytt also enactyd by the auctorite aforeseyd that all Mayers bayles Shreffys & all oder hed officers schall make open proclamacion of thes Presente in every markett & feyre to be holden wythin theyre sewall Jurysdyccions & auctorytes; And also that the Justices of the Gaole delyvere Assyces & Justices of Peas do cause the same to be proclaymyd in their severall circuytes & cessyons before them holden. And also that no Straunger borne out of the Kynges Obeysaunce not beyng denysen shall nott convey nor do to be conveyed in to any parties out of the Kynge obeysaunce any long bowes arowes or shaftys wythout the Kyngye specyall lycence, uppon payne of forfayture of the same, where so ever they shall be takyn wythin thys the Kynge power, & uppon payn of imprisonament without bayle or maympryse unto suche tyme he or they so beyng in Ward have made a resonable fyne to the Kyng for this or their offences afore the Justice of Peace or ij of hem in theyr Sessyons in the same Countie where he or they shalbe comytted to Warde to fynde suffycyent suertye for the payment of the same fyne. Item that no maner person nott beyng borne wythin the Kynge obeysaunce, nat made denysen, use wythyn the Kynges obeysaunce shotyng wyth long bowes wythout the Kynges lycence uppon payn of forfayture suche bowes arowes & shaftes as they shalbe founden soe shotyng wyth; And every of the Kynges Subjectes may have auctorite to take & sease the same forfaytures to hys owne use; as in the sayde Acte more playnly apperyth: whyche acte was made to endure to thys Present parliament. And for asmoche as the seyd acte ys good & necessary for uppholdyng of Archery for the defence of this realme be ytt therfore ordeynyd establysshed & enacted by the Kyng our Soveraygne Lord & the Lordys spirituall & temporall and the Commons in this present pliament assembled & by auctoryte of the same that the seyd acte & every thyng therin conteynyd as ys afore rehersyd shall from hensforth stand & be in full strenght vertue & effecte for ever more.

---

[52] The intent

## 19. Acts concernyng the brynging in of Bowestaves in to this Realme. (1514)

*As in 1483, legislation relating to the ownership of bows required provisions to ensure a supply of bow staves.* **12 Ed.4 c.2** *and* **1 Ric.3 c.11** *had been effective provided they were implemented, but the stipulation that they applied only to foreign merchants had somehow become overlooked. The issue may have arisen from the sometimes ambiguous nature of overseas trade in the late fifteenth- and early sixteenth-centuries before the registration of ships became formalised. If an English ship carried goods on behalf of an Italian or Flemish merchant, as many did, should it count as English or foreign for the purposes of the legislation?*

### 6 Henry 8. c.11

Where by acte of parliament holden at Westminster the xxiii$^{th}$ daie of Octobr in the iij$^{de}$ yere of the reigne of King Richard the iij$^{de}$ in dede and not in right King of Englond, it was enactid[53] that noo merchaunt of Venyce nor other wont to resorte in to this Realme with merchandises of those parties bring in to this said Realme any merchaundises, but if the same merchaunt bring with every butte of Malmesey, and with every butte of Tire, x bowstaves of good and hable stuffe under payne of forfaiture of xijs. iiijd.[54] for every butte of the forsaid Wynes so brought and not the nombre of the said bowstaves with the said butte; the one half therof to the King and the oder half thereof to the partie that for the same woll sue, as by the said Acte and ordenaunce more playnely apperith: Thentent[55] of which Acte and estatute and the myndes of the Makers thereof was that the said estatute shuld not extend to any of the Kinges Subjectes borne within this his Realme of England Wales or Irlond but only unto merchauntes of Venyce and other merchauntes estraungers wount to resorte in to this Realme with merchaundises of those parties; And this notwithstonding dyverse the Kinges Subjectes borne within this his Realme of Englond of late have bene inquieted vexid and troubled in the Kinges Eschequier for

---
[53] See **Doc. 13**. In fact the act in question was passed in the first year of Richard III's reign, not the third as stated.
[54] 12 shillings 4 pence
[55] The intent

bringing of Malmeseys into this Realme withoute bowstaves contrie to the true entent of the said acte and estatute, Wherfore be it enactid ordeyned judged and declared by the King oure Soveraigne Lord the Lordes spirituall and temperall and the Comons in this present parliament assembled and by thauctorite[56] of the same, that the said Acte made in the said iij$^{de}$ yere of the said late King Richard extend not to any of the Kinges Subjectes borne within this his Realme Wales or Irlond, but that they and every of theym be forprised oute of the said Acte for any penaltye to be levyed in any wise upon theym or any of their executours or Admynystratours, but that they and every of theym be discharged by thauctoritie of this parliament of almaner[57] of accions sutes billes of complayntes taken sued or to be taken and sued in the Kinges Eschequier or any other of his Courtes or any other Courte or Courtes place or places for any penaltie or Summes of Money comprised in the said Acte or for or concernyng any thyng specified in the said Acte. This Acte to endure to the next parliament.

---

[56] The authority
[57] All manner

## 20. An Acte concerninge Crosbowes and Handguns. (1541)

*The first law limiting the use of crossbows was passed in the reign of Henry VII in 1503 (19 Hen.7 c.4), and further laws expanding and restating the limitations were passed in 1511 and 1514. In 1523 a new act was passed placing limitations on who could legally own and use a crossbow and, for the first time, the same restrictions were also applied to handguns.*

*From the point of view of the crown and parliament there were two major issues with crossbows, and later handguns. First, it was thought that men who shot crossbows and guns would be less likely to own and practice with bows. Later, as we shall see, debate raged over the relative merits of bows and guns as weapons of war,[58] but there was no doubt in the sixteenth century that English bows were superior weapons to crossbows. More importantly, crossbows and guns required far less practice than bows, so although crossbows had their place, such as in the defence of fortifications, there was little to be gained by men shooting them for leisure. Secondly, crossbows and guns were better weapons for poachers, highway robbers, tavern brawlers, assassins and other sorts of rogues, and as such were not to be encouraged into the hands of the baser sort of person. Gentlemen and landowners were more trustworthy and less likely to serve as archers in a military context, so cold be trusted to use crossbows and guns. The common sort definitely could not.*

*None of the acts concerning crossbows contribute to our knowledge or understanding of archery, so the first four have not been included in this volume. However, as the issue of crossbow and gun ownership is tangentially linked to the decline of archery the fifth and fullest of them is printed here.*

### 33 Henry 8. c.6

Where in the Parliament holden at Westminster the fyftenthe daye of Januarie in the twenty fyve Yere of the Kinges most gracious Raigne, and there contynued and kepte untill the thirtieth daye of Marche then next ensuynge, amonge diverse and sondrie holsome and lawdable Acte Statute and ordynances one Statute and Ordynance was made and ordeyned for

---

[58] See **Docs 49-51**

the avoydinge and eschewinge of shotinge in Crosbowes and Handguns; synce the makinge of whiche Acte diverse malicious and evill disposed persons not only presumynge wilfullye and obstynatlye the violacion and breach of the saide Acte, but also of their malicious and evill disposed myndes and purposes have wilfully and shamefully comytted perpetrated and done diverse detestable and shamefull murthers roberies felonyes ryottes and routes with Crosbowes little shorte handguns and little hagbuttes, to the great perill and contynuall feare and daunger of the Kinges most lovinge subjectes and also diverse Kepers of Forestes Chases and Parke aswell of our saide Soveragne Lorde as other his Nobles and Commons and diverse Gentlemen Yomen and Servingmen nowe of late have layde aparte the good and laudable excise of the longe bowe, whiche alwaye heretofore hathe bene the suertie savegarde and contynuall defence of this Realme of Englande, and an inestimable dread and terror to the Enemyes of the same, and nowe of late the saide evill disposed persons have used and yet doe daylie use to ryde and goe in the Kinges highe Wayes and elswhere, havinge with them Crosbowes and little handguns, ready furnished with Quarrelle Gunpowder fyer & touche to the great perill and feare of the Kinges most lovinge Subjectes : For Reformacion wherof be it enacted ordeyned and established by the Kinge our Soveraigne Lorde the Lordes spirituall and temporall and the Commons in this present Parliament assembled and by thauctoritie[59] of the same, in maner and fourme followinge That ys to saye; that noe person or persons of what estate or degree he or they be, excepte he or they in their owne right or in the right of his or their Wyeffe to his or their owne uses or any other to the use of any suche person or persons, have landes tenementes fees annuyties or Offices to the yerely value of one hundred poundes, from or after the laste daye of June next comynge, shall shote in any Crosbowe handgun hagbutt or demy hake, or use or kepe in his or their houses or elswhere any Crosbowe handgun hagbut or demy hake, otherwise or in any other manner then ys hereafter in this present Acte declared, uppon payne to forfeyt for everie tyme that he or they so offendinge contrie to this Acte tenne poundes.

---

[59] The authority

AND furthermore be it enacted by thauctoritie aforesaide that no person or persons, of what estate or degree soever he or they be, from or after the saide laste daye of June shall shote in carye kepe use or have in his house or els where any handgune other then suche as shalbe in the stock and gonne of the lenghe of one hole Yarde, or any hagbutt or demyhake other then suche as shalbe in the stock and gune of the lenghe of thre quarters of one Yarde, uppon payne to forfeyt for everie tyme that he or they shall carie use or have anye suche Gun being not of the lenghe of one whole Yarde or hagbutt or demyhake beinge not of the lenghe of thre quarters of a Yarde, Tenne poundes sterlinge. And that it shalbe laufull to everie person and persons, which have landes tenementes fees annuyties or offices to the yerelye value of one hundred poundes as ys aforesaide, to seise and take everie suche Crosbowe, and also everie handgun beinge in stock and gune shorter in lenghe then one whole Yarde and everie hagbutt and demyhake beinge shorter in lenghe then thre quarters of a Yarde, or any of them; from the Kepinge or possession of everie suche Offendor contarie to the forme of this Acte, and the same Crosbowe or Crosbowes to kepe and reteyne to his or their owne use, and also the same handguns hagbutte and demyhakes so seised and taken within twenty dayes next after the same seisure or takinge to breake and distroye, upon peyne of fourtye Shillinges for everie Gune so seised and not broken and destroyed, and the same so broken and destroyed to kepe & reteyne to his or their owne use.

AND be it further enacted by thauctoritie aforesaide, that noe person or persons, other then suche as have lande tenementes rentes fees annuyties or Offices to the yerely value of one hundred Poundes as ys aforesaide, from or after the saide laste daye of June, shall carrie or have, in his or their Jorney goinge or ridinge in the Kinges highe waye or elswhere, any Crosbowe bent or Gune charged or furnished withe Powder fier or touche for the same, Except it be in tyme and Service of Warre, upon payne to forfeyt for everie suche Offence tenne poundes; this present Acte or any thinge therin conteyned to the contarie notwithstandinge.

AND be it further enacted by thauctoritie aforesaide, that no person or persons from the saide laste daye of June shall in anywise shote in or withe anye handgune demyhake or hagbutt at any thinge at lardge, within any Cittie Boroughe or Markett Towne or within one quarter of a myle of anny Cittie Boroughe or Markett Towne, excepte it be at a Butt or Banck of earth in place convenient, or for the defence of his person or house, upon payne to forfeyte for everie suche Shott tenne poundes; this present Acte or anny thinge therin conteyned to the contrarie notwithstandinge.

AND be it further enacted by thauctoritie aforesaide, that noe person or persons of what estate or degre soever he or they be, shall from or after the saide laste daye of June comaunde any of his or their servaunte to shote in any Crosbowe handgune hagbutt or demyhake of his or their saide Masters or of any other persons, at any deare fowle or other thinge excepte it be only at a butt or bank of Earth or in the tyme of Warre as ys abovesaide, upon payne to forfeyt for everie suche offence tenne poundes : The one moytie of all which forfeytures and penalties in this present Acte above specified shalbe to the Kinge our Soveraigne Lorde his heires and Successors, and thother moytie thereof to the partie that will sue for the same by bill playnt accion of Debte or Informacion in anny of the Kinges Courtes of Recorde in whiche suyte noe Essoyne proteccion nor Wager of lawe shalbe allowed.

Provided alwaye and be it enacted by thauctoritie aforesaide, that it shalbe laufull from henceforthe to all Gentlemen Yeomen and Servingemen of everie Lorde or Lordes spirituall or temporall and of all Knightes Esquiers and Gentlemen, and to all the Inhabitauntes of Citties Boroughes and Markett Townes of this Realme of Englande, to shote withe any handgune Demyhake or hagbutt at anye butt or bank of Earth onlye in place convenient for the same, so that everie suche handgune Demyhake or hagbutt be of the severall lenghes aforesaide and not under; and that it shalbe laufull to everie of the saide Lorde and Lordes Knightes Esquiers and Gentlemen, and the Inhabitauntes of everie Cittie Boroughe and Markett Towne, to have and kepe in everie of their houses any suche handgune or handgunes of the lenghe of one whole Yarde, or any hagbutt or Demyhake of the lenghe of thre quarters of a Yarde as ys aforesaide and not under, to thintent to use and shote in the same at a butt or banke of Earthe onlye, as ys abovesaid, wherbye they and everie of them by thexercise[60] thereof in forme abovesaid may the better ayde and assist to the defence of this Realme when nede shall requyre; this present Acte or any thinge therein conteyned to the contrie notwithstandinge.

AND be it further enacted by thauctoritie aforesaide, that it shalbe laufull to everie person and persons whiche dwelleth and inhabiteth in anye house standinge and being sett distant twoo furlonges from any Cittie Boroughe or Towne, to kepe and have in his saide house for the onelye defence of the same handgunes hagbuttes and demyhakes beinge of the severall lenghes aforesaide and not under, & to use and exercise to shote in the same at any butt or bancke of earthe nere to his house and not otherwise; Any thinge conteyned in this Acte to the contrie notwithstandinge.

AND furthermore the Kinges most lovinge Subjectes the Lordes spirituall and temporall and the Commons in this present Parliament assembled, most humblye doe beseche the Kinges Majestie that it be further enacted by thauctoritie aforesaide, that all lettres patentes Fraternyties, and also all other placardes lycences and billes assigned heretofore had made or signed by his Highnes or by any other authorised by his Highnes lettres patentes under his Great Seale to give licence and placardes to shote in Crosbowes & handgunes or any of them, shalbe from and after the saide laste daye of June frustrate voyde and of none effecte.

And also that it may be further enacted by thauctoritie aforesaide that the saide Statute made in the saide xxv[th] Yere of the Kinges most gracious Raigne, and all other Statute heretofore made and pvided for thavoydinge[61] and restreynt in shotinge of Crosbowes and handguns or for any of them, or for the usinge and kepinge of the same, be from henceforth utterlie voyde and of none effecte: Provided alwayes that everie processe suyte or Informacion conceaved commenced and nowe dependinge for any Offence done contarie to the forme of the saide Statute made in the said xxv[th] Yere of the Kinges moste noble Raigne, or of

---

[60] The exercise
[61] The avoiding

any other Statute made or provyded for and concerninge the shotinge in Crosbowes and handguns, not repealed, and for the kepinge of the same, shalbe as good and effectuall to the parties that have comenced the same and shall stande and be in suche forme effecte and condicion as if this Acte had never bene made.

Provided also that this Acte or any thinge therin conteyned be not in any wise hurtfull or prejudiciall to any person or persons nowe beinge or that hereafter shalbe appoynted by the Kinges Highnes, to kepe receyve or take any Crosbowes or Handguns that shalbe forfeyted or taken within the precincte or libertye of the Kinges forrestes parkes or chaces, but that he or they may laufully kepe and reteyne the same Crosbowes or Handguns from tyme to tyme untill suche tyme as the further pleasure of the Kinges Highnes in that behalfe be to every suche person shewed & declared.

Provided also that this Acte extende not to the makers of Crosbowes or Handguns, but that they may laufully kepe Crosbowes and Handguns Hagbuttes and Demyhakes in their houses, and shott in the same onlye for provinge & assayinge of them at a butt or bank of earthe in the place convenient and not otherwise, so that the saide Handguns Hagbuttes & Demyhakes be of the severall lenghes in Stock and Gune as ys above lymitted.

Provided also that this Acte nor any thinge therin conteyned extende not or be prejudiciall to any Marchauntt whiche have or shall have any Crosbowes Handguns Hagbuttes and Demyhakes or any of them to sell within this Realme and to none other use, so that the same Handguns Hagbuttes and Demyhakes be of the severall lenghes in Gune and Stocke as ys above lymitted and not under.

Provided also that noe manner of parson rune in any daunger or take hurte by reason of any penaltye or forfeiture conteyned in this Acte untill suche tyme as proclamacion be made of the same Acte, within the Countye where the partie that shall or maye offende contrie to this Acte dwelleth, by the space of twentye dayes nexte after the makinge of the saide proclamacion.

Provided also that yf any manner of person bringe or cause to be brought withe him into his lodginge or in or to any other mans house any Crosbowe or Handgune, that then the penaltye and forfeyture, yf any suche be or hereafter shalbe forfeited by reason of this Acte, to rune and be onely upon the bringer of the saide Crosbowe and Handgune and not to the owner of the same lodginge or house, yf the saide howner of the said lodging or house cause the saide bringer thereof to take & carrie awaye the saide Crosbowe or Handgune agayne withe him at his departinge; anye thinge in this Acte made to the contarie notwithstandinge.

AND be it also enacted by thauctoritie of this present parliament that if any person or persons, from or after the laste daye of June next comynge, see or fynde any person or persons offendinge or doinge contrie to the forme and effecte of this Acte, that then it shalbe laufull to everie suche person or persons perceyvinge fyndinge or seinge anye suche person or persons so offendinge contarie to the fourme of this acte, to arrest and attache every suche offendor or offendors and to bringe or convey the same to the next Justice of Peace of the same Countye where the said offendor or offendors shalbe founde soe offendinge; And that the same Justice of Peace upon a due examinacion and proeff thereof before him had or made by his discrecion shall have full power and aucthoritie to sende or commytt the same offendor or offendors to the next Gaole, there to remayne till suche tyme as the saide penaltye or forfeyture shalbe trulye contented and paide by the saide offendor; the one moytie of the same penaltye to be paide to the Kinges Highnes and thother moytie thereof to the first bringer or conveyer of the saide offendor to the same Justice of Peace.

AND be it further enacted by thauctoritie aforesaide, that yf any person or persons doe at any tyme hereafter obteyne gett or purchase, of the Kinges Majestie his heires or successors, any placarde licence or bill assigned to shote in any Crosbowe Handgun Hagbutt or Demyhake contarie to the tenor purporte and effecte of this present acte, that then there shalbe conteyned in everie suche placarde licence and bill assigned, at what beaste fowles or other thinges the saide person or persons so obteyninge any suche placarde licence or bill assigned shall shote, withe any Crosbowe Handgune Hagbutt or Demyhake, or els that everie suche placarde licence and bill assigned hereafter to be obteyned gotten or purchased shalbe clerely voyde frustrate and of none effecte: And also that everie suche person or persons so obteyninge any suche placarde licence or bill assigned, before they shote in any suche Crosbowe Handgun Hagbutt or Demyhake, in any suche manner or forme as shalbe mencioned in any suche placarde licence or bill assigned, shalbe bounden in the Kinges Courte of Chauncerie by recognizaunce in the some of twenty poundes to the Kinges use withe and upon condicion that he so obteyninge or havinge the saide licence placarde or bill assigned, shall not shote in any Crosbowe Handgune Hagbutt or Demyhake at any other beaste or fowles then in any suche placarde licence or bill assigned shalbe conteyned and specified, and els all suche placardes licence and billes assigned so hereafter to be made to any person or persons not beinge so bounden by recognizaunce in the Courte of Chauncerie as is aforesaide, to be utterlie voide and of none effecte.

AND be it further enacted by thauctoritie aforesaide, that it shalbe laufull to all Justice of Peace in their sessions and to all Stewardes and Baylieffes in their sevall leete and lawe dayes to enquyre heare and determyne every suche offence after the saide laste daye of June to be comytted and done contrie to the tenor of this present Acte; So that alwayes noe lesse fyne then tenne poundes be assessed upon everie suche presentment and convicion made accordinge to the due course of the lawe; the same fyne so by the same Justice of Peace upon everie suche presentment and convicion made before them in their Sessions, to be payde and levyed onely to the Kinges use; and the one moytie of everie fyne to be assessed by the Stewardes or Baylyffes of any leete or lawe daye, upon everie presentment and convicion before them, to be payde and levyed to the use of the Kinge our Soveraigne Lorde, and of the other moytie the one halfe to the owner of the saide leete or lawe daye by distresse or accion of debte, and thother halfe of the same seconde moytie of the same fyne, to be to the partie that will pursue for the same in any of the Kinges Courte by bill playnte informacion or accion of debte, in the whiche none Essoyne proteccion nor wager of lawe shalbe allowed.

AND be it further enacted, that yf any Jurie beinge sworne and charged to enquyre for the Kinge our Soveraigne Lorde before anye Justice of the

Peace or Stewardes of leete or lawdayes, of any offence comytted or done contrie to this present Acte, doe wilfullie conceale any of the same offence, that then the saide Justice Stewardes or Bayliffes before whom any concealment shalbe had and done, shall have auctoritie by vertue of this present Acte from tyme to tyme to chardge and sweare an other Jurie of twelve or mo good and substantiall honest persons to enquire of everie suche concealment, and if any suche concealment be founde and presented by the saide Jurie so chardged to enquyre of the same, that then everie one of the saide fyrste Jurie that so did conceale the same, shall leese and forfeyt for everie suche concelement of every suche offence twenty shillinges; All whiche forfeytures and penaltyes of twentye shillinges for everie such concealment of everie suche offence so found and presented before the same Justice of Peace shall holye be levyed and payde to the Kinges use, and the moytie of all the same forfeytures and penaltyes of twenty shillinges, so founde and presented before the Stewardes or Bayliffes of any leete or lawdaye, shalbe levied and paide to the use of the owner of the saide leete or lawdaye by distresse or accion of debte, and thother moytie thereof to be to the partie or parties that will sue for the same by accion informacion bill or playnte in any of the Kinges Courtes, in the whiche accions informacions billes or playntes no wager of lawe essoyne nor proteccion shalbe allowed.

Provided alwaies and be it enacted by thauctoritie aforesaide, that yf any person or persons hereafter in any parte do offende or do contrie to the purvewe and remedy of this Acte, whereupon cause of Accion for the same offence shalbe geven to the Kinge his heires or successors or to any other person or persons that will sue by vertue of this Acte for the punyshment of the saide offence or forfeytures, that yf the Kinge our Soveraigne Lorde his heires or successors within one yere next and ymediatlye after suche offence and forfeytures had and made do not pursue their accion or accions so given by this Acte or cause examinacion upon suche defaultes and offence to be had and made before their counsaile, or other presentmentes thereof to be had accordinge to the meanynge of the same Acte, and everie other person whiche hereafter by vertue of this Acte maye have accion or accions suyte or informacion upon this Statute within halfe a yere next and ymediatlye after suche offence or forfeitures had and made do not comence their suytt informacion accions or presentmentes of and upon the said forfeyte by accion or otherwise as in this present Acte ys lymited and declared, that then aswell the Kinge our Soveraigne Lorde his heires and successors, after one yere next after suche offence and forfeytes had and made yf no suyte in his or their name be taken by accion or otherwise as ys before expressed before the same yere ended & determyned, as everie other person after halfe yere next after like Offence had and done in the fourme aforesaide yf noe suyte thereupon be taken by none of them in fourme above declared, be utterly excluded and debarred of their saide suytes accions Informacions and examinacions to them gyven by vertue of the saide Acte, and the partyes and every of them so offendinge shalbe of all suche Offence and forfeyte clerely dischardged and quytt; Any thinge in this Acte comprised to the contarie notwithstandinge.

Provided alwayes and be it enacted by thauctoritie aforesaide that this present Acte ne any thinge therin conteyned shall in anywise extende or be prejudiciall unto the Kinges Subjectes resident or inhabitinge nere unto the Coaste of the Sea in any parte of this Realme, their houses beinge not above fyve myles distant from the same Coste, nor also to any of the saide Subjecte inhabitinge within twelve myles of the borders of Scotlande, nor to any the Kinges Subjectes Inhabitauntes of the Towne and Marches of Callice, nor to any of the Inhabitauntes of the Isles of Jersey Gernesey Anglesey and the Isles of Weight and Man, but that it shalbe laufull for everie of the saide Inhabitauntes at all tymes hereafter to have exercise and use their handguns hagbutte and demyhakes of the lenghes abovesaide within the lymytte and Isles abovesaide, so that it be at noe manner of Dere heron Shoveler fesant partriche wild Swanne or Wilde Elke or any of them; this present Acte or any thinge therin conteyned to the contarie notwithstandinge.

Provided also that this Acte ne any thinge therin conteyned be in anywise hurtfull or prejudiciall to any servante or person that hereafter, from the saide laste daye of June, shall bend beare carrie charge use or assaye anye Crosbowe or any handgun demyhake or hagbutt of the lenghes abovesaide, by the commaundment of his Lorde and Master so that the saide servante or person doe not shote at any fowle Dere or other Game of what Kynd or nature soever they be; nor also to any suche servante person or persons that shall after the saide last daye of June beare or convey any Crosbowe handgun hagbutt or Demyhake of the lenghes aforesaide to any place or places, by the commaundment of his lorde or master that maye shote by auctoritie of this Acte, to be amended repayred delyvered or assayed; so that the saide Servaunte or other person so bringinge or conveyinge the saide Crosbowe handgun hagbutt or demyhake have redye to shewe to every person requiring the sight thereof one licence in Writinge sealed or subscribed by his saide Lorde or Master to carrie and convey the same Crosbowe handgun hagbutt or demyhake to thintent to be amended repayred assayed or delivered as ys aforesaide.

Provided alwaies that this Acte or any thinge conteyned therein shall not extende to any Owner of any Shippe, for having or kepinge of any handgun hagbutt or demyhake of the sevall lenghes in this Acte expressed or under, only to be had and occupied within their Shippe or other Vessell, or for the carriage and recarriage of them or any of them on lande, or kepinge of them for the onlye exercise and occupyinge of them within their saide Shippe or Vessell; Anye thinge in this Acte to the contarie in any wise notwithstandinge.

## 21. An Acte for Mayntenance of Artyllarie and debarringe of unlauful Games. (1541)

*The last of the Henrican archery acts was by far the fullest piece of legislation governing archery in the medieval or Tudor periods. It is essentially a compilation and expansion of most of the previous acts, codifying them into a single piece of legislation. It covers the same topics as previous acts: the ownership of bow, compulsory regular archery practice, the price of bows, the erection of butts, etc.*

*Some of the specific details and requirements found in earlier acts were changed and updated. For example, where the 1511 act, 3 Hen. 8 c.3,[62] stipulated that bowyers must make two mean wood bows for every yew bow, the new act increased that number to four mean bows for each yew bow for bowyers working ouside London. The price of yew bows for children was limited for the first time.*

*Two significant new clauses were added to the latest act. The first established 220 yards as the minimum range for practicing with prick- or flight-arrows. This distance is frequently, and erroneously, cited as some kind of medieval or Tudor standard which archers were required to reach, often with a heavier livery arrow. In fact the statute says no such thing. No particular range was specified for practicing with heavy arrows, and no particular ability to hit a target at any range was required. The second was a curious clause which allowed bowyers, stringers, fletchers, and arrowsmiths living in London or its suburbs but not Freemen (guild members) of the City to be ordered to move their trade to provincial towns which were lacking in manufacturers of archery equipment.*

### 33 Henry 8. c.9

Moste humbly complayninge shewe unto your Highnes your dayly Orators the Bowers Fletchers Stringers and Arrowehedmakers of this your Realme, that where for the advauncement and mayntenance of Archerie the better to be maynteyned and had within the same, and for the avoydinge of diverse and many unlaufull Games and Playes occupied and practised

---

[62] See **Doc. 17**

within this Realme to the great hurte and lett of Shotinge and Archerie, diverse good and laufull Statutes have bene devised enacted and made, amongest whiche one was made in a parliament holden at Westminster in the thirde yere of your moste gracious raigne, and the same Acte made perpetuall in the parliament there holden in the sixte yere of your saide raigne; the whiche good and laudable Acte notwithstandinge diverse and many subtill & inventatyve and craftye persons, intendinge to defraude the same estatute, sithence the makinge thereof have founde and dayly fynde many and Sondrie newe and crafty Games and Playes, as logatinge in the Feilde, slydethrifte otherwise called shovegrote, aswell within the Cittie of London as else where in many other and divers partes of this Realme, kepinge houses playes and allyes for the mayntenance thereof, by reason whereof Archerie ys sore decayed and dayly is lyke to be more mynished, and diverse Bowers and Fletchers for lacke of Worke gone and inhabyte them selves in Scotlande and other places out of this Realme, there workinge and teachinge their Science, to the puyssaunce of the same to the greate comforte of estraungers and detryment of this Realme.

And where also your Graces subjectes Bowyers Fletchers and others Artifycers afore named from tyme to tyme resorte repayre and come out of all places of this your Realme unto the Cittie of London for lacke of livinge, and doe inhabite nygh the same Cittie or in the suburbes of the same Cittie and in the streetes and lanes of the same Cittie, beinge no fremen of the same Cittie nor bearinge nother scott lott nor other chardge within your saide Cittie as other Citizens and fremen of the same Cittie doe and are bounde to doe and by their othes are sworne to doe, and whiche Cittizens and fremen of your saide Cittie of the mysteries and crafte before rehersed whiche have bene brought upp as prentices from their youthe dwellinge within the Freedome of your saide Cittie of London are alwayes in readynes to furnyshe your Graces affayres when they shalbe comaunded; by reason of the whiche resortinge and aboade of suche forrens and Straungers of the mysteries and craftes before rehersed in the suburbes streetes and lanes of the sam Cittie, other Citties Townes Villages and Places within this Realme remayne and be unfurnyshed of Artyficers and Crafte men before rehersed, to the great decaye of the Archerie of this Realme; And forasmuche as it appeareth by the preamble of the saide estatute enacted in the saide thirde yere, whiche was established and made perpetuall in the foresaide syxte yere of your most gracious raigne, That your Highnes callinge to your most noble and gracious remembraunce that, by the feate and exercise of the Subjectes of this your Realme in shotinge in longe Bowes, there hathe contynually growen and bene within the same great nomber and multytude of good Archers, whiche hathe not only defended this Realme and the Subjectes thereof agaynste the cruell malice and daunger of their outward Enemyes in tyme heretofore paste, but also withe little nomber and puyssaunce in regarde have done many notable Actes and discomfytures of Warre agaynst the Infidels and others, and furthermore subdued and reduced diverse and many Regions and Countries to their due obeysaunce, to the great honor fame and suertie of this Realme and Subjecte, and to the terrible dread and feare of all straunge Nacyons anythinge to attempte or doe to the hurte or damage of them, yet nevertheles Archerie and Shotinge in longe bowes was little used, but dayly did mynishe decaye and abate more and more, for that muche parte of the commonaltye and poore people of this Realme, wherby of olde tyme the great nomber and substaunce of archers hathe growen and multiplyed, were not of power or abylitie to buy them longe bowes of Ewe to excise shotinge in the same and to susteyne the contynuall chardge thereof, And also by meanes and occacion of customable usage of Tennys Playe Bowles Cloyshe and other unlaufull Games, prohibited by manye good and beneficiall estatutes by auctoritie of Parliament in that behalfe provided and made, great ympoverishment hathe ensued, and manye haynous murders robberies and fellonyes were comytted and done, and also the devyne service of God by suche misdoers & holye and festyvall dayes nor heard or solempnized, to the highe displeasure of Almyghtie God ; as by the foresayde preamble more playnely maye appeare: IT MAYE therefore be enacted by your Highnes the Lordes spirituall and temporall and the Commons in this present parliament assembled and by thauctoritie[63] of the same, that every man beinge the Kinges subjecte, not lame decrepitt nor maymed nor havinge any other lawfull or reasonable

---

[63] The authority

cause or ympedyment, beinge within thage of threscore yeres,[64] excepte spiritual men Justice of one Benche and of the other, Justices of the Assise and Barons of the Eschequer, shall from the Feaste of Pentecoste[65] next comynge use and exercise shotinge in long bowes, and also have a bowe and arrowes contynuallye readye in his house to use himselfe and doe use himselfe in shotinge. And also the Father Governours and Rulers of suche as be of tender age do teache and bringe them up in the knowledge of the same shotinge; And that everie man havinge a man childe or men children in his house shall provide ordeyne and have in his house for everie man childe being of thage[66] of seven yeres and above till he shall come to thage of seventene yeres, a bowe and two shaftes, to enduce and learne them and bringe them upp in shotinge, and shall delyver all the same bowes and arrowes to the same younge men to use and occupye; And yf the same younge men be servauntes that then their Maisters shall abate the money that they shall paye for the same bowes and arrowes of their wage; And after all suche younge men shall come to thage of xvij yeres everie of them shall provyde and have a bowe and fower arrowes contynually for himselfe, at his proper costes and charges or els of the guyfte or provision of his freindes, and use and occupie the same in shotinge as is before rehersed; And if the Master suffer any of his servauntes takinge wage beinge in his housholde and under thage of xvij yeres, or the Father suffer anny of his sonnes beinge in houshoulde and under thage of xvij yeres to lacke a bowe and two arrowes contarie to the fourme of this estatute by the space of one moneth together, Then the master or father in whom such negligences shalbe, shall for everie suche defaulte forfeyt vj s. viijd;[67] And that every servaunte passinge thage of xvij yeres and under thage of threscore yeres and takinge wage, whiche can or is able to shoote and shall lacke a bowe and fower arrowes by the space of one moneth together, shall for everie suche defaulte forfeyte and lose vi s. viijd.

Be it further enacted by aucthoritie aforesaide, that noe Man under thage of xxiiij yeres shall shoote at any standinge prick excepte it be at a Rover

---

[64] The age of three score years
[65] Seventh Sunday after Easter
[66] The age
[67] 6 shillings 8 pence

whereat he shall chaunge at every shoote his marke, uppon payne for everye shoote doinge the contarie fower pence; And that noe person above the saide age of xxiiij yeres shall shoote at any marke of xj score yardes or under, withe anye prickshafte or fleight, under the peyne to forfeyt for everie shoote vi s. viijd. And that noe person under thage of xvij yeres, excepte he or his father or mother have landes or tenementes to the yerely value of tenne poundes or be worthe in moveables the some of fortie markes sterlinge, shall shote in any bowe of Ewe whiche shalbe bought for him after the feast of the Purificacion of our Ladye[68] next comynge under the peyne to loose and forfeyt vi s. viij d. And also that Butts be made on this syde the feaste of Saincte Michaell Tharchaungell[69] next comynge in everie Cittie Towne or Place, by the Inhabitauntes of everie suche Cittie Towne and Place, accordinge to the Lawe of auncyent tyme used; And that the Inhabitauntes and Dwellers in everie of them be compelled to make and contynue suche buttes uppon payne to forfeyt, for everie thre monethes so lackinge, twentye shillinges; and that the saide Inhabitauntes shall exercise them selfes withe longe bowes in shotinge at the same and els where in holye dayes and other tymes convenient.

AND to thintent[70] that everie person maye have bowes of meane price, Be it enacted by thauctoritie aforesaid, that everie bowyer dwellinge out of the Cittie and suburbes of London shall, after the saide feaste of the Purifycacion of our Ladye next comynge, for every bowe that he maketh of Ewe, make fower other bowes mete to shote in, of Elme wyche hasill ashe or other Wood apte for the same, under the peyne to lose and forfeyt for everie suche bowe so lackinge iijs. iiijd.[71] And everie bowyer dwellinge within the saide Cittie or Suburbes of London shall after the saide feast of the Purificacion of our Ladye next comynge, for everie bowe of Ewe that he shall make, shall also make two other bowes apte for shotinge, of Ayshe Elme Wyche hasill or other Wood meet for the same, under lyke peyne and forfeyture.

---

[68] 2 February
[69] Feast of St. Michael the Archangel, 29 September
[70] The intent
[71] 3 shillings 4 pence

AND be it also enacted by thauctoritie aforesaide, that noe Bowyer shall sell any bowe of Ewe for any person beinge betwene thage of eight yeres and fourtene yeres above the price of xij d.[72] And that the same bowyers shall have Bowes of Ewe of all prices from vi d. the pece to xij d. the pece for youthes betwene the saide ages of vij yeres and xiiij yeres, and like wise have bowes of Ewe for youthes betwene thage of xiiij yeres and xxj yeres, and shall sell the same at reasonable prices; And moreover that no Bowyer shall sell or put to sale to any the Kinges subjecte any bowe of Ewe of the taxe called Elke[73] above the price of iij s. iiij d. under the peyne to forfeyt xx s,[74] for everie bowe soulde to the contarie above the saide price of iij s. iiij d. as appeareth by a Statute made in the xxij[th] yere of the Raigne of Kinge Edwarde the fourth, the fourth Chapter. And that all bowe staves of Ewe hereafter to be brought into this Realme shalbe soulde open and not in bundelle nor close, to the intent the buyers of them may have perfecte knowledge of the goodnes of them & give the better price for them yf they be soe worthe.

AND furthermore be it enacted by thauctoritie aforesaide that Fletchers of London and the Suburbes of the same, may at their libertye sell seasonable tymber to every Fletcher of the Countrie, without fallinge into anye penaltye or daunger to any of their Wardens for so doinge; And that all ordnances and other lawes made or to be made by their Wardens or otherwise to the contarie shalbe henceforthe clerelye frustrate and voyde.

AND also be it enacted by thauctoritie aforesaid, that the Bowyers Fletchers Stringers and Arrowhed makers, repayringe and resortinge unto the saide Cittie or the Suburbes of the same and there makinge their dwellinge or abydinge, beinge not Fremen of the said Cittie bearinge neither scott nor lott within the saide Cittie, shall at all tymes by the appoyntment of your Grace most honorable Counsaile the Lorde Chauncelor of Englande for the tyme beinge Lorde Tresorer or the Lorde Privie Seale or one of them, goe and inhabyte suche Citties Burroughes and Townes as be destitute of such Artyficers and there to exercise occupie and

---

[72] 12 pence
[73] Yew is often referred to as 'tax,' from the Latin 'taxus.' The meaning of 'elke' here is unclear.
[74] 21 shillings

practise their saide craft and facultyes for the mayntenance of Artillerie and Archerie; and if any suche person, to whom warnynge shalbe so given by the Kinges most honorable Counsell the Lorde Chauncelor the Lorde Treasorer or the Lorde Privie Seale as ys aforesaide, to departe unto other Townes or place of the saide Realme of Englande from the saide Cittie of London the suburbes streetes lanes and places nere the same, refuse to accomplishe the same, that then he or they so refusinge shall forfeyt for everye daye that he shall make his abode contrarie to this acte fourtye shillinges.

BE It also enacted by thauctoritye aforesaide, that no Straunger borne out of the Kinges obeysaunce not beinge Denizen shall convey or do to be conveyed, geve sell or exchaunge, into any partes out of the Kinges obeysaunce any longe bowes arrowes or shaftes without the Kinges speciall lycence, uppon payne of forfeyture of the same wheresoever they shalbe taken or the value thereof within the Kinges power, and uppon peyne of ymprisonement without bayle or maynprice unto suche suche tyme as he or they so beinge in Warde have made a reasonable fyne to the Kinge for his or their offence, afore the Justice of Peace or two of them in the Sessions in the same Countye where he or they shalbe commytted to Warde, or fynde sufficient suertye for the payment of the same fyne. And that noe manner of person not beinge borne within the Kinges obeysaunce, not made denizon, use within the Kinges obeysaunce shotinge withe longe bowes without the Kinges licence, uppon of forfeyture suche bowes arrowes and shaftes as they shalbe founden so shotinge withe ; and everie of the Kinges subject may have authoritie to take and seise the same forfeytures to his owne use, and that Justices of Assise & of Gayle delyverie Justices of Peace and Stewardes of Fraunchises leets and lawedaies have power to enquyre of all the Premisses in their Sessions leetes and lawdayes and heare and determyne the same, and also by their discrecion examyne all persons lackinge and not havinge bowes shaftes and arrowes accordinge to the fourme aforesaide.

BE it also enacted by thauctoritie aforesaide, that noe manner of person of what degree qualytie or condicin soever he or they be, from the Feast of the Nativitye of S. John Baptist[75] now next comynge, by himselfe factor Deputye servaunte or other person, shall for his or their gayne lucre or lyvinge, kepe have houlde occupie exercise or maynteyne any common house alley or place of bowlinge Coytinge Cloyshe Cayles halfe bowle Tennys Dysing Table or Cardinge, or any other manner of Game prohibite by anye estatute heretofore made, or any unlaufull newe game nowe invented or made, or any other unlaufull newe game hereafter to be invented founde had or made, upon payne to forfeyt and paye for everie daye kepinge havinge or mayntayninge, or sufferinge any suche Game to be had kepte executed playde or maynteyned, within anye suche house garden Alley or other place contrie to the fourme and effecte of this Estatute fourtie shillinges; And also everie person usinge and hauntinge any of the saide houses and places and there playenge, to forfeyt for everie tyme so doinge vi s, viij d. And yf any person hereafter sue for any placarde to have comon Gamynge in his house contarie to this Estatute, That then it shalbe conteyned in the same placarde what game shalbe used in the same house and what persons shall playe thereat, and everie placarde graunted to the contarie to be voyde, and also that the partye obteyninge any suche placarde before he put the same in execucion shalbe bounde withe sufficient suertyes withe him by Recognizaunce in the Chauncerie in a certen some to be appoynted by the discrecion of the Lorde Chauncelor of Englande that he shall not use the saide placarde contrie to the fourme thereof.

Be it further enacted by thauctoritie aforesaide, that it shalbe lawfull to all and everie the Justices of Peace in everie Shier, Maiors Sheriffes Bayliffes and other Head Officers within everie Cittie Towne and Boroughe within this Realme, from tyme to tyme aswell within libertyes as without as nede and case shall requyre, to come enter and resorte into all and everie houses places and allies where suche Games shalbe suspected to be houlden used exercised or occupied contarie to the fourme of this Estatute, And as well the Kepers of the same as also the persons there hauntinge resortinge and playinge to take arrest and ymprison, and them so taken and arrested to keep in prison, unto such tyme as the Kepers and

---

[75] 24 June

maynteyners of the saide playes and Games have founde suerties to the Kinges use to be bounde by Recognizaunce or otherwise no longer to use kepe or occupye any suche house playe Game Alley or Place: And also that persons there so founde be in like case bounden, by themselfes or els withe suerties by the discrecions of the Justices Mayors Sheriefes Bayliffes or other head Officers, no more to playe haunte or exercise from thenceforthe in at or to anye of the saide places or at anye of the saide Games.

Also be it further enacted by thauctoritie aforesaide, that the Maiors Sheriffes Baylieffes Constables and other head Officers within everie Cittie and Towne within this Realme where any suche Officers shall fortune to be, aswell within the Franchises as without, shall make due search, wekelye or at the furthest at all tymes hereafter once everie monethe, in all place where any suche houses Alleyes playes or places shalbe suspected to be had kepte and mayneteyned: And if the saide Mayors Sheriffes Bayliffes Constables and other head Offycers within their Cities Burroughes and Townes, aswell within Fraunchises as without, doe not make due searche at the furtherst once everie moneth yf the case soe requyre accordinge to the tenor of this Acte, and doe not execute the same in all thinges accordinge to the purporte and force of the same, That then everie suche Mayor Sherief Bayliff Constable or other head Officer to paye & forfeyte for everie Moneth not makinge suche searche nor executinge the same fourty shillinges.

Be it also enacted by thauctoritie aforesaide, that noe manner of Artyficer or Crafte man of any handy crafte or occupacion, husbandman apprentice laborer servaunte at husbandrye jorneyman or servaunte of artyficer marriners fysshermen watermen or any servyngman, shall from the saide Feast of the Natyvitie of Sainte John Baptiste playe at the Tables Tennys Dyce Cardes Bowles Clashe Coytinge Logatinge, or any other unlawfull Game, out of Christmas, under ye peyne of twentye shillinges to be forfeyt for everie tyme, And in Christmas to playe at anye of the saide Games in their maisters houses or in their maisters presence: And also that noe manner of person shall at any tyme playe at any bowle or bowles in open place out of his garden or orcharde, under the peyne for everie tyme so offendinge to forfeyt vi s viij d: And that all Justice of Peace Mayors Bayliffes Sherieffes and all other hed Officers and everie of them, fyndinge or knowinge any manner person or persons usinge or excisinge any unlaufull games contrie to this present estatute, shall have full power and auctoritie to commytt everie such offendor to Warde, there to remayne without bayle or mayneprise untill suche tyme that they so offendinge be bounden by obligacion to the Kinges use, in such somes of money as by the discrecions of the saide Maior Justice Bayliffe or other head Offycers shalbe thought reasonable, that they or any of them shall not from henceforthe use suche unlaufull games.

Be it further enacted by thauctoritie aforesaide, that all other Statute made for the restraynt of unlaufull games or for the mayntenance of Artillerie, as touchinge the penaltyes or forfeytures of the same, shalbe from hensforthe utterlye voyde; And for all informacions pleyntes accions or suyte that shalbe taken or sued uppon anye parte of this estatute shalbe commenced within the yere after the offence comytted and done, or otherwise no advantage or suyte thereof to be taken; And where any suche forfeytures shall happen to be founde within the precincte of anye fraunchise leete or lawe daye, then the lorde of the same fraunchese leete or lawedaye to have the one moytie thereof, And thother moytie thereof to anye of the Kinges subjecte that will sue for the same in anye of the Kinges Courtes by accion informacion bill or otherwise, in whiche accion or suyte the Defendaunte shall not be admitted to wage his lawe nor any proteccion nor essoyne shalbe allowed; And where suche forfeyture shalbe founden out of the Precincte of any franchise leete or lawe daye, that the moytie of all suche forfeytures shalbe to the Kinge our Soveraigne Lorde and thother moytie thereof to any of the Kinges subjectes that will sue for the same by bill playnte accion informacion or otherwise in anye of the Kinges Courtes, in whiche suyte or accion the defendaunte shall not be admytted to wage his lawe nor any proteccion or essoyne shalbe allowed.

AND to thintent that everie person maye have knowledge of this acte and avoyde the daunger and penaltyes of the same, be it enacted by thauctoritie aforesaide That all Mayors Bayliffe Sheriffes and other head Officers shall fower tymes in the yere, That ys to saye once everie quarter, make open proclamacion of this present Acte in everie markett to be houlden win their sewall Jurisdicions and auctorities, And also that the Justice of Gaole Delyverie Assises and Justices of Peace do cause the same to be proclaymed in their severall Circuytes and Sessions before them houlden: And that this Estatute shall begynne to take his effecte concernynge the penaltyes of the same from the saide Feast of Sainct John Baptiste nowe next comynge and to contynue and endure for ever.

Provided alwaye and be it enacted by thauctoritie aforesaide, that yf any person or persons have taken by lease, whether it be by wordes writinges or otherwise, any house alley or place wherin anye suche unlawfull game nowe ys and at any tyme of suche lease made was used, that then everie suche lease shall, at the libertye of him or them to whom such lease is made, their executors admynistrators or assignes, from the saide feast of the Natyvitie of S. John Baptiste be utterlye voyde, Excepte it be for breache of covenante or agrementt or payment of rent due att the saide Feast or att any tyme before; so that at the same Feaste, or within one moneth next after the same, the saide lessee geve knowledge to suche lessor or lessors their heires or assignes that hee will noe longer occupye the same, And that then it shalbe laufull to the Inheritor lessor or owner thereof or to his heires or assignes in the same house Alley or place to reenter.

Provided also and be it enacted by thauctoritie aforesaide, that it shalbe laufull for everie maister to licence his or their servaunte to playe at Cardes Dice or Tables withe their saide maister or withe any other Gentleman repayringe to their saide maister, openly in his or their house or in his or their presence, accordinge to his or their discrecion; and that it shalbe laufull to everie suche servaunte, for everie tyme so beinge commaunded or licenced by his saide maister as ys aforesaide, to playe at Carde Dyce or Tables withe his saide maister or other Gentleman so to him repayringe; Any thinge in this Acte to the contarie notwithstandinge.

Provided also and be it enacted by thauctoritie aforesaide, that it shalbe laufull to everie Nobleman and other, havinge mannors lande tenementes or other yerelye profittes for terme of lyef in his owne right or in his wyeffe righte to the yerelye value of a hundred poundes or above, to comaunde appoynte or licence by his or their discrecion his or their servauntes or famylye of his or their house or houses for to playe, within the precyncte of his or their Houses Gardens Or Orchardes, at Cardes Dyce Tables Bowles or Tennys, aswell amongest themselfes as other repayringe to the same house or houses, And that they so playinge by comaundment appoyntment or licence as ys aforesaide, shall not incurr anye daunger or penaltye conteyned in this Acte for the same; This Acte or anye thinge therin conteyned to the contarie thereof in anywise notwithstandinge.

Provided alwaie and be it enacted by thauctoritie aforesaide, that all Informacions accions and suytes nowe dependinge in any of the Kinges Courtes for or concerninge anye penaltye or forfeyture conteyned in any of the saide Statute by this Acte repealed, and noe Judgement therin yet given, the same Informacions accions and suyte shalbe remayne and stande as good and effectuall in the lawe to all intents construcions and purposes as yf this Acte had never bene had ne made; Any thinge in this Acte conteyned to the contrie in anywise notwithstandinge.

## 22. An Acte for the having of Horse Armour and Weapon. (1557)

*The Statute of Winchester[76] had provided the legislative basis for requiring men to own their own arms and armour, essential to the functioning of the county militia system, since 1285. After nearly three centuries, however, the requirements for lances and mail shirts were fairly outdated, and although they were updated in practice so that militia requirements of the sixteenth century more closely resembled the equipment stipulated in 10 Hen.7 c.9 (Ireland)[77] the English legislation badly needed updating. The 1557 act, therefore, overhauled and updated the requirements of the Winchester statute.*

### 4 Philip and Mary. c.2

For the better furniture and defence of this Realme, Be it enacted by the Kinge and Quenes Majesties, withe thassent[78] of the Lordes Spirituall and Temporall and the Commons in this present Parliament assembled, and by aucthorite of the same, That asmuche of all and every Acte and Statute, concerning onelye the keping or finding, of Horse Horses or Armoure or of any of them, heretofore made or provided, and all and everye forfeiture and penaltie concerning onelye the same, shalbe from hensfoorthe utterly voide repealed and of none effect.

And Be it further enacted by thaucthorite[79] aforesaid, That every Nobleman Gentleman and other Temporall Person, after the Rate and Proportion hereafter declared, shall have and kepe in a readines suche Horses Geldinges Armoure and other Furniture for the Warres, at the least, and in suche sorte and maner as ys and shalbee in this Acte hereafter expressed and declared, that is to saye: All and every parsone Temporall having anye Honoures Lordeshipes Manours Houses Landes Meadowes Pastures or Woodde of Estate of Inheritance or Freeholde, to the clere yerely value of one thowsande powndes or above, shall from and after the first daye of Maye whiche shalbe in the yere of our Lorde God one

---

[76] See **Doc. 1**
[77] See **Doc. 15**
[78] The assent
[79] The authority

thowsande five hundrethe fiftie and eight, have finde kepe sustayne and mayntayne within this Realme of Englande, of their owne proper and at their owne proper Costes and Expenses, Syxe Horses or Geldinges hable for Dimilances, wherof three of them at the least to be Horses withe sufficient Harnesses Steele Sadels and Weapon requisite and apperteyning to the sayd Demylances Horses or Geldinges; and tenne light Horses or Geldinges hable and mete for Light Horsemen, withe the Furniture of Harneis and Weapon requisite for the same; And also Fourtye Corpselettes furnished, Fourtye Almayne Rivettes, or in stedd of the said Almayn Rivette, Fourtie Coates of Plate Corpselette or Brygandynes furnished, Fortye Pikes xxx Long Bowes Thirtye Shefes of Arrowes xxx Steele Cappes or Sculles xx Black Billes or Halberdes xx Haquebuttes and xx Morians or Sallettes: And everye persone Temporall, having any Honours Lordshippes Manours Houses Landes Meadowes Pastures or Wooddes of any suche Estate as ys aforesaid to the clere yerelye value of one thowsande Marckes or above, and under the clere yerelye value of a thousande pownde, shall have finde susteyne and mayntayne within this Realme, of their owne proper and at their owne proper Costes and Expenses, Fowre Horses or Geldinges hable for Demyelances, wherof twoo at the least to be Horses withe sufficient Harnesses and Weaponne and Saddels meete and requisite to the sayd Demielaunces Horses or Geldinges, and Syxe light Horses or Geldinges hable and meete for Light Horsmen, withe Furniture of Harneis and Weapon requisite for the same; And also of Armour and Weapon xxx Corpselettes furnished xxx Almayn Rivettes, or in steade of the said Almayne Rivettes xxx Cotes of Plate Corpselettes or Brigandynes furnished, xxx Pykes xx Long Bowes xx Sheffes of Arrowes xx Steele Cappes or Sculles x Black Billes or Halbertes x Haquebuttes and Tenne Morians or Sallettes : And everie person temporall having Honors Lordeshipes Manors Houses Landes Meadowes Pastures or Wooddes of any suche Estate as is aforesaid, to the clere yerelye value of CCCC li,[80] or above, and under the clere yerelye value of a thowsande Marckes, shall have finde kepe susteine and mayntayne as is aforesaid, twoo Horses, or one Horse and one Gelding, able for Demilance withe sufficient Furniture of Harnes Steele Sadles and

---

[80] £400

Weapon for the same as is aforesaid, and Fowre Geldinges hable for Light Horsmen withe sufficient Harnes and Weapon for the same, and also xx Corpselettes furnished, xx Almayne Rivettes furnished, or in stede of Almayne Rivettes twentye Cotes of Plate Corselettes or Brigandines furnished xx Pikes xv Long Bowes xv Sheffes of Arrowes xv Steele Cappes or Sculles Sixe Haquebuttes and Six Morians or Sallettes: And that everie persone temporall, having Lordeshipes Mannors Houses Landes Meadowes Pastures or Woodes of any suche Estate as is aforesaid, to the clere yerely value of CC li.[81] or above, and under the clere yerelye value of CCCC li. shall from the said first daye of Maye have kepe sustayne and mayntayne, one greate Horse or Gelding hable for a Demielance withe sufficient Furniture of Harneis steeled Sadle and Weapon for the same, and Twoo Geldinges able for Light Horsemen with Harneis and Weapons sufficient as is aforesaid for the same, and also Tenne Corseletes furnished Tenne Almayne Rivettes, or in the place of Almaine Rivettes Tenne Cotes of Plate Corselettes or Brigandines furnished, x Pikes viij Long Bowes viij Sheffes of Arrowes viij Steele Cappes or Sculles Three Haquebuttes and Thre Morians or Sallettes: And everie person Temporall having any Lordeshipes Manours Houses Landes Meadowes Pastures or Woodes of any suche estate as is aforesaid, to the clere yerely value of one C li,[82] or above, and under the yerely value of CC li, shall from and after the saide first daye of Maye have kepe and mayntaine as ys Aforesayd twoo Geldinges able and mete for Light Horsemen, withe sufficient Harneis and Weaponnes requisite for the same, and also three Corselettes furnished, three Almayne Rivettes, or in stede of them, so many Cotes of Plate Corsellettes or Brigandines furnished, iij Pikes, iij Long Bowes, three Sheffes of Arrowes, iij Steele Cappes or Sculles, two Haquebuttes and twoo Morians or Sallettes: And also every person Temporall having Lordeshipes Manours Houses Landes Meadowes Pastures or Woodes of any suche Estate as is aforesaid, to the clere yerelye value of one hundrethe Marckes or above, and under the yerely value of one C li. from the said first daye of Maye, shall have kepe maintayne and susteyne one Gelding able and mete for a Light Horseman with the Harenes and weapon sufficient and requisite for the same, two Corseletes

---

[81] £200
[82] £100

furnished, twoo Almaine Rivettes, or in stede of the same, twoo Cotes of Plate or Brigandines furnished, twoo Pykes, twoo Long Bowes, twoo Shefes of Arrowes, twoo Steele Cappes or Sculles, one Hacquebutt, one Moryan or Sallett: And also everye persone Temporall, having Lordeshipes Manours Howses Lande Meadowes Pastures or Woodes of any suche Estate as is aforesaid, to the yerelye value of xl li.[83] or above, and under the yerely value of one hundrethe Marckes, shall from and after the said firste daye of Maye, have maintayne and kepe twoo Corselettes furnished, twoo Almayn Rivettes, or in stede of the same twoo Cotes of Plate Corselettes or Brigandines furnished, twoo Pikes, one Long Bowe, one Shefe of Arrowes, one Steele Cappe or Sculle, twoo Hacquebuttes, twoo Morians or Sallettes: And also every person Temporall having Lordeshippes Manors Howses Landes Meadowes Pastures or Wooddes of any suche Estate as is aforesaid, to the clere yerelye value of Twentie powndes or above, and under the yerelie value of Fowrtye powndes, shall from the said first daye of Maye, have kepe and maintaine one Corselet furnished, one Pyke, one Hacquebut, and one Moryan or Sallet, one Long Bowe, one Sheife of Arrowes, and one Steele Cappe or Skull; And also every person Temporall having Lordeshippes Manours Howses Landes Meadowes Pastures or Woodes of any suche Estate as is aforesaid, to the clere yerelye value of Tenne powndes or above, and under the yerelye value of Twentie powndes, shall from and after the said daye have kepe and sustaine one Almaine Rivet, Coate of Plate, or Brigandine furnished, one Haquebutt, one Murrien or Sallet, one Long Bowe, and one Sheife of Arrowes, and one Steele Cappe or Sculle: And also every person Temporall having Lordeshipes Manours Howses Landes Meadowes Pastures or Wooddes of suche Estate as is aforesaid, to the clere yerelye value of Five powndes or above, and under the yerelye value of Tenne powndes, shall from and after the said first daye of Maie have kepe and sustaine one Cote of Plate furnished, one black Bill or Halbert, one Long Bowe, one Sheife of Arrowes, & one Steele Cappe or Sculle: And also everye person Temporall, having Gooddes or Cattelles to the value of One thowsande Marckes or above, shall from the sayd first daie of Maye have finde kepe sustaine and maintaine as is aforesaid one

---

[83] £40

Horse or Gelding able for a Demielaunce withe sufficient Harneis Steele Saddle and Weapon convenient and requisite for the same, and one Geldinge able and meete for a Light Horseman, withe Harneis and Weapon sufficient and requisite as is aforeseid for the same, or xviij Corselettes furnished in steade of the sayd Horse and Geldinge and furniture of the same, at his choise: And also shall from the same daye have finde kepe and maintaine of Armour and Weapon, twoo Corselettes furnished two Almaine Rivettes, or for the same Almaine Rivettes twoo Cotes of Plate twoo Corselettes or two Brigandines furnished, twoo Pikes, fowre Long Bowes, fower Sheifes of Arrowes, fowre Steele Cappes or Sculles, and three Hacquebuttes, withe three Morians or Sallettes: And also every person Temporall having Gooddes or Cattelles to the values hereafter in this presente Acte specified and declared, shall from and after the said first daye of Maye have finde kepe susteine and maintaine suche Geldinges Armour Weapon and Furniture for Warre as is hereafter declaredd, that ys to saye; Having to the value of fowre hundrethe powndes or above, and under the value of one thowsande Marckes, one Geldinge able and mete for a Light Horseman, withe sufficient Harneis and Weapon requisite and meete for the same, or nyne Corselettes furnished, at his Elecion, and also shall have finde and kepe one other Corselet furnished, one Pyke twoo Almayn Rivettes or Plate Cotes or Brigandines furnished, one Haquebutt, twoo Long Bowes, two Sheifes of Arrowes, and twoo Steele Cappes or Sculles: And having in Gooddes and Cattelles to the value of CC li, or above, and under CCCC li, one Corselet furnished, one Pike, twoo Almayn Rivettes Plate Cotes or Brigandines furnished, one Haquebut, one Murian or Sallet, twoo Long Bowes, and twoo Sheifes of Arrowes, and twoo Sculles or Steele Cappes: And having in Gooddes and Cattelles to the value of C li. or above, and under CC li. one Corselet furnished and one Pike, one paire of Almaine Rivettes, one Plate Cote or paire of Brigandines furnished, two Long Bowes, two Sheifes of Arrowes, and twoo Sculles: And having as is aforesaid, in Goodes and Cattelles to the value of Fourtye powndes or above, and under a C li. two paire of Almon Rivettes, or twoo Cotes of Plate or Brygandines furnished, one Long Bowe, and one Sheife of Arrowes, one Steele Cappe or Scull, and one blacke Bill or Halberte: And having as ys aforesaid in Goodes and Cattelles to the value of xx li. or above, and under the value of xl li, one paire of Almain Rivettes, or one Cote of Plate, or one paire of Brigandines, twoo Long Bowes, two Sheifes of Arrowes, two Sculles or Steele Cappes, and one Black Bill or Halbert: And having as is aforesaid, to the value of Tenne powndes or above, and under xx li, one Long Bowe, one Sheife of Arrowes, withe one Steele Cappe or Sculle, and one Blacke Bill or Halberte: And also that every person Temporall, not beinge above chardged by this Acte, having or that hereafter shall have anye Annuitee or Annuitees or yerely Fee or Fees for terme of Lyef or of any State of Enheritance, or any Copieholde or Copieholdes for terme of Lyef or of anye Estate of Enheritance, to the clere yerely value of xxx li, or above, shall bee chardged and chardgeable withe suche Furniture of Warre as is aforesaid, in every Degree Qualite and Condicion according to the Proporcions and Rates before expressed lymited and appointed for Gooddes and Cattelles.

And Be it further enacted by thaucthoritee aforesaid, That every person whiche by vertue of thacte[84] made in the Parlament holden at Westminster in the xxxiij yere of the Reigne of King Henrye theight, was bownde (by reason that his Wief shoulde weare suche kinde of Apparell or other Thing as in the same Statute ys speciallye mentioned and declared,) to kepe or finde one greate stoned trotting Horse, and is not by this Acte before chardged to have mayntayne and kepe any Horse or Geldinge, shall from the said first daye of Maie, have kepe and mayntayne one Gelding able and meete for a Light Horsman, withe sufficient Harneis and Weapon for the same, in suche maner and fourme as everye Temporall person having Lordeshippes Howses Landes Meadowes Pastures or Wooddes of suche Estate as ys aforesaid, of the clere yerely value of one hundrethe Marckes, is chardged or appointed to finde have and maintaine by this presente Acte.

And Be it further enacted by thaucthorite aforesaid, That if any person chardgeable by this Acte as ys aforesaid, shall, by the space of any three whole Monethes after the sayd first daye of Maye, lacke or wante the said nomber and kindes of Horses Geldinges Armour Weapon and Furniture aforesaid, or any of them, after suche Rate Proporcion Maner and Fourme

---

[84] The act

as is in this Acte above lymited declared and appointed, That then every suche person shall forfaite and lose, for every suche three Monethes that he shall so lacke and want the same nomber and kindes of Horses Geldinges Armour Weapon and Furniture or any parte therof, for every Horse or Geldinge so lacking, Tenne powndes, And for every Demielance and Furniture of the same, Three powndes, and for every Corselet and Furniture of the same, xl s.[85] and for every Almayn Rivet Cote of Plate or Brigandine and the Furniture of the same, xx s.[86] and for every Bowe and Sheife of Arrowes Bill Halbert Haquebut Steele Cappe Scull Murryen and Sallet x s.[87] thone[88] Moietee of whiche said Forfeitures shalbee to the Kinge and Quene our Sovereigne Lorde and Ladye, and to Theires[89] and Successoures of the same our Sovereyne Ladie, and thother Moietie to him or them that will sue for the same in any Courte of Recorde by Bill Playnt Accion of Dett or Informacion in the whiche Bill Playnt Accion of Dett or Informacion, no Wager of Lawe Essoigne or Protecion shall be allowed or admitted.

AND Be it further enacted by thaucthoritee aforesayd, That thenhabitantes[90] of everye Citie Bourghe Towne Parishe and Hamelett within this Realme, other then suche as arre speciallye chardged before in this Acte, shall have finde kepe sustayne and mayntayne, at their comen Chardges and Expenses, suche Harneis and Weapon and as muche therof as shalbe appointed by the Commissioners of our said Sovereigne Lorde and Ladie, and of theires and Successoures of the same our Sovereigne Ladie, for the Musters or Veue of Armour within suche Citie Boroughe Towne Parishe or Hamelett, ther to be kepte in suche Place as by the sayd Commissioners shalbe appointed: And the nomber and kindes therof to be writton and comprised in a Payre of Indentures to be made betwen the said Commissioners or twoo of them at the leaste, and xij. viij. or iiij. of the cheifest of every suche Citie Bourghe Town Parishe or Hamelett, wherof

---

[85] 40 shillings
[86] 20 shillings
[87] 10 shillings
[88] The one
[89] The heirs
[90] The inhabitants

one parte to remaine withe the Cheife Officer of the same Citie Boroughe Towne Parishe or Hamelett and thother parte to remayne with the Clarck of the Peace of the Shire or Cowntie wher every suche Citie Bourghe Parishe or Hamelet shall stand or bee; And if the same Inhabitauntes of every suche Citie Bourghe Towne Parishe or Hamelett, other then suche as arr speciallye as is aforesaid chardged, shall lack or want suche Harneis or Weapons or any parte therof, as shall bee unto them appointed by the said Commissioners for the Musters or Vewe of Armour as is aforesaid, by the Space of any three Monethes together next after any suche Appointment made, that then the sayd Inhabitantes shall forfeite for every the said three Monethes for every suche Harneis or Weapons so lacking, after the Rate above lymited, thone Moietie therof to be our said Soverayne Lorde and Ladye and to theires and Successoures of our said Sovereygne Ladie, and thother Moietie to him or them that will sue for the same in eny of the Courtes of Recorde of our saide Sovereigne Lorde and Ladie, and of theires and Successors of the same our Sovereigne Ladie, by Bill Plaint Accion of Det or Informacion, wherin no Wager of Lawe Essoine or Proteccion shalbe admitted or allowed.

AND Be it further enacted by thaucthorite aforesayd, That the Lorde Chancellor of Englande for the time being, shall have full power and aucthorite by vertue of this presente Acte, from time to time to grante out Commissions under the Greate Seale of Englande, to the Justices of Peace within everie Shire or Countie of this Realme, or to so many of them as by his discretion shalbe thought mete and convenient, for the appointing and lymiting of the saide Harneses and Weapons, to be fownde kepte and mainteined in everye suche Citie Bourghe Towne Parishe and Hamelet at the Commen Chardges of thinhabitantes therof as is aforesayd.

Provided alwaies, That this Acte or any thing therin conteined shall not extende to take awaye or dischardge any Tenaunt or Fermour of his Service or Covenant towardes his Lorde, for the finding of Horse Armor or Weapon, or for doing of Service by himself or any other, whiche by the Tenure of his Lande or Ferme he is bownde to doo at the tyme of making of this Acte; but that he shall yelde paye and doo the same in as large ample maner and fourme as though this Acte had never been had ne made.

AND Be it further enacted by thaucthoritee aforesaid, That the Justices of Peace of everie Shire shall have power and aucthorite, by vertue of this Acte, from tyme to tyme to make searche and vewe of and for the said Furnitures of Horses Geldinges Armor and Weapon to be fownde mainteined and kept by any person abovesaid, having Lordeshippes Manors Howses Landes Meadowes Pastures or Woodes to the clere yerely value of CC li, or under, and not above the yerely value of CCCC li or to bee fownde mainteined or kepte by any person or persons chargeable by this Acte by reason of his or their Goodes Cattelles Annuities Fees or Copieholdes as is aforesayd ; and to heare and determyne at their Quarter Sessions all and every the Defaultes comitted or doone contrary to this Acte within the Countie where suche Sessions shall be kept, by Inquisicion Presentment Bill or Informacion before them exhibited, or by Examination of twoo lawfull Witnes at the discretion of the same Justices, and to awarde proces theruppon, as thoughe they were indicted before them by verdicte of twelve Men or more: And upon the convicion of The Offendor, by Informacion or Suite of any other then the King or the Quene, or of theires or Successoures of the Quene, to make Estretes of thone Moitee of the said Forfeitures to be levied to thuse of our said Sovereigne Lorde and Ladye, or of theires or Successoures of the same our Soverein Ladie, as they use to doo of other Fines Issues and Amertiamentes growing in the Sessions of Peace, and to awarde Execucion of thother Moitee for the Complaynante or Informer ageynst thoffender by Fieri Facias or Capias, as the Kinges Justices at Westminster maye doo and use to doo; And yf any suche convicion shall hereafter happen at thonelye Sute of our sayd Soveraine Lorde and Ladie or of theires or Successors of the same our Soveraine Ladie, that then thole[91] Forfeitures to bee estreated and levied to their Uses onelye.

AND Be it further enacted by thaucthoritee aforesayd, That whensoever any person shall at anny tyme heereafter bee convicted by vertue of this Acte for anny defaulte or thing mentioned in this Acte, that then the same personne shall not otherwise or eftesoones bee vexed trobled sued or

---

[91] The whole

convicted for the same defaulte or thing, wherfore he shalbee so convicted.

And Be it moreover enacted by thaucthorite aforesaid, That if any Souldiour shall at any time hereafter make Sale of his Horse Harneis and Weapon or any of them, contrary to the fourme of the sayd Statute made in the seconde and thirde yeres of the reigne of the late King Edwarde the Sixthe, concerning true Service to bee doone by Captaynes and Souldiours; that then not onelye the same Souldiour shall incurr the Penalties of that Statute, but also the sayd Sale made by suche Souldiour, to anny person or persones knowing him to bee a Souldior, shall be voide and of none effecte, against him or them that fownde or set forthe the said Horse Harneis and Weapon, or any of them, to or for the Furniture of suche Souldior to serve withe the same.

Provided alwayes, that no person shalbe empeached or troobledd for any Offence doone contrary to this Acte, oneles Presentment or Sute therof be had made or taken within one yere next after thoffence doon; Any thing in this Acte to the contrarye therof in any wise notwithestanding.

Provided alwaie, and be it enacted by thaucthoritee aforesaid, That if at any time hereafter it shall fortune any person or persons aforesaid to be sued or impeached for any Forfeiture or Penaltie for not having susteining or keping suche Furniture of Corselettes Pikes Hacquebuttes or Morians as by this Acte ys before lymited rated and appointed, and for his or their excuse and answer shall alleadge and pleade that the same Furniture so lacking coulde not by him or them conveniently bee had gotten or provided, for wante and lacke of the same within this Realme, according to the tenour and purporte of this Acte; the same matter of wante and lacke as is aforesaid, shalbe allowed and taken for a good and sufficient aunswer and barre in the Lawe in cace it be true; and yf the same be denyed or traversed, that therupon an Issue shalbe joyned, and that the triall shalbe, of everye such Issue onelye, had by the certificate to be made by the Lord Chancellor Lorde Treasurer the Lorde President of the Councell the Lorde Stewarde of the Kinge and Quenes most Honorable Householde the Lorde Privie Seale the Lorde Admirall and the Lord Chamblaine of the sayd Howseholde, or by three of them in writing under their Seales, or the

Seales of three of them; This presente Acte, or any Statute Lawe or Usage heretofore hadd to the contrary notwithestanding.

Provided also and be it enacted by thaucthoritee aforesaid, That no person or persons chargeable by vertue of this Acte, to or for the finding or having of any Horse Gelding Armour Weapon or Furniture for the Warre as is aforesaid, shalbe charged withe the same, or withe any of them, bothe for his Manors Houses Landes Meadowes Pastures and Woodes, and also for his Goodes Cattelles Fermes Leases Copiholdes Rentes Anuitees.

Provided also and be it further enacted by thaucthoritee aforesaid, That this Acte or any thing therin conteined shall not in any wise extende or be adjudged or interpreted to abrogate repeale or make voide any Parte Sentence Matter Clause Article or Thing, conteined or specified in the Statute made in the xxxiij yere of the reigne of the late noble Prynce of worthye memorie King Henry theight, for or concerning the having of Long Bowes and Arrowes, and thusing order exercising and maintenance of Artilarie and shoting in Long Bowes; but that the same Statute and everie Article Clause Sentence and thing therin conteined and specified, touching or in any wise concerning the having of Long Bowes Arrowes usinge order exercising or maintenance of Archerye and shoting in Long Bowes, shall stande and remayne in force and be observed perfourmed and kepte according to the tenor effecte and true meaning of the said Acte, upon the paines conteined in the same, as if this Acte had not been hadd ne made; This present Acte or any thing therein conteined to the contrary in any wise notwithestanding.

Provided also, that if it shall fortune the said Furniture of Armour aforesaid, or any parte therof, at any time hereafter to be loste or spent in any service of defence of this Realme, or els the Horses or Geldinges aforesaid to bee killed or distroied, or els by some other occasion to be deade, that in suche case or cases no person or persones shalbe chardged withe any Forfeiture or Penaltie aforesaid, for not having suche quantitie or nomber of Armour Horses or Geldinge as is aforesaid, so that he or they within one yere next after suche losse or want doo supply the same againe in all pointes, according to the true meaning and purporte of this Acte ; Any thing in the same Acte to the contrarye notwithstanding.

Provided also, that the wante of any Gauntelette or Gauntelettes shall not be demed accompted or taken for anny lacke or wante of Furniture for a Corpselette: Anny woordes before expressed sounding to the contrarie notwithestanding.

Provided also, and be it enacted by the aucthorite aforesaid, That every person and persons chardged withe the finding of any Haquebut, and his or their Servant or Servantes shall and maye exercise and use shoting in the same Haquebut, at suche marckes as arr limited and appointed by the Statute made in the xxxiii yere of the reigne of King Henrye theight, at their owne proper Games, so that they carye not or use not the same Haquebut in any Highe waye, oneles it be coming or going to or from the Musters, or marching towardes or from the Service of Defece of the Realme; Any Clause or Article in the said Acte of the xxxiij yeere to the contrary notwithestanding.

Provided alwaies, that this Acte ne any thing therin conteyned, shall extende to chardge any persone or persones dwelling or abiding within the Countries of Northe Wales and Sowthe Wales, and withein the Countie Palentine of Lancaster and Chester or either of them, withe the finding or having of any Haquebutt; but that they and every of them shall and maye at their will libertie and pleasure, have and kepe, in stede and place of every Haquebutt charged by this Acte, one Long Bowe and one Sheife of Arrowes, over and besides suche other Armour and Munition, as is by the Lawes of this Realme limited and appointed; Any thing in this Acte to the contrarye notwithestanding.

Provided alwaies, that the Lorde Chauncellor of Englande or Keper of the Greate Seale for the tyme being shall and maye from time to tyme by vertue of the King and Quenes Highnes Commission, name assigne and appoint Commissioners in every City Bourghe and Towne Corporate, wherin there bee Justices of the Peace, aswell in Englande as in Wales, so many of the same Justices of Peace, withe suche and as manye other persons to be joyned withe them, dwelling out of the said Cities Boroughes and Townes Corporate, as he or they shall thincke mete, to take viewe of Armour in every of the same Cities Boroughes and Townes Corporate according to this present Acte, and also to assigne what Harneis and

Armour shall bee provided and kepte by the Inhabitantes of every suche Citie Boroughe and Towne Corporate as is aforesaid, according to this presente Acte.

## 23. An Acte for Bowyers and the pryces of Bowes. (1566)

*Although the bow as a military weapon was definitely in decline by 1566 it still remained an important part of the national arsenal. The provision of reasonably-priced bows which several earlier pieces of legislation had been intended to encourage was still vital to the continued practice with bows by commoners, but the weaknesses of some of the earlier acts had become apparent, and the bowyers act of 1566 was an attempt to rectify them. London bowyers, who had obeyed the law and produced two mean wood bows for each yew bow now found that they had large stocks of mean wood bows which they were unable to sell, so the law was changed and now stipulated how many mean wood bows they had to keep in stock rather than how many they had to make. It also updated the maximum price of various sorts of bows for the first time since 3s 4d had been established 84 years earlier. Inflation was a problem throughout the Tudor period, especially in the middle of the century, and it has been estimated that the price of some commodities rose by 400% between 1485 and 1603. The new price scale for bows allowed bowyers to keep up with inflation.*

### 8 Elizabeth 1. c.10

Moost humbly complainyng sheweth unto your Highnes and to your High Courte of Parlyament, your obedient Subjectes the Bowyers dwelling and inhabityng within the Citie of London and the Suburbes of the same; That where in the Parlyament of the late Kyng of moost famous memorye Kyng Henry the Eight, begunne and holden at Westmynster the xvi[th] daye of January in the xxxiij[th] yere of the Raigne of the sayd late Kyng, and there continewed untill the first daye of Aprill then next following, there was one Acte and Statute then made and provided intituled, An Acte for the Mayntenaunce of Artyllerie and debarring of unlawfull Games; in which Acte and Statute amongest other Thinges there is one Braunche conteined and specyfied, the Tenour whereof is as heereafter followeth, That is to saye; And to thintent[92] that everie person maye have Bowes of meane pryce, bee it enacted by the aucthoritie aforesayd, that everie Bowier

---

[92] The intent

dwelling out of the Citie of London shall after the Feast of the Puryficacion of our Ladie then next comyng, for everie Bowe that he maketh of Ewe, make three[93] other Bowes meete to shote in of Elme Wichsasell[94] Asshe and other Woodde apte for the same, under the payne to lose and forfaite for every suche Bowe so lackyng, Three Shillinges and Fower pence; And every Bowyer dwelling within the Citie and Suburbes of London shall after the sayd Feast of the Purifycacion of our Ladie then next commyng for everie Bowe of Ewe, make two other Bowes apt for shoting, of Asshe Elme Wychsasell or other Woodde meete for the same, under lyke Payne and Forfayture as by the sayd Estatute more playnlie it doth and maye appere; And althowgh the sayd Braunche of the sayde Statute bee needefull and expedient to remayne and continewe for such Bowyers as do dwell and inhabyte in the Countrey and other Places out of the Citie of London and the Suburbes of the same, Yet forasmuche as there be very fewe or no Bowes of Elme Wichhasell or Asshe or of any other Wood then onely of Ewe used or occupyed by any person within the sayd Citye and Suburbes of the same, therefore the sayd Braunche of the sayd Acte and Statute before rehearsed was not ne is needefull to be had and made for the Bowyers dwelling within the sayd Citie and Suburbes; And yet neverthelesse your sayd Subjectes for the avoidyng of the Daungers and Penaltie conteyned in the sayd Braunche are daily enforced to make suche great number of Bowes of Elme Wychhasell and Asshe, that they cannot in convenient tyme utter and sell the same, but are constrayned to kepe suche Bowes by them so made, untill they be putrifyed and not meete for any good Use or Purpose; By reason whereof muche of the sayd Wood of Elme Wichhasell and Asshe is daily wasted and consumed in making of the sayd Bowes, and your sayd Subjectes by by suche Losses as they daily susteine in making suche Bowes greatly impoverished, and the Commonwealthe therby nothing advanced but rather hindered: And where also in the severall Statutes of the noble Kyng of famous memorie Kyng Edward the Fourthe, made in the xxij[th] yere of his Raygne, and in the thyrd yere of the Raigne of

---

[93] 33 Hen. 8, c.9 actually specifies the bowyers outside London were to make *four* bows of mean wood for every yew bow, not three as stated here.

[94] 'Witch hazel' was an alternative name for wych elm in the sixteenth century, rather than the flowering plant now known as witch hazel. The earlier statute appears to suggest bows made of wych elm or hazel rather than 'wych hazel.'

Kyng Henry the Seventh, Graundfather to our sayd Soveraigne Ladie the Queenes Majestie, and in the sayd xxxiij[th] yere of the Raigne of our sayd late Sovaigne Lord Kyng Henry the Eight, Father to our sayd Soveraigne Ladie, there is mencion made of the prices of Bowes, which at those severall tymes was appointed to be but three shillinges fower pence and not above to sell the best; at which sayd tymes suche Bowes might well have ben so solde to any person or persons according to the Rates and Prices expressed in the sayd severall Actes, untill nowe withiin this twentie yeres the pryces of Bowestaves have diversly ben raysed and enhaunced from fyve poundes a hundreth to twelve poundes or thereaboutes; For which Causes the pryces conteyned in the sayd severall Statutes cannot be observed, and yet your Majesties sayd Subjectes the Bowyers are presently in daunger of the sayd severall Statutes concernyng the pryces of Bowes, which they humbly beseche your Majestie with thassent of your Hygh Courte of Parliament maye be releassed unto them and the penalties appointed for the same: Bee it therefore enacted ordeined and establyshed by the Queenes Majestie our Soveraigne Ladie with thassent of the Lordes Spirituall and Temporall and the Commons in this present Parliament assembled and by the aucthoritie of the same, That the sayd Estatutes of Kyng Edwarde the Fourthe and Kyng Henry the Seventh, concernyng the prices of Bowes, and all the braunches conteyned in the sayd Statute of Kyng Henry the Eight, so farre fourthe as the same extendeth to the prices of Bowes therein expressed only, from the first daye of this present Parliament and so for ever be thereby clearely repealed and made voide and frustrate to all Intente Construccions and Purposes; And also all and every Clause and Sentence of the said Statute of Kyng Henry the Eight before recited, tending to the making of Bowes of Elme Wichhasell Asshe and other Woode besydes Ewe before rehearsed or any penaltie therein conteined for any the sayd last rehersed Premisses from hensfourth for ever shall not be entended construed or taken to extende to any Bowyer nowe dwelling or inhabityng or which hereafter shall happen to dwell or inhabite within the Cityes of London and Westmynster or the Suburbes of any of them, or in the Borough of Southwarke in the Countie of Surrey; The said Statutes or any Thing in them or any of them conteined in any wyse to the contrarie notwithstanding.

And bee it further enacted by the aucthoritye aforesayd, That all and everie the sayd Bowyers within the sayd Cityes and Suburbes of London and Westmynster and Borowgh of Sowthwarke, shall from hensforte from tyme to tyme and at all tymes hereafter, provide and have in his or their Custodie the number of fiftie good and able Bowes of Elme Wichhasell or Asshe at the least, well and substancyally made and wrowght, upon payne that everie of the sayd Bowyers which by the space of twenty dayes shall not have in his Custody such number of the sayd Bowes of Wichhasell Elme or Asshe redye made and meete to be solde and used as aforesayd, shall hereafter for everie Bowe lacking of the number aforesayd, forfayte tenne shillinges, the one moitye of which forfayture shalbe to oure sayd Soveraigne Ladie the Queenes Majestie, and the other moitye thereof shalbe to him or them using the Arte of An Armourer Fletcher or maker of Bowestringes that will sue for the same by Action of Debt Byll Playnt or otherwise in any Courte of Recorde, in which Action and Sute no Protection or Wager of Lawe shall in any wise be admitted or allowed for the Defendaunt.

Provided allwayes and be it enacted by the aucthoritie aforesayd, That if any Bowyer after the fyrst daye of Maye next commyng, do sell any Bowes meete for mens shoting, being outlandishe Ewe and of the best sorte, over and above the pryce of six shillinges eight pence, or do sell any Bowes meete for mens shoting, being of the seconde sorte, over and above the pryce of three shillinges fower pence, or shall sell any Bowes meete for men as is aforesayd being of the course sorte called Livery Bowes for and above the price of two shillinges a peece, or that shall after the sayd fyrst daye of Maye sell any Bowes being Englishe Ewe over and above the pryce of two shillinges the peece, That then the seller or sellers of suche Bowes shall forfayte for every Bowe so solde over and above the pryce aforesayd, fortye shillinges, the one moitye thereof to the Queenes Majestie her Heires and Successours, and the other moitie to the partie using the Art of an Armourer Fletcher or maker of Bowestrynges that will sue for the same in any Courte of Recorde, by Action of Debt Byll Playnt or otherwise, wherein no Wager of Lawe Essoigne or Protection shalbe admitted or allowed ; Anything in thys Acte or in any other Acte conteyned to the contrary in any wise notwithstanding. This Acte to continewe untill the last daye of the fyrst Session of the next Parliament.

99

## 24. An Acte for the bringing of Bowestaves into this Realme. (1571)

*As in the 1480s, when limiting the retail price of bows meant subsequent legislation ensuring a sufficient supply of bow staves,[95] so the Elizabethan establishment of new prices for bows required renewed efforts to keep bowyers supplied with affordable raw materials. The earlier acts requiring foreign merchants to include a certain number of bow staves in their cargo had been good, but enforcing them ha d proven problematic because there was no real incentive for individuals to police the trade. The last of the Elizabethan archery acts circumvented the problem by rewarding anyone who would bring a case in law against merchants who failed to bring the requisite number of staves with half the fine imposed. Charles I reissued some of the medieval and Henrican archery acts in the seventeenth century, but archery ceased to perform a meaningful military purpose in England seventeen years after this act was passed, and no further new pieces of legislation to support the practice of archery or the provision of archery equipment were passed in the Tudor period.*

### 13 Elizabeth 1. c.13

Where as the use of Archerie not onely hathe ever ben but also yet is by Gods special Gyfte to the English nation a singuler Defence of this Realme, and an occasion of many noble Victoris and both a very wholesome Exercise for the Health and Strengh of Mens Bodies, and a Maynteynance of a greate number of the Queenes true Subjects and Artificers as Bowyers Fletchers Stringers Arrowheadmakers, and other of this Realme; and for that among other Causes of the Decaye of Archerie, one great Cause is, the excessive pryce of Bowe Staves, which groweth principally by the Scarcitie of Bowe Staves brought into this Realme: For Reformation whereof, Bee yt enacted by thaucthoritie[96] of this present Parliament, That all the Statutes made in the Twelf yere of the Raigne of Kyng Edward the Fourth, concerning bringing in of certayne number of Bow Staves according to the Wayght or Value of other Wares to be brought into this Realme, shall from henceforth be duely put in Execusion; And bee yt enacted and declared by

---

[95] See **Docs 12** and **13**
[96] The authority

this present Statute, That al Merchaunt Straungers using to bring Wares into this Realme from the East Partes, aswel from the threescore twelve Hanse Townes be comprised & meant under the name of and bound as the merchauntes mentioned & bound by the said Statute to bring in Bowe Staves upon lyke paynes and forfeytures as by the said Statutes are appoynted.

And where the greatest Cause of not putting the said Statute in execution hathe ben, that the Forfaitures thereby lymited are by the said Statute geven only to the Queenes Majestie her Heires and Successors, without any Reward to the person that shall sue for the same; Bee yt enacted, That from henceforth al the Forfaytures appoynted by the said Statutes shalbe imployed in fourme folowing, that is to saye, Thon[97] Halfe thereof to the Queenes Majestie her Heyres & Successors, thother Halfe to such person as shall sue for the same in any Court of Record, wherein no Essoyne Protection nor Wager of Lawe for the Defendaunte shalbe admitted or alowed.

And yt may please the Queenes most excellent Majestie, That it be on her Highnes Parte straightly charged and comaunded, that all the Statutes nowe remayning in force for repressing of unlawfull Games, and for the Mayntenance and Use of Archerye shalbe duely put in Execution for ever under the Paynes in the said Statutes contayned.

---

[97] The one

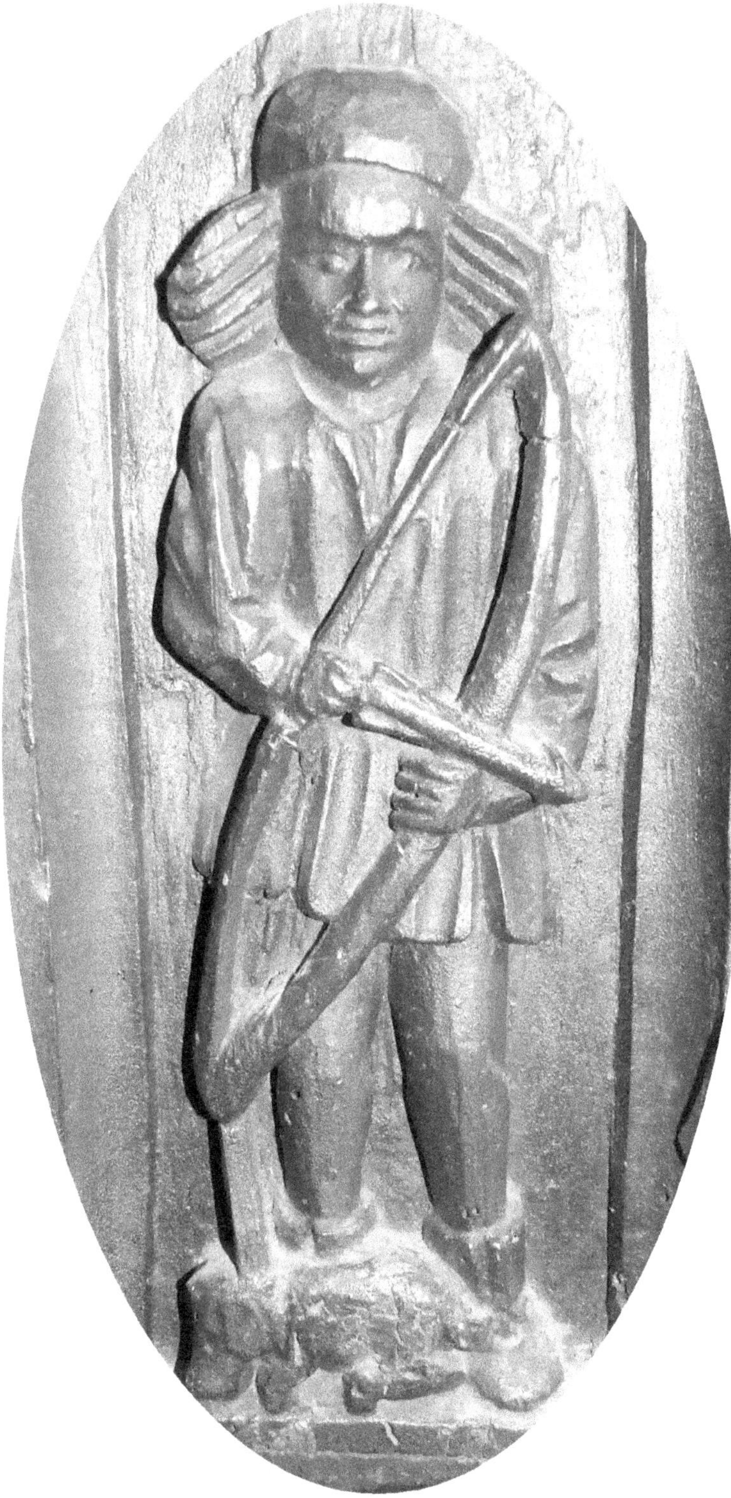

# Part 2

MISCELLANEOUS SOURCES.

## 25. The Welsh Longbow? 1194

*It is often said that the 'English' bow was, in fact, a Welsh invention adopted and perhaps adapted by the English. The claim probably stems from the pride Shakespeare's Fluellen exhibits before Henry V, and the undoubted presence of Welsh archers at Agincourt. Proponents of the Welsh origin are wont to cite Giraldus Cambrensis (Gerald of Wales), who wrote of the prowess of Welsh archers a century or so before the widespread adoption of the bow by English armies. Recruitment records for Henry V's 1415 campaign in France show that the majority of the archers present at Agincourt were recruited in England, and Shakespeare's historical accuracy hardly matches his poetic ability. It is worthwhile, therefore, examining what Giraldus actually said about the Welsh bow: the description that he gives both of the bow itself and the nature of its use are very different indeed to the 'English' bow of later years.*

*Extract from Giraldus Cambrensis,* Descriptio Cambriae, *translated by Sir R.C. Hoare.*

It seems worthy of remark, that the people of what is called Venta are more accustomed to war, more famous for valour, and more expert in archery, than those of any other part of Wales. The following examples prove the truth of this assertion. In the last capture of the aforesaid castle, which happened in our days, two soldiers passing over a bridge to take refuge in a tower built on a mound of earth, the Welsh, taking them in the rear, penetrated with their arrows the oaken portal of the tower, which was four fingers thick; in memory of which circumstance, the arrows were preserved in the gate. William de Braose also testifies that one of his soldiers, in a conflict with the Welsh, was wounded by an arrow, which passed through his thigh and the armour with which it was cased on both sides, and through that part of the saddle which is called the alva, mortally wounded his horse. Another soldier had his hip equally sheathed in armour, penetrated by an arrow quite to the saddle, and on turning his horse round, received a similar wound on the opposite hip, which fixed him on both sides of his seat. What more could be expected from a balista? Yet the bows used by this people are not made of horn, ivory, or yew, but of wild elm; unpolished, rude, and uncouth, but stout; not calculated to shoot an arrow to a great distance, but to inflict very severe wounds in close fight.

*Welsh archer from a 13$^{th}$ century manuscript.*

## 26. Recalcitrant Archers, 1326[98]

*Given the feudal nature of military recruitment in the medieval period, in which every man was liable to be ordered to serve the king as required, it is not surprising to find that not all men were keen. Desertion from the army was an issue which most medieval commanders faced, but occasionally the unwilling conscripts simply failed to arrive at the appointed muster. The eventual fates of the 28 Sussex men who refused the order to muster in 1326 are unknown.*

13 Sept 1326. To the Sheriff of Sussex.

Order to attach and imprison until further orders John son of Alan de Bredherst, John Crullyng, Robert Colier of Herst Mounceaux, Richard Franceis, John Michiel the elder, Robert Aillewyne, Thomas Ailwyne, Simon Ailwyne, Walter Stodhird, Robert Tothe, Robert Wyldebor, Thomas Wilon, John Bosgate, William de Holetye, Henry Seller', Roger de Horne, Richard Bely, Thomas le Man of Bisshoppeston, William le Pike, Richard atte Ford, John Osbarn, William Taillour, Philip atte Crouche, John Ballard, Peter Caperoun, John Hervy, Simon de Burghham, and Adam de Ydenne, and to certify the king in writing of his proceedings herein, as the arrayors of men-at-arms and footmen in that county have signified to the king that they have caused the aforesaid men to be chosen in execution of the king's order to cause a certain number of footmen, archers, and others to be chosen and sent to him at Porcestre, in order to set out upon the sea in his service, and that they have enjoined the aforesaid men to be at Porcestre on the appointed day in person, and that the men have wholly refused to do so.

---

[98] *Calendar of Close Rolls*, Edward II, vol. 4, p. 647

## 27. The Battle of Crecy, 1346

*Giovanni Villani,* Nuova Cronica.[99]

*The Battle of Crecy in which an English army under Edward III defeated a numerically superior French army commanded by Phillipe de Valois is one of the key events which has contributed to the legend of the medieval English archer. It was the subject of numerous accounts in a variety of medieval chronicles, most written decades after the battle. Of all the chronicle accounts that by the Italian Giovanni Villani was probably the first: Villani died just two years after the battle, in 1348, so his account is probably the earliest and is certainly near-contemporary. It's impossible to know from where Villani got his information about the battle, but his writing demonstrates a keen interest in international affairs and he certainly kept abreast of the latest news. Crucially, his account includes details not found in other near contemporary accounts, and is eminently readable. Eye-witness accounts of the battle have survived, the letters of Edward III for example, or Richard de Wynkeley, but they uniformly fail to mention the archers who have since been hailed as the real heroes of the day, so Villani's account is not just the first written for public consumption, but is also the first to describe the archers' role.*

> Philippe de Valois, king of France, who with his army was following Edward, king of England, and his army, having discovered that they had pitched camp near Crécy and were ready for battle, advanced towards him, firmly believing he had caught him already weary and defeated by the discomforts and hunger suffered during the march. The king of France had three times more mounted men-at-arms than his opponent, having 12,000 horse and nearly an uncountable number of foot soldiers, while the king of England had 4,000 horsemen and around 30,000 English and Welsh archers, plus many Welsh infantry with axes and short spears. The king of France, having arrived a horse's gallop from the English camp, at the hour of Nones on Saturday, 26 August 1346, divided his army into three divisions. In the first he had 6,000 Genoese crossbowmen and other Italians, led by Carlo Grimaldi and Antone Doria, and with the crossbowmen were also King John

---
[99] Translated from the Italian by Maria Rossi, with unhelpful pointers from E.T. Fox.

of Bohemia, Sir Charles, his son, elected king of the Romans, and other barons and knights for a total of 3,000 cavalry. The second division was led by Charles, count of Alençon, with many counts and barons amounting to 4,000 horsemen and many foot sergeants. The third division was the king of France, with the other aforementioned kings, counts and barons, and all the rest of the army that were an uncountable number of horse and foot. Just before the armies clashed, two great crows appeared above the deployed armies, crying and crowing; then down came a shower of rain and, when it ended, the battle commenced. The first division with the Genoese crossbowmen advanced towards the king of England's wagon-fort[100] and started shooting their quarrels. But immediately they were subjected to counter-shot: the carts and below them were protected from bolts by fabric and drapes, and in the king of England's divisions inside the wagon-fort and in the others already deployed, stood 30,000 English and Welsh archers. Every time the Genoese shot a bolt from their crossbow, that bolt would be answered by three arrows from their bows, which formed a storm cloud in the sky. And these did not fall without hitting men and horses. To these one must add the shots from the bombards, so loud and threatening that it seemed God himself was thundering, with great killing of men and gutting of horses. But worse for the French forces, the tight narrow fighting area was as wide as the opening of the wagon-fort, the second division led by the count of Alençon hit and pushed the Genoese, pushing them towards the carts, so that they could neither hold their ground nor shoot their crossbows, being constantly hit by the arrows of those on top of the carts and blasted by the bombards, so that many were killed or wounded. For this reason, the aforesaid crossbowmen, crammed together and pushed towards the wagon-fort by their own knights, turned and fled. The French knights and their sergeants, seeing them run, believed they had betrayed and so killed them with few surviving. Edward, Prince of Wales, son of the king of England was leading the first mounted division, around 1,000 men, with 6,000 Welsh archers. Seeing the first division of the French king's crossbowmen take to their heels, he and

---

[100] Earlier in his text Villani described the English defences: 'the king of England ordered his archers, of which he had many, on top of the carts and below them, together with bombards firing small iron balls, in order to frighten the French horses and cause them to fly.'

his men mounted their horses and, exiting the wagon-fort, attacked the king of France's cavalry, the front line of which included the king of Bohemia and his son, the count of Alençon, the count of Flanders, the count of Blois, the count of Harcourt, Sir Gianni d'Analdo, and many other counts and great lords. The fight here was hard and bloody, so that he was reinforced by the second English division led by the earl of Arundel, so that together they routed the first and second French divisions, mainly thanks to the Genoese flight. And in that clash were killed the king of Bohemia, the count of Alençon, and many counts, barons, knights, and sergeants. Seeing his men flee, the king of France attacked the English with his third division and all the rest of his army, performing in person wonderful feats of arms, managing thus to push the English back to the wagon-fort. The English would have been defeated had not King Edward devised an able maneuver, as he came out from the wagon-fort through an opening he ordered made among the carts, allowing him to swing round the enemy and attack him from the rear, coming to his men's relief by hitting the enemy hard in the flank, his Welsh and English infantry archers and spearmen ripping open the horses' bellies. But what really created confusion among the French was the mass of their own men on horse and on foot, who in their haste to defeat the English went on pushing and hitting each other, so that they piled one horse on top of the other, thus resembling what happened with the Flemings at Kortrijk. In particular, they were impeded by the dead Genoese of the first division lying on the ground, and the mountains of dead and fallen horses covering the field, hit by arrows and bombards so that not one French horse was unhurt and many were killed. The fearsome battle lasted from before Vespers to two hours into the night, and in the end the French, unable to resist any longer, took to their heels. Wounded, the king of France escaped to Amiens, together with the bishop of Amiens, the count of Alzurro, and the son of the royal chancellor, together with sixty men-at-arms under the dauphin of Vienne's standard, because all his banners and royal standards had fallen on the field. As scattered groups fled on horse and on foot under the cover of darkness, they were robbed and killed by their own peasantry, and in this way many perished without even being pursued. On the following day, a Sunday, those French who had fled during the night rallied on a small salient near a wood, numbering

8,000 mounted and on foot. Among these was Charles, emperor-elect, who had survived the first rout and had gone there not knowing where else to run. The king of England sent the earls of Warwick and Northampton to attack these with many men on horse and on foot. As they had already been defeated, they did not stand for long and, fleeing, many were killed and captured, while Charles escaped to the abbey of Ourscamp, where the cardinals were, having been wounded three times. And that Sunday morning there arrived on the field the duke of Lorraine, nephew of the king of France, and leading reinforcements numbering 3,000 horse and 4,000 foot from his own country, being ignorant who had been the defeated the night before. Seeing those French whom, as we said, out of fear were arrayed on the little ridge, he charged the English, but was defeated and died with about one-hundred of his knights, and killed also most of his foot soldiers while the others dispersed. In this bloody and unfortunate battle for the king of France, practically all those present who have written about it agree that about 20,000 cavalry and infantry were killed, and horses of innumerable quantity, of which more than 1,600 between counts, barons, knights banneret, and knights bachelor, without including the more than 4,000 mounted esquires, and as many captured; and nearly all those who escaped suffered arrow wounds. Among the slain great lords were John of Bohemia with five German counts of his retinue, that of Majorca, the count of Alençon, brother of the king of France, the count of Flanders, the count of Blois, the duke of Lorraine, the count of Sancerre, the count of Harcourt, the count of Albemerle and his son, the count of Salm in Germany, who was with the king of Bohemia, Carlo Grimaldi and Antone Doria from Genoa, and many other nobles whose names we have not discovered. King Edward remained for two days on the battlefield, where he had the mass of the Holy Spirit celebrated, to thank God for his victory, and a mass for the dead. He had the ground consecrated so as to bury the dead, friend and foe alike, while the wounded he had separated from the dead and treated, giving money to the common people before dismissing them. The dead lords he had nobly buried in a nearby abbey, and among others he gave great honor and celebration to the king of Bohemia, as befitted a king's body, and for his love bemoaning his death and dressing in black with his barons, sending the body back to his son, Charles, who was at the

Ourscamp Abbey, and from there his son carried it to Luxembourg. And this done, King Edward, with his lucky victory, because few of his men died compared to the French, departed from Crécy on the third day to Montreuil. 'O santus santus santus dominus deus Sabaot,' which is Latin for 'Holiest of Holy, Our Lord, God of the army, how great is Your power, on heaven and on earth,'[101] especially in battles, which sometimes, actually often, makes it so that those less powerful defeat the great armies to show His power to strike down pride and arrogance, and to clean the sins of the kings, the lords and the people. And in this defeat, God well shows His power since the French were three times the size of the English. But this peril for the king of France was not without a just reason, since the king, among his many sins, even setting aside the wrong done to the king of England, and others of his barons' lands and heritage, had more than ten years earlier sworn before Pope John XXII to take the cross and to depart to Outremer and to retake the Holy Land within two years. He collected the tithes and subsidies, but he used them to make unjust war against Christian lands. For these reasons the Armenian and Syrian Christians who, because of a hope for the king of France had begun to fight the Saracens in Syria, were killed and enslaved by the Saracens of Outremer.[102] And this explains it all.

---

[101] In fact it is Latin for 'O holy, holy, holy Lord God of Hosts.'
[102] Technically 'Outremer' refers to the Christian-controlled areas of the Middle East, but in practice it was used often to refer more generally to the Holy Land.

## 28. Recruitment and clothing, 1346[103]

*After the victory at Crecy Edward III led his army to Calais and laid siege to the town. The defenders withstood the siege for nearly a year until August 1347 when a French army marched to end the siege and relieve the town. When they arrived at Calais, however, they found a very strong Anglo-Flemish force in an entrenched position, so retreated without action. The failure of the relief force left the defenders no option but to capitulate and the town was surrendered to the English. Calais remained in English hands until recaptured by the French in 1558.*

*Among the most prominent of Edward III's commanders was his son, Edward, Prince of Wales: the 'Black Prince.' Shortly after the English army invested Calais the prince wrote to the officers of his principality, ordering them to send more troops. These men, archers as well as spearmen, were uniformed in green and white.*

> Sept. 12. Westminster.
>
> To Sir Thomas de Ferreres, justice of Cestre,[104] or Roger de Hopwell, his lieutenant. With the help of God the prince has prospered in his present expedition and is now come before Caleys[105] to besiege it. He needs more Welshmen to help him in the siege and the expedition which he purposes to make after it, and therefore orders Sir Thomas to cause 200 Welshmen to be chosen, tried, and arrayed in the county of Flynt, as well within the liberty of the bishop of St. Asaph as elsewhere, and to have them armed, half with lances and other suitable arms and half with bows and arrows, so that they be at Dovre[106] on Saturday the morrow of Michaelmas next. Griffith ap Jor' ap Meyler is to be their leader. This order is to be carried out without sparing anyone for gift or favour; and Sir Thomas is not to be so negligent or tardy in this matter as he was in the last array of archers of Cheshire. The prince has ordered his clerk, Master John de Brunham, the

---

[103] *The Register of Edward the Black Prince* (London, 1930), vol. 1, pp. 14-15
[104] Chester
[105] Calais
[106] Dover

younger, to pay the Welshmen's wages until they reach him, and will have them clothed in uniform at London.

These letters were delivered to Master John de Brunham on 14 September.

The like order was given to the justice of South Wales or his lieutenant, for 200 Welshmen of South Wales to be at Dovre at the octave of Michaelmas.

*Sept. 12. Westminster.*

Order to Richard atte Hogh, sheriff of Flynt, to choose and make trial of the 200 Welshmen referred to in the above order to Sir Thomas de Ferreres.

This letter was delivered to Master John de Brunham at London on 14 September. Sept. 14.

Order to the prince's clerk, Master John de Brunham, the Westminster, younger, to buy suitable green and white cloth for the abovementioned Welshman from Flynt, and deliver to each of them a short coat and a hat of both colours, the green on the right; also to pay by indenture to their leader a certain sum in advance on account of his and their wages until they reach the prince.

The like to George de Upton, chamberlain of South Wales, in respect of the Welshmen from South Wales.

## 29. Provision of Equipment for Archers, 1355[107]

*The provision of equipment for archers varied greatly over the medieval period. In some cases they were expected to furnish their own bows and arrows, and indeed the Statute of Winchester[108] required them to be able to do so. In other cases their commander made up any shortfall in their equipment, and in others still they were provided with arms and clothing by the authorities. In this example forty archers destined for the Channel Islands were provided not only with a bow and a sheaf of arrows each, but also a tunic.*

20 June 1355. To John Lovel, late sheriff of Middlesex.

Order to deliver by indenture Westminster, forty bows and forty sheaves of arrows appointed for archers tried and arrayed in that county for the king's service, and in the sheriff's custody, to Roger, yeoman of William Stury for the munition of the archers about to set out with him to the islands of Gerneseye, Jereseye, Serk and Aurneye, so that the departure of those archers may not be postponed, as the king has ordained twenty archers of that county and twenty archers of Surrey to set out with Roger to those islands.

[Same date] To Richard Lacer.

Order to deliver by indenture forty tunics, appointed at another time for archers chosen and arrayed for the king's service in Surrey and afterwards delivered to the keeping of John Randolf, deceased, whose wife Richard has married, to Roger yeoman of William Stury for the clothing of the forty archers of Middlesex and Surrey about to set out with him in the king's service to the parts of the islands of Gerneseye, Jereseye, Serk and Aurneye.

---

[107] *Calendar of Close Rolls*, Edward III, vol. 10, pp. 135-136
[108] See **Doc. 1**

## 30. Provision of Bows, Arrows, and Strings, 1359[109]

*The Breton War of Succession (1341-1365) was one of the theatres of the Hundred Years' War in which England and France took opposing sides in what was, essentially, a Breton civil war. Olivier de Clisson, known as 'The Butcher,' was the son of the infamous Jeanne de Clisson whose husband had been executed by Philip VI of France and who achieved her revenge at sea through piracy and supplying English forces in France. In 1359 Olivier de Clisson accompanied Edward III and John de Montfort in a* chevauchée *campaign in Brittany.*

*This order for the provision of archery equipment is interesting because of the ratio of bows to strings and arrows. Three strings per bow seems reasonable enough, but the provision of only one sheaf of arrows for every three bows is curious, and presumably the shortfall was to be made up from supplies taken from elsewhere. It is unclear what bows were 'painted' with, but a number of medieval illustrations show bows with a green back.*

> 8 October 1359. To William de Rothewell, clerk of the king's privy wardrobe in the Tower of London.
>
> Order to deliver by indenture to Oliver de Clikzon, who is about to set out to Brittany to stay there in the king's service, 500 bows, to wit, 200 painted and 300 white, 100 sheaves of arrows, and 1,500 bowstrings, to be taken to the said parts for furnishing the archers in his company.

---

[109] *Calendar of Close Rolls*, Edward III, v. 10, p. 481

## 31. Threat of Invasion, 1361[110]

*When medieval commanders required a fixed number of men for a planned campaign they may have found themselves able to choose the best archers from the men available,[111] but in an emergency, such as when threatened with invasion, quantity of men was more important than their quality and every man who could wield a bow (or spear, or pollaxe etc) was ordered to muster for the defence of the realm.*

> March 2 1361, To the arrayers in the county of Southampton of men at arms and archers.
>
> Whereas the king has sure intelligence that his enemies of France are actually at sea with a host of men at arms, armed men, archers and others, horse and foot, in a great navy, and purpose to invade the realm at Suthampton, Portesmuth, Sandewich or elsewhere: order, upon their allegiance and under pain of forfeiture, for defence of the realm against attack, immediately upon sight of these presents, to assemble and array all men at arms, armed men, archers and other fencible men, as well knights and esquires as others, within liberties and without, and bring them in their company, furnished with competent arms, to the sea coast where any such peril may threaten, so bearing themselves that those parts may by their care be preserved, and their behaviour deserve commendation.

---

[110] *Calendar of Close Rolls*, Edward III, vol. 11, pp. 97-98
[111] See **Doc. 34**

## 32. Edward III to the Lord Lieutenant of Kent, 1363[112]

*This letter, which has been cited frequently but rarely printed, is of particular interest because it appears to be the earliest reference to mandatory archery practice. It is not a statute, but such a clear instruction from the king to a lord-lieutenant was as good as a parliamentary statute in real terms, and although it applied only to Kent we might assume that similar letters reached the lords-lieutenant of other regions at the same time. It is interesting, too, that as early as 1363, when the Hundred Years' War was not even thirty years old and the great victory at Agincourt was still 52 years in the future, commanders were already concerned about the decline of English archery. Twenty-five years after this letter was written mandatory archery practice and the prohibition of certain games were entered into law by* 12 Ric.2 c.6.[113]

The King to the Lord-lieutenant of Kent, greeting:

Whereas the people of our realm, rich and poor alike, were accustomed formerly in their games to practise archery - whence by God's help, it is well known that high honour and profit came to our realm, and no small advantage to ourselves in our warlike enterprises - and that now skill in the use of the bow having fallen almost wholly into disrepute, our subjects give themselves up to the throwing of stones and of wood and of iron; and some to handball and football and hockey; and others to coursing and cockfights, and even to other unseemly sports less useful and manly; whereby our realm - which God forbid - will soon, it would appear, be void of archers:

We, wishing that a fitting remedy be found in this manner, do hereby ordain, that in all places in your county, liberties or no liberties, wheresoever you shall deem fit, a proclamation be made to this effect: that every man in the same county, if he be able-bodied, shall upon holidays, make use, in his games, of bows and arrows and so learn and practise archery.

---
[112] Rymer, *Foedera*, vol.3
[113] See **Doc. 3**

Moreover we ordain that you prohibit under penalty of imprisonment all and sundry from such stone, wood and iron throwing; handball, football, or hockey; coursing and cock-fighting; or other such idle games.

## 33. London Archers, 1369[114]

*In 1347 Edward III captured Calais, and in 1360 the Treaty of Brétigny was signed, bringing the first stage of the Hundred Years' War to a close and ceding Calais to England. Anglo-French conflict ensued in Spain when England and France supported opposing sides in the Castillian civil war and this, together with resistance to an unpopular hearth-tax imposed in English-controlled Aquitaine and the accession of Charles V of France in 1364, led to the treaty being repudiated in 1369. The fresh outbreak of war necessitated the raising of troops to augment the Calais garrison.*

Assessment of Wards made by Simon de Mordone, the Mayor, and the Aldermen, on Monday after the Feast of St. John ante portam Latinam,[115] 43 Edward III., for sending sixty armed men[116] and sixty archers to the town of Calais, the King having paid to Robert de Kaytone, the Common Serjeant, their wages for forty days, viz., 12d. a day for every armed man and 6d. for every archer, and the Mayor and Aldermen and good men of the Wards paying for their arms, bow and arrows, and clothing as follows:—

Tower: 3 armed men and 3 archers, £9.

Billyngesgate: the like, £9.

Bridge: 4 armed men and 4 archers, £12.

Douegate: 3 armed men and 3 archers, £9.

Portesokne: 1 armed man and 1 archer, 60s.

Bisshopesgate: the like, 60s.

Candelwykestret: 2 armed men and 2 archers, £6.

Algate: 1 armed man and 1 archer, 60s.

---

[114] *Letter Books of the City of London, 1352-1374*, ff. 225-226
[115] 6 May
[116] Spear- or bill-armed infantry.

Langebourne: 2 armed men and 2 archers, £6.

Cornhill: the like, £6.

Bradestret: the like, £6.

Walbroke: 3 armed men and 3 archers, £9.

Vintry: the like, £9.

Bassyeshawe: 1 armed man and 1 archer, 60s.

Farndone Within: 3 armed men and 3 archers, £9.

Farndone Without: the like, £9.

Crepulgate Within: the like, £9.

Crepulgate Without: 1 armed man and 1 archer, 60s.

Queenhithe: 2 armed men and 2 archers, £6.

Cordewanerstret: 5 armed men and 5 archers, £15.

Bredstret: 2 armed men and 2 archers, £6.

Aldresgate: 1 armed man and 1 archer, 60s.

Castle Baynard: 2 armed men and 2 archers, £6.

Colmanstret: 1 armed man and 1 archer, 60s.

Cheap: 5 armed men and 5 archers, £15.

Lymstret: 1 armed man and 1 archer, 60s.

Names of armed men and archers sent for the defence of Calais at the King's request by the Mayor and Aldermen on 10th May, 43 Edward III.

Simon de Ware, vintainer,[117] answers for himself and his vintaine, and has under him, viz.:—

---

[117] Junior officer commanding a small force, nominally of 20 men. In this case the vintenars did command precisely 20 men each, including themselves: 10 archers and 9 'armed men,' suggesting that the vintenars were also 'armed men.'

*Armed men*: Thomas Heywode, Nicholas Wittele, William Chesman, Edmund de Bury, Thomas Kayhoo, John Spyndeler, Thomas Yakeslee, William atte Wode, John Luddyngtone.

*Archers*: William Freynshe, Peter Chaundeler, Henry Betrynge, Walter Savage, William de York, William Saundre, William Koc, William fitz Johan, Robert Iklyngtone, William Shrouesbury.

Hugh Warmer, vintainer, answers for his vintaine, and has under him, viz.:—

*Armed men*: Thomas Wrong, John Bristowe, John Clapham, Thomas Sely, John Asshe, John Andreu, Nicholas Berde, Adam Ratteseye, John Basset.

*Archers*: John atte Marche, Richard Shirbourne, John Burel, William Love, Adam Blakemore, Roger Gaunt, Thomas Hert, Nicholas Brode, John Clerc, John Waller.

Hugh Brenge, vintainer, answers for himself and his vintaine, and has under him, viz.:—

*Armed men*: Richard Pottere, Thomas Belchambre, Elias Shiptone, John Haunfeld, John Marchaunt, Jordan Sperwe, John Braybourne, John Moburlee, Nicholas Bradeleye.

*Archers*: Nicholas Crumpe, John Lowys, Vincent de Cornewaille, Robert Roundel, Thomas Hervy, Nicholas Proudfot, John Cornewaille, William Lowys, Ralph Longe, Henry Felix.

Robert Terry, centainer,[118] and James Shaldebourne, vintainer, answer for themselves and their vintaine, and have under them, viz.:—

*Armed men*: John Sheldone, John Castre, Andrew Geet, Robert Suttone, William Stigenheye, William Wattes, John Fuller, Henry de Ware.

---

[118] Officer in command of nominally 100 men, in this case apparently 120 men.

*Archers*: John Beket, Walter Kirkeby, John Noke, Robert West, Richard Newe, John atte Doune, Richard atte More, Ralph Clyfford, John Daventre, John Skylman.

William de Notyngham, vintainer, answers for himself and his vintaine, and has under him, viz.:—

*Armed men*: Henry Pountfreyt, Henry Grandone, John Wappelode, John de Thorpe, Robert Somerville, William Braunceby, John Parker, Walter Devenisshe, William Neuman.

*Archers*: John Horold, Peter Gardiner, Roger Chount, John Appel, Adam Lentale, Simon Driffeld, Richard Clakke, Edward Malemayn, John Kaynel, William Brys.

William Frenyngham, vintainer, answers for himself and his vintaine, and has under him, viz.:—

*Armed men*: Robert Lyncolne, Thomas Shirbourne, John Rocheford, John Morce, Adam Heyward, John atte Broke, John Bury, John Peek, Thomas Lancastre.

*Archers*: John Herward, John Baroun, John Rankediche, John Blaket, Roger Spere, Thomas Portour, John Frere, John Shrouesbury, John Brad, William Coggeshale.

## 34. Recruitment of Archers, 1386[119]

*As noted above,[120] in times of emergency every able-bodied man with a bow might be levied for the defence of the realm, but when smaller numbers of men were required for a specific campaign the county arrayers might be instructed to select 'archers of the best.' The number of archers which could be raised by this selective method appears to have been relatively small - only 3,620 from 23 counties - and it is unclear whether the local officials always did choose the best men as instructed, or whether they sometimes put other considerations first. The arrayers and sheriffs did not necessarily select the men personally, but in many cases relied on parish constables or other local officials to carry out the orders. The constables had to balance the order for the best archers against the smooth-running of their parish, not denuding any farm or business of all its able-bodied men, and the protection of essential parish tradesmen.*

October 2 1386. To the arrayers of men at arms etc. in Yorkshire, and to the sheriff of York, lately appointed to choose and try four hundred archers of the best in that county, and when armed and arrayed to set them in twenties and hundreds, and cause them to be brought to the king at London, so as to be there at the feast of Michaelmas[121] last, ready to march in his army against Charles the king's adversary of France and his allies, if they shall invade the realm. Notice that it is and was the king's intent that those archers should be brought to London at the cost of the county, there to be levied by the arrayers and sheriff ; and order so to bring them without delay.

The like to the arrayers and sheriffs in the following counties :

Surrey, in regard to 100 archers.

Middlesex, 100 archers.

Hertfordshire, 100 archers.

Cambridgeshire, 100 archers.

Huntingdonshire, 100 archers.

---

[119] *Calendar of Close Rolls*, Richard II, vol. 3, p. 187
[120] See **Doc. 31**
[121] 29 September

Lincolnshire, 400 archers.

Warwickshire, 150 archers.

Leycestershire, 150 archers.

Staffordshire, 200 archers.

Derbyshire, 150 archers.

Oxfordshire, 200 archers.

Berkshire, 200 archers.

Somerset, 200 archers.

Dorset, 100 archers.

Devon, 100 archers.

Notynghamshire, 150 archers.

Salop, 100 archers.

Northamptonshire, 200 archers.

Bedfordshire, 60 archers.

Bukinghamshire, 60 archers.

Herefordshire, 100 archers.

Gloucestershire, 200 archers.

## 35. The Battle of Agincourt, 1415 (1)

*Gesta Henrici Quinti, c.1418*

*Like Crecy, the battle of Agincourt attracted numerous chroniclers to write accounts in the century or so following the event. Perhaps the most widely quoted was written by Jean de Wavrin[122] who, although writing some thirty years or more after the event, had been a witness to the battle from the French side. Less well-known is the account published in the* Gesta Henrici Quinti, *an anonymous work whose author was one of the chaplains to Henry V's army and who was present at the battle on the English side. Internal evidence suggests that the* Gesta *was written before 1418, making it the earliest of the chronicle accounts. The author tells us himself that he observed the battle from the baggage lines and was able to following the to and fro of the fighting. A clergyman rather than a soldier, he nevertheless comes across as familiar with military matters and a fairly reliable witness to that remarkable day.*

We left there on our march towards the River of Swords,[123] leaving on the following Wednesday the walled town of ...[124] a league to the left. When on the next day, namely Thursday, we were descending the valley towards the said River of Swords, it was announced to the king by scouts and patrols on horseback that an enemy force many thousands strong was on the other side of the river, about a league away on our right.

Therefore we crossed the river as fast as we could, and when we reached the top of the hill on the other side, we saw emerging from further up the valley the grim ranks of Frenchmen, about half a mile from us. Being of an incomparable number in relation to us, they took up position in columns, ranks and squadrons somewhat more than half a mile opposite us, filling a very broad field, as if they were an innumerable multitude of locusts, and occupying the moderately sized valley that lay between them and us.

---

[122] See **Doc. 36**
[123] R. Ternoise
[124] The name of the town is missing from the original manuscript. Benjamin Williams, who first published the *Gesta* in 1850, postulated Doullens and most historians have agreed with him since.

Meanwhile our king roused his army in a most civil and unperturbed manner, and positioned them in lines and wings, as if they were to enter battle immediately. Then each and every man who had not earlier cleansed his conscience by confession took up the arms of penitence. There was no shortage then of men except of priests. Among the other things that I then noted as being said, Sir Walter Hungerford implored the king to have, with the small company that he had there, ten thousand of the best English archers, who would indeed have wanted to be there with him. To him the king said, 'You are talking foolishly, because by the God of heaven, on whose grace I have depended, and in whom I have the firm hope of victory, I would not want to have even one more man than I have, even if I could. For these are the people of God I have here, and it is an honour for me to have them at this time. Or do you not believe that His omnipotence, with these His humble few, can overcome the pride of the French that opposes Him, who boast of their great number and strength?', as if he were saying, He can if He wishes to. And in my opinion nothing unfortunate could happen through the great justice of God to a son of His with such great faith, just as nothing happened to Judas Maccabeus until he fell into a lack of faith and then deservedly into ruin.

When for a while the opposing ranks had seen and considered our measure and smallness of number, they brought themselves to a field that lay beyond a wood, which was near on the left between us and them, where our route towards Calais was. Our king, supposing that the men would thus either encircle the wood, so that they could come upon him via that route, or else would go round through the more distant woods that neighboured it and surround us on every side, immediately removed his columns and positioned them in constant opposition to them.

When eventually after some delay we had almost reached sunset, the Frenchmen perhaps saw that war was not going to be waged, as this was not appropriate around nightfall, and entered the hamlets and scrub nearby, intending to rest until morning.

When it at last reached nightfall, and darkness had overcome us and them, and we were still standing on the field and listening to the enemy in their quarters, as each of them shouted, as is their custom, for their comrade, servant and friend, who had perhaps become separated from them in so great a crowd, and our men had similarly begun to do the same, the king ordered silence throughout the whole army, on the penalty of losing horse and harness, in the case of a nobleman who committed the offence, and of a right ear in the case of an archer and anyone of lower rank, without any hope of obtaining forgiveness for anyone who should presume to violate the king's edict. And immediately he retreated in silence to the hamlet nearby, where we had some houses, although very few in number, along with gardens and groves for our respite, and there was rain in abundance for almost the whole night.

While our enemy contemplated our quietude and silence, thinking that our small number had been seized by fear and had perhaps proposed flight in the night, they lit fires and manned watches throughout the fields and passes. And it was said that they thought themselves so safe from us that they played dice for our king and noblemen that night.

And on the following day, namely Friday on the Feast of St Crispin and Crispinian, 25 October, as dawn rose, the French positioned themselves in ranks, squadrons and wedges, and took their place in front of us on the field named Agincourt, across which was our route to Calais, and they were of a most terrifying number. Cohorts of cavalry stood in many hundreds on both sides of their vanguard in order to burst through our battle line and our force of archers. And that vanguard of soldiers on foot consisted of all the choicest noblemen: it was a forest of lances and a grave multitude of gleaming shields and cavalry at their sides, and was approximately thirty times greater than ours. But their rearguard and wings, squadrons and wedges were all on horseback, as if prepared for flight rather than to remain in place, and in respect to ours they were of an incomparable number.

While our king meanwhile readied himself for the field, after the praises of God and masses had been heard not far from our resting place, he set up one line of battle but with all of his small retinue, positioning the vanguard, which the duke of York commanded, as the wing on the right, and the rearguard, which Lord Camoys commanded, as the wing on the left, and mixed in wedges of archers into each battle line, and made them plant their stakes amidst them, as had been previously arranged to prevent the cavalry from bursting in. The astuteness of the enemy perceived this by means of scouts that went between them, and either on that account or for some other reason I know not (but God does), they kept themselves back from us opposite and did not march against us.

When they had spent much of the day in delays of this kind, and each army had stood still and not moved a step against each other, the king saw that the multitude were deferring the attack which he had expected from them, and thus stood across our route, either to break up our deployment or to instil our hearts with fear of their numbers, or as if to obstruct our movement and await more allies who chanced to be on their way, or at least, knowing the shortage of our victuals, to defeat us with hunger, whom they did not dare to defeat with the sword. Our king decided to move against them, sending word for the army's baggage so that it would be at the rear of the battle and not fall prey to the enemy. He had previously decided that this baggage, together with the priests who were to celebrate rites and zealously pray for him and his men, should wait in the hamlet and closes where he had been the night before, until the end of the battle, and at which the French brigands were looking at from almost every side, intending to attack it as soon as they had seen the armies of both sides engage; and they fell on its tail, where because of the laziness of the king's servants the royal baggage was, as soon as the battle began, and plundered the king's valuable treasure, his sword and crown among other valuables, together with all his furniture.

Once the king thought that almost all the baggage had reached his rear, in the name of Jesus, at whom every knee bends of those in heaven, on earth and in hell, and in the name of the glorious Virgin and St George, he marched against the enemy and the enemy marched against him.

At that time, for as long as the conflict of battle lasted, I who write this was sitting on a horse amidst the baggage at the rear of the battle. With the other priests who were present we humbled our souls in the presence of God, and recalled ...[125] which the church was reading at that time, and we

---

[125] Text missing in manuscript

said in our hearts, 'Remember us, Lord! Our enemies have congregated together and boast of their strength. Grind down their bravery and destroy them, so that they can know that there is no one else who fights for us except you, Lord.' We also exclaimed in fear and panic with our eyes raised to heaven that God would take pity on us and the crown of England and not allow the speeches and tears which the church of England had shed, and was very probably shedding for us as that hour in their customary processions, to perish, but to admit them to the bosom of His mercy, and not allow that devotion which our king had undertaken regarding divine worship, the extension of the church, and the peace of the kingdoms to be suppressed by his enemies, but rather to make Him more exalted in future by his manifest munificence, and mercifully free him from these dangerous events, as from others.

## Chapter 13

When the time came near for the enemy's offensive, the French cavalry that had been positioned on the sides made attacks against our archers who were on either side of our army. But soon, as God willed, they were compelled to retreat amidst the showers of arrows, and to flee to the rearguard, with the exception of a very small number of men who ran amidst the archers and the groves, not without slaughter and wounding; and indeed, with the exception of the many men whom stakes driven into the ground and the barrage of missiles aimed at both horses and knights held back from fleeing far away. Whereas the enemy missiles which were aimed at the rear of the armed men and on their sides, after the first but hasty movement, harmed very few people, they retreated at the strength of our bows. When the armed men made an attack on both sides over about the same distance, the sides of both battle lines, namely ours and the enemy's, immersed themselves into the groves that were on each side of the armies. But the French nobility, who had previously advanced with all of their front, so that they had nearly come into contact with us, either out of fear of the weapons whose force had passed through the sides and visors of the helmets, or to penetrate our strong points more quickly through to the standards, divided themselves into three squadrons, invading our battle line at the three places where the standards were; and in the first mingling of lances they marched against our men with such a ferocious attack that they forced them to retreat by almost the length of a lance.

Then indeed those of us who had been ascribed to the clerical militia and who were looking on fell upon our faces in prayer before the throne of God's utmost mercy, calling out in the bitterness of our spirit, so that God would still remember us and the crown of England, and save us from this iron furnace and the dire death that awaited us by the grace of His utmost liberality. But God did not forget the multitude of prayers and speeches of England, through which, as it is piously believed, our men quickly regained their strength and, by boldly resisting them, repelled them continually until they recovered the ground they had lost.

Then a most bitter battle raged, and our archers notched the ends of their arrows[126] and sent them against their flanks, continually renewing battle. When their arrows had been used up, they took up axes, stakes, swords and the heads of lances that lay between them, and laid the enemy low, ruining and transfixing them. For the almighty and merciful God, who is always miraculous in His work, and who wanted to show his mercy to us, whom it pleased that the crown of England, which has long been invincible, to remain under the power of our gracious king, His soldier, and his small retinue, as soon as the battle lines had been joined together and the battle begun, increased our power that the shortage of our provisions had previously debilitated and weakened, removed the terror from them, and gave them a fearless heart. And it seemed to our elders that the English had never attacked their enemy more bravely, intrepidly or wilfully.

The same just judge himself, who wanted to transfix the proud multitude of the enemy with the thunderbolt of vengeance, turned them away from His face, and broke their powers: the bow, shield, sword and battle line. Nor had it ever been seen before, so far as any chronicle or history relates, that so many most chosen and strong soldiers had put up resistance so sluggishly, so disorderly and fearfully or in so unmanly a fashion. For fear

---

[126] Nocked their arrows?

and trepidation took hold of them, as was said among the army, since there were some of them, even of the more noble men, who surrendered themselves on that day more than ten times. But no one had time to take them as prisoners but almost all of them without discretion, as soon as they were laid low on the ground, were instantly consigned to death, either by those who laid them low or by those that followed them, by some hidden judgment of God, it is unknown.

For God transfixed them with another incurable blow. For when some of them were killed as battle was joined, and had fallen at the front, the undisciplined violence and pressure of the crowd at the rear was so great that the living fell upon the dead, and even those falling upon the living were killed, such that, in the three places where there was a strong force and the line of our standards, the heap of those who had been killed and those who lay crushed between them grew so great that our men climbed the piles which had grown higher than a man's height, and slaughtered their adversaries at the rear with their swords, axes and other weapons. When at last after two or three hours their vanguard had been transfixed and broken up, and the remainder were forced into flight, our men began to disperse those heaps and to separate the living from the dead, intending to keep them to serve as slaves.

But then at once, for what wrath of God it is unknown, a shout arose that the rearguard of the enemy's cavalry was of an incomparable number and fresh, and that they had restored their position and battle line in order to overcome us in our small numbers and weary state. And the prisoners were killed at once, without any heed to the difference between people, excepting the dukes of Orleans and Bourbon and other illustrious men who were in the king's battle line, along with a very few others, by the swords of either their captors or others that followed them, lest they should be ruinous to us in the ensuing battle.

But after a short while the enemy ranks, according to the will of God, once they had tasted the bitterness of our weapons and our king had drawn close to them, abandoned to us a field of blood along with carriages and their draughthorses, many being filled with provisions, weapons, lances and bows. And thus when, on God's orders, the strength of that people had been dissipated and the rigours of the war had finished, we who had obtained victory returned through the masses, mounds and piles of dead men, and saw and inspected them, but not without the pain and tears of many, because so many outstanding and most powerful soldiers – had only God been with them – had sought their own deaths in such a manner from us, completely against our wishes, and had thus vainly destroyed and broken up the glory and honour of their own dwelling place. And if that was a site for compunction and piety in us as strangers passing by, how much more lamentation and wailing did it cause for the local people, who were watching and seeing the military of their country being destroyed and despoiled in this manner! And I truly believe that there is not a heart of flesh or even one of stone that, if it had seen and considered the terrible deaths and bitter wounds of so many Christians, would not have broken itself and dissolved into tears out of grief. Indeed, however illustrious or respectable they were, the men, having been despoiled earlier by our English pillagers, did not have on our retreat any more covering, except only to cover their nature, than that which nature had woven for them on first entering the light.

Would that those Frenchmen would quickly attain peace and harmony with the English, and desist from their injustices and wicked ways, by which they are have been abducted, confused and led astray, lest that saying of the prophet be a reproach to them: 'Does not God, who is a just, brave and patient judge, grow angry every day? Unless you are converted, He will brandish his sword, stretch and ready his bow, and in it he has prepared the vessels of death'. And if they do not come to their senses soon, let them experience what follows: "Behold, He is bringing justice to birth, He has conceived grief, He has given birth to iniquity, He has opened up a lake and dug it, and has fallen into the trap He made. His grief shall be turned onto His head and His iniquity shall descend upon his crown'. For God is merciful and a long-suffering spectator, but once He has used up the remedies of His mercy and long suffering, He is a stern avenger, and many times takes away the powers of brave men whom justice does not attend. This is clear in the multitude of our men, all of whom indiscriminately He gave up to flight, capture or the sword by means of our small number who were striving for justice.

## 36. The Battle of Agincourt, 1415 (2)[127]

*Jean de Wavrin*

*Jean, or Jehan, de Wavrin was the illegitimate son of a French nobleman who sat on the sidelines at Agincourt while his father and older brother fought and died in the French host. In subsequent years the fractured nature of French politics put Wavrin in Burgundian service where he developed a strong affection for the English. His account of the battle of Agincourt was written sometime between 1445 and 1469, by which time his memories of the day would have been influenced by both his own later experiences and the accounts of the battle written by others. Nevertheless, his lively account is important first-hand testimony and provides details not found in the* Gesta Henrici Quinti.

It is true that the French had arranged their battalions between two small thickets, one lying close to Azincourt, and the other to Tramecourt. The place was narrow, and very advantageous for the English, and, on the contrary, very ruinous for the French, for the said French had been all night on horseback, and it rained, and the pages, grooms, and others, in leading about the horses, had broken up the ground, which was so soft that the horses could with difficulty step out of the soil. And also the said French were so loaded with armour that they could not support themselves or move forward. In the first place they were armed with long coats of steel, reaching to the knees or lower, and very heavy, over the leg harness, and besides plate armour also most of them had hooded helmets; wherefore this weight of armour, with the softness of the wet ground, as has been said, kept them as if immovable, so that they could raise their clubs only with great difficulty, and with all these mischiefs there was this, that most of them were troubled with hunger and want of sleep. There was a marvellous number of banners, and it was ordered that some of them should be furled. Also it was settled among the said French that every one should shorten his lance, in order that they might be stiffer when it came to fighting at close quarters. They had archers and cross-bowmen enough,

---

[127] Sir William Hardy and Edward Hardy (trans), *A Collection of the Chronicles and Ancient Histories of Great Britain, now called England, by John de Wavrin* (London, 1883), pp. 209-216

but they would not let them shoot, for the plain was so narrow that there was no room except for the men-at-arms.

Now let us return to the English. After the parley between the two armies was finished, as we have said, and the delegates had returned, each to their own people, the King of England, who had appointed a knight called Sir Thomas Erpingham to place his archers in front in two wings, trusted entirely to him, and Sir Thomas, to do his part, exhorted every one to do well in the name of the king, begging them to fight vigorously against the French in order to secure and save their own lives. And thus the knight, who rode with two others only in front of the battalion, seeing that the hour was come, for all things were well arranged, threw up a baton which he held in his hand, saying 'Now strike!' which was the signal for attack; then dismounted and joined the king, who was also on foot in the midst of his men, with his banner before him. Then the English, seeing this signal, began suddenly to march, uttering a very loud cry, which greatly surprised the French. And when the English saw that the French did not approach them, they marched dashingly towards them in very fine order, and again raised a loud cry as they stopped to take breath.

Then the English archers, who, as I have said, were in the wings, saw that they were near enough, and began to send their arrows on the French with great vigour. The said archers were for the most part in their doublets, without armour, their stockings rolled up to their knees, and having hatchets and battle-axes or great swords hanging at their girdles; some were barefooted and bare-headed, others had caps of boiled leather, and others of osier,[128] covered with harpoy or leather.

Then the French, seeing the English come towards them in this fashion, placed themselves in order, every one under his banner, their helmets on their heads. The constable, the marshal, the admirals, and the other princes earnestly exhorted their men to fight the English well and bravely; and when it came to the approach the trumpets and clarions resounded everywhere; but the French began to hold down their heads, especially

---

[128] Wicker.

those who had no bucklers,[129] for the impetuosity of the English arrows, which fell so heavily that no one durst uncover or look up.[130] Thus they went forward a little, then made a little retreat, but before they could come to close quarters, many of the French were disabled and wounded by the arrows; and when they came quite up to the English, they were, as has been said, so closely pressed one against another that none of them could lift their arms to strike their enemies, except some that were in front, and these fiercely pricked with the lances which they had shortened to be more stiff, and to get nearer their enemies.

The said French had formed a plan which I will describe, that is to say, the constable and marshal had chosen ten or twelve hundred men-at-arms, of whom one party was to go by the Azincourt side and the other on that of Tramecourt, to break the two wings of the English archers; but when it came to close quarters there were but six score left of the band of Sir Clugnet de Brabant, who had the charge of the undertaking on the Tramecourt side. Sir William de Saveuse, a very brave knight, took the Azincourt side, with about three hundred lances; and with two others only he advanced before the rest, who all followed, and struck into these English archers, who had their stakes fixed in front of them, but these had little hold in such soft ground. So the said Sir William and his two companions pressed on boldly; but their horses tumbled among the stakes, and they were speedily slain by the archers, which was a great pity. And most of the rest, through fear, gave way and fell back into their vanguard, to whom they were a great hindrance; and they opened their ranks in several places, and made them fall back and lose their footing in some land newly sown; for their horses had been so wounded by the arrows that the men could no longer manage them. Thus, by these principally and by this adventure, the vanguard of the French was thrown into disorder, and men-at-arms without number began to fall; and their horses feeling the arrows coming upon them took to flight before the enemy, and following their example many of the French turned and fled. Soon afterwards the English archers, seeing the vanguard thus shaken, issued from behind their

---

[129] Shields.

[130] This suggests that, at this stage of the battle at least, the archers were lobbing arrows long-range at a high trajectory, rather than flat-shooting.

stockade, threw away their bows and quivers, then took their swords, hatchets, mallets, axes, falconbeaks and other weapons, and, pushing into the places where they saw these breaches, struck down and killed these Frenchmen without mercy, and never ceased to kill till the said vanguard which had fought little or not at all was completely overwhelmed, and these went on striking right and left till they came upon the second battalion, which was behind the advance guard, and there the king personally threw himself into the fight with his men-at-arms. And there came suddenly Duke Anthony of Brabant, who had been summoned by the King of France, and had so hastened for fear of being late, that his people could not follow him, for he would not wait for them, but took a banner from his trumpeters, made a hole in the middle of it, and dressed himself as if in armour; but he was soon killed by the English, Then was renewed the struggle and great slaughter of the French, who offered little defence; for, because of their cavalry above mentioned, their order of battle was broken; and then the English got among them more and more, breaking up the two first battalions in many places, beating down and slaying cruelly and without mercy; but some rose again by the help of their grooms, who led them out to the melee; for the English, who were intent on killing and making prisoners, pursued nobody. And then all the rear guard, being still on horseback, and seeing the condition of the first two battalions turned and fled, except some of the chiefs and leaders of these routed ones. And it is to be told that while the battalion was in rout, the English had taken some good French prisoners.

And there came tidings to the King of England that the French were attacking his people at the rear, and that they had already taken his sumpters and other baggage, which enterprise was conducted by an esquire named Robert de Bornouille, with whom were Rifflart de Plamasse, Yzembart d'Azincourt, and some other men-at-arms, accompanied by about six hundred peasants,, who carried off the said baggage and many horses of the English while their keepers were occupied in the fight, about which robbery the King was greatly troubled, nevertheless he ceased not to pursue his victory, and his people took many good prisoners, by whom they expected all to become rich, and they took from them nothing but their head armour.

At the hour when the English feared the least there befell them a perilous adventure, for a great gathering of the rear guard and centre division of the French, in which were many Bretons, Gascons, and Poitevins, rallied with some standards and ensigns, and returned in good order, and marched vigorously against the conquerors of the field. When the King of England perceived them coming thus he caused it to be published that every one that had a prisoner should immediately kill him, which those who had any were unwilling to do, for they expected to get great ransoms for them. But when the king was informed of this he appointed a gentleman with two hundred archers whom he commanded to go through the host and kill all the prisoners, whoever they might be. This esquire, without delay or objection, fulfilled the command of his sovereign lord, which was a most pitiable thing, for in cold blood all the nobility of France was beheaded and inhumanly cut to pieces, and all through this accursed company, a sorry set compared with the noble captive chivalry, who when they saw that the English were ready to receive them, all immediately turned and fled, each to save his own life. Many of the cavalry escaped; but of those on foot there were many among the dead.

When the King of England saw that he was master of the field and had got the better of his enemies he humbly thanked the Giver of victory, and he had good cause, for of his people there died on the spot only about sixteen hundred men of all ranks, among whom was the Duke of York, his great uncle, about whom he was very sorry. Then the king collected on that place some of those most intimate with him, and inquired the name of a castle which he perceived to be the nearest; and they said, 'Azincourt.'

'It is right, then,' said he, 'that this our victory should for ever bear the name of Azincourt, for every battle ought to be named after the fortress nearest to the place where it was fought.'

## 37. Fletchings, 1417[131]

*Statutes relating to the making of bows, wood for arrow shafts, and the quality of arrowheads have been given above.[132] This document is included to illustrate the mechanisms by which sufficient feathers to fletch the vast numbers of arrows required for foreign campaigns were acquired.*

10 Feb 1417 To the sheriff of Kent.

Order upon sight etc. by his bailiffs and others whom he shall appoint in singular the towns and other places of Kent, for the king's money to be paid of the issues of that county, to cause six wing feathers to be taken of every goose, except those called 'brodeges,' fittest for new making of arrows for the king's use, and to cause the same to be brought to London before 14 March next; as the king is shortly to sail to France for recovery of his rights and the heritage of the crown, long withheld and wrongfully occupied by the adversary of France, as all men know; and considering how that God of his ineffable goodness and not for the king's merit gave him the victory by his archers among others with their arrows, his will is to make provision for a sufficient store thereof with what speed he may for better furtherance of his present expedition .

Like writs to the sheriffs of the following counties :

Wiltesir.

Bedford and Bukingham.

Surrey and Sussex.

Oxford and Berkshire.

Middlesex.

Norfolk and Suffolk.

Lincoln.

Somerset and Dorset.

---

[131] *Calendar of Close Rolls*, Henry V, vol. 1, p. 336
[132] See **Docs 4** and **6**

Cantebrigge and Huntingdon.

Norhampton.

Essex and Hertford.
Roteland.

## 38. Inventory of arrows, 1422.[133]

*The inventory of Sir John Dinham's[134] arrows, entrusted to the care of his servant William Michell at Nutwell, Devon, is full of incredible detail about the heads, fletching, and whipping. It is clear that these are not munition-quality arrows - peacock ('pocokke') fletchings striped with gold leaf are unlikely to have been issued widely - but it is also unlikely that 598 arrows and 33 bolts were all for Dinham's personal use. We might assume fairly safely that this stock of arrows was intended to supply Dinham's retainers, in which case the large number of peacock-fletched arrows may have been a sign of his wealth and status.*

*In addition to the peacock fletchings white and grey goose and swan are also mentioned, along with gold, red, and black silk, and 'gold of Cypress' bindings or whippings, and black and white horn nocks. Most interesting of all perhaps are the descriptions of the heads, which fell into four types: spearheads ('sperhedys'), byker, duckbill ('dokebyll'), broad hooked ('brode hokede'), 'pere,' and broad ('brode'). Broad hooked heads and broad heads may have been of the same or similar design, the former for arrows and the latter for bolts, and were probably similar to what we would still call a broadhead with a swallowtail form. The meaning of 'pere' heads is entirely unclear, but given their association with bolts rather than arrows may refer to crescent-shaped hunting heads with a 'pair' of points, but this is no more than speculation. Spearheads were probably fairly narrow heads such as the kind now known as swaged or 'Tudor' bodkins. 'Dokebyll' is a most descriptive term and must surely be applied to head with a flattened-diamond section with curved edges such as a Type 10[135] arrow head. 'Byker' is a word that appears often in medieval military texts, an early form of 'bicker,' applied to the exchange of missiles in the opening stages of battle, often between archers. This would suggest that the arrows referred to*

---

[133] Archives and Cornish Study Service, AR/37/34
[134] Regrettably there is no place here for a biography of Dinham, who must have been one of the most interesting yet obscure characters in medieval England. His father was murdered by two robbers who were arrested and incarcerated at Ilchester. When one of them escaped Dinham tracked him to Exeter cathedral where he was seeking sanctuary. Dinham risked excommunication by entering the cathedral, smashing through the door to the room in which the murderer was taking refuge, dragged the man forcibly out of the cathedral, and killed him.
[135] Museum of London typology

*here* were military arrows, and perhaps lighter flight arrows for long-range shooting.

Ferst a doseyn of pocokke arwys nywe ybounde yn tweyne placys wyth golde & sylke and wyth whyte horne nokkys yhedyth wyth sperhedys; and 1 doseyn of pocokke arwys nywe wyth whyte horne nokkys, ylayde yn thre placys wyth golde foyle yn the federys, yhedyth wyth sperhedys; and xiii arwys of pocokke, the scheftys nywe and the federys olde, yhedyth wyth sperhedys; and 1 doseyn arwys of whyte gose, ybounde wyth rede & blak sylke, yhedyth wyth byker; and 1 doseyn arwys of whyte gose, ybounde wyth golde & rede & blak sylke, yhedyth wyth byker; and xxiiii scheftys of whyte gose, ybounde wyth golde & rede sylke; and xlviii scheftys of whyte gose, ybounde wyth rede & blak sylke, alle of on sorte; and ix hole schevys & xx arwys olde & febell of grey gose, alle of on sorte, yhedyth wyth dokebyll hedys; and vi arwys of pocokke, olde & ybounde wyth golde of seprys & rede & blak sylk, wyth blak horne nokkys, yhedyth wyth dokebyll; and 1 doseyn of pocokke arwys wyth blak horne nokkys, ybounde wyth golde & rede & blak sylke, yhedyth wyth dokebyll; and xxi pocokke arwys, the nokkys ypoudart therof, olde & forwered yhedyth wyth dokebyll; and xxii pocokke arwys olde & febell, the nokkys ypoudart, ii therof tobroke, yhedyth wyth dokebyll; and xxiiii pocokke arwys wyth blak horne nokkys, olde & forwered yhedyth wyth dokebyll; and xxii pocokke arwys olde and forwered, som wyth blak horne nokkys & som onne honne & som tobroke, yhedyth wyth dokebyll; and 1 doseyn of pocokke arwys, som the nokkys ypoudart & som onne poudart, yhedyth wyth dokebyll; and xxvi scheftys of diverse federyng, som therof pocokke, som whyte gose, som grey gose; and vi whyte arwys yhedyth wyth byker; and v smale pocokke arwys yhedyth wyth byker; and xvii brode hokede arwys of pocokke, olde and febell, alle of on sorte; and xii brode hokede arwys of pocokke of another sorte; and xii brode hokede arwys of pocokke of another sorte; and iiii brode hokede arwys of pocokke ylayde yn the federys, alle wyth golde foyle; and x brode hokede arwys of whyte swanne; and xiii boltys of pocokke of on sorte; and viii boltys of pocokke of another sorte, v therof pere hedys and thre brode hedes; and xii nywe sperhedys.

## 39. English Archers in Foreign Service, 1434[136]

*English archers were in demand as mercenaries in European armies throughout the later medieval period. Most famously Sir John Hawkwood, leader of the White Company, had begun his own military career as an archer in the service of Edward III and risen through the ranks to command and fame. Sir Walter of England's mercenary band was no White Company, but they continued the tradition of the mercenary 'free companies' that saw service across European battlefields in the fourteenth and fifteenth centuries. Venice in the fifteenth century was one of the most powerful of the Italian city-states. Until 1430 Venice had been fighting a fierce war against the Ottoman Empire, and at the time of Sir Walter's arrival with his mercenaries was about to embark on the fourth stage of fighting in Lombardy and along the Dalmatian coast where it was acquiring territory and cities, giving Venice almost undisputed control over the northern Adriatic. There are no surviving details about the deployment of Sir Walter and his men, but it is probable that they fought in either Lombardy or Dalmatia.*

Doge Francesco Foscard

Takes into his service Sir Walter of England, Knight, with one hundred archers, himself being included in this number, and in which he is to have two spears,[137] they to comprise mounted bowmen; the rest of the archers to be footmen. For the two spears he is to receive the same stipend as the Doge's other men-at-arms, with no additional pay for himself. The foot-archers to have fifteen light livres each. The archers, both mounted and on foot, to have bows and all other necessary and usual weapons. These archers must be from England and Ireland, or from other subjects of the King of England, and not from foreign parts. When Sir Walter has engaged them, and had them reviewed in arms, he shall receive two [months'] pay; being bound to effect the engagement and review within 15 days, either in Venice or at Padua, according to the Doge's order.

---

[136] *Calendar of State Papers, Venetian*, vol. 1, 1202-1509, item. 248
[137] Possibly 'spear' here refers to a small unit of troops, similar to a 'lance' consisting of a knight and his retainers.

## 40. Bows in Close Defence of a House, 1449[138]

*This delightfully surreal letter relates to an ongoing feud in which the Pastons were involved and begins by describing the difficulty of defending a house with long bows, before Margaret Paston remembered that she also needed her husband to do some shopping for her while he was in London.*

*Most English-language sources are easy enough to follow, but Margaret Paston's writing is idiosyncratic in the extreme so a modernised transcript as well as the original text is included below.*

Margaret Paston to John Paston, 1449 (undated)

RYT wurchipful hwsbond, I recomawnd me to zu, and prey zw to gete som crosse bowis, and wyndacs to bynd them with, and quarrels; for zour hwsis her ben so low that ther may non man schet owt with no long bowe, thow we hadde never so moche nede.

I sopose ze xuld have seche thyngs of Ser Jon Fastolf, if ze wold send to hym ; and also I wold ze xuld gete ij. or iij. schort pelleaxis to kepe with doris, and als many jakkys, and ye may.

Partryche and his felaschep arn sor aferyd that ze wold entren azen up on them, and they have made grete ordynawce with inne the hwse, as it is told me. They have made barris to barre the dorys crosse weyse, and they have made wykets on every quarter of the hwse to schote owte atte, bothe with bowys and with hand gunnys ; and the holys that ben made forr hand gunnys, they ben scarse kne hey fro the plawncher, and of soche holis ben made fyve. There can non man schete owt at them with no hand bowys. Purry felle in felaschepe with Willyum Hasard at Querles, and told hym that he wold com and drynk with Partryche and with hym, and he seyd he xuld ben welcome, and after none he went thedder for to aspye qhat they dedyn, and qhat felaschep they hadde with them ; and qhan he com thedder, the dors were fast sperid and there wer non folks with hem but Maryoth, and Capron and hys wyf, and Querles wyf, ad another man in

---

[138] James Gairdner (ed.), *The Paston Letters, 1422-1509, A New Edition* (London, 1872), vol. 1, pp. 82-83

ablac zede sum qhate haltyng, I sopose be his words that it was Norfolk of Gemyngham; and the seyd Purry aspyde alle this forseyd thyngs. And Marioth and his felaschep had meche grette langage that xall ben told zw qhen ze kom hom.

I pray zw that ze wyl vowche save to don bye for me j. li. of almands and j. li. of sugyr, and that ze wille do byen sume frese to maken of zour child is gwnys ; ze xall have best chepe and best choyse of Hayis wyf, as it is told me. And that ze wyld bye a zerd of brode clothe of blac for an hode fore me of xliiij.d or iiij.s a zerd, for ther is nether gode cloth ner god fryse in this twn. As for the child is gwnys, and I have them, I wel do hem maken.

The Trynyte have zw in his keping, and send zw gode spede i alle zour materis.

[*Right worshipful husband, I recommend me to you, and pray you to get some crossbows, and windlasses to bind them with, and quarrels; for your house here been* [is] *so low that there may no man shoot out with no long bow, though we had never so much need.*

*I suppose you should have such things of* [from] *Sir John Fastolf, if you would send to him; and also I would you should get ij. or iij. short polleaxes to keep indoors, and as many jacks, and you may.*

*Partryche and his fellowship are sore afraid that you would enter upon them, and they have made grete ordnance* [defences] *within the house, as it is told me. They have made bars to bar the doors cross wise, and they have made wickets on every quarter of the house to shoot out at* [from], *both with bows and with hand guns; and the holes that* [have] *been made for hand guns, they been* [are] *scarce knee high from the plawncher* [floor], *and of such holes been made five. There can no man shoot out at* [from] *them with no hand bows. Purry fell in fellowship with William Hasard at Querles, and told him that he would come and drink with Partryche and with him, and he said he should be welcome, and after noon he went thither for to espy what they did, and what fellowship they had with them; and when he came thither, the doors were fast sperid* [fastened] *and there were no folks with him but Maryoth, and Capron and his wife, and Querle's wife, and another man in black said somewhat halting, I suppose by his words that it was Norfolk of Gemyngham; and the said Purry espied all these foresaid things. And Marioth and his fellowship had much great language that shall be told [to] you when you come home.*

*I pray you that you will vouchsafe to do but for me j. li. [1 lb] of almonds and j. li. of sugar, and that you will do buy some frieze to make of your child's gowns; you shall have the cheapest and best choice of Hay's wife, as it is told me. And that you would buy a yard of broadcloth of black for a hood for me of xliiij.d or iiij.s a yard, for there is neither good cloth nor good frieze in this town. As for the child's gowns, and I have them, I will do them make.*

*The Trinity have you in his keeping, and send you God speed in all your matters.* ]

## 41. Bridport Muster Roll, 1457

*The muster roll compiled at Bridport, Dorset, on 4 September 1457 is a fairly well-known document which has been previously transcribed and printed elsewhere. Previous printings, however, have suffered from a number of transcription errors and, in some case, a failure to differentiate between the equipment each person produced and the equipment they were ordered to acquire. Some errors may still remain in the present transcription, and a number of words are either damaged or illegible in the original document.*

*In 1457 England suffered a large number of French raids along the South coast and it is believed that the muster of arms was taken in Bridport in that year in response to the threat. It illustrates the arms and equipment available to provincial levied troops at the end of the Hundred Years' War and the beginning of the Wars of the Roses, and it shows us that despite repeated statutes and instructions concerning the provision of arms and armour even at what might be considered the height of the 'long bow age' a significant number of men still did not own either a bow or the other required armaments.*

*The roll lists 196 men and 4 women. The women were not expected to fight and probably attended the muster either in place of their husband or because they were the head of their household. 82 of the people named in the roll arrived at the muster with no military equipment at all, and between them all they could manage only 89 bows and 82 sheaves of arrows. A few men owned more than one bow, but even if they shared out their spare bows among their unarmed neighbours still a maximum of 45% of the Bridport men were armed with a bow. Ordinarily this might not have presented a problem: as we have seen,[139] for most military campaigns only a few men from each parish or county were selected for service. However, when threatened with invasion or localised raiding the position was different, and every man might be required. The shortage of bows under those circumstances might have been a very real issue, and the statutes requiring both bow-ownership and regular practice are easier to understand.*

---

[139] See **Docs 33** and **34**

# Bridport Muster Roll, 4th September 1457

Taken by William Oliver, Robert Scarlet, and Thomas Stockfyshe

| Name | Equipment | Ordered to provide |
|---|---|---|
| Thomas Chere | | |
| John Wodedale | | |
| Robert Capper | Sword | Bow, sheaf of arrows |
| William Bridport | | |
| William Strekbryge | Bow | 22 arrows, sallet, dagger |
| William Pele | Jack, sallet, sword, dagger | Sheaf of arrows |
| John Tye | Jack, sallet, sword, dagger, glaive, bow, 2 sheaves of arrows | |
| Thomas Tracy | Jack, sallet, sword and buckler, bow, sheaf of arrows | |
| William Bremmytt | Jack, sallet, bow, sheaf of arrows, sword and dagger | |
| Elyot Dgound[?] | | |
| Alex Younge | Jack, sallet, bow, sheaf of arrows, sword, buckler, dagger | |
| John Dollyng | Bow, sheaf of arrows | |
| William Smyth | Sword, buckler, sallet, dagger | Jack, bow, sheaf of arrows, |
| Thomas Smith | | |
| Robert | | |
| John [damaged] | 2 bows | Pavise |
| Henry Mill | [damaged] dagger | Pavise |
| John [damaged] | | |
| WIlliam Gill Smith | Bow, sheaf of arrows, sword, mail shirt, sallet | |

| | |
|---|---|
| John Quyke | |
| William Weykys | Jack, sallet, bow, sheaf of arrows, sword, dagger |
| John Boley | |
| William Churchfile | Jack, sallet, bow, sheaf of arrows, sallet |
| Jacob Bertam | Jack, sword, buckler, bill, bow | Sheaf of arrows, sallet |
| Henry Lanpus | |
| Henry Maxmys | Jack, sallet, bow, sheaf of arrows, sword, dagger, leg harness |
| John Harys | Brigandine, bow, sheaf of arrows, poleaxe, jack |
| John Bennet | 'Barbo' [bevor?], bow, sheaf of arrows, 'pell' [javelin?] |
| Nigel Hoze | Brigandine |
| John Batt | [indecipherable] |
| Thomas Boyly | Jack, sallet, glaive, bow, sheaf of arrows |
| John Steyr | Jack, sallet, sword, axe, 2 bows, 2 sheaves of arrows, mail shirt |
| John Pelltow | Jack, bow, sheaf of arrows, sword, dagger | Axe and [indecipherable] |
| John Crokeson | Jack, sallet |
| Richard Burgh | 2 jacks, 2 sallets, 3 bows, 3 sheaves of arrows, sword, 2 poleaxes, 2 glaives, 2 daggers |
| Haulynd B | |
| Robert Helyr | Jack, sallet, 2 bows, |

| | | |
|---|---|---|
| | sheaf of arrows, dagger, glaive, sword | |
| John Gryally | 2 jacks, 2 sallets, bow, sheaf of arrows, pair of gauntlets | |
| William Todeyr | | |
| Thomas Pellters | | |
| [damaged] | | |
| [damaged] | Whole white harness, 2 jacks, 2 sallets, 2 bows, 2 sheaves of arrows, 2 daggers | |
| [damaged] | | Bow, sheaf of arrows, glaive, ax |
| John [damaged] | | |
| [damaged] | | |
| Robert Smyth | Jack, sallet, bow, sheaf of arrows, dagger, sword, buckler | |
| John Gamwell | Bow, sheaf of arrows, sallet, pair of gauntlets, dagger | Jack |
| John Todelyn | Sword, glaive, axe, 'kyvett hiame' | |
| Richard Wyse | Axe | |
| William Tadywood | Pavise, spear | Dagger |
| Peter Poleyn | Sword, poleaxe | Bow, sheaf of arrows, pavise |
| Robert Tarell | | |
| John Lucas | | |
| Alice Gare | 3 pairs of 'ares', 'plet' | |
| Thomas Gamme | Poleaxe, staff | Pavise, bow, sheaf of arrows |
| John Durgens | | |
| John Elebeth | | |

| | | |
|---|---|---|
| William [damaged] | | |
| John Hyder | | |
| William Waley | | |
| Thomas | Sheaf of arrows, dagger | |
| [damaged] | | |
| [damaged] | Sheaf of arrows, dagger | |
| [damaged] | Glaive, sword, buckler, dagger | Bow, sheaf of arrows |
| [damaged] | | Bow, sheaf of arrows |
| [damaged] | Glaive, sword | pavise |
| [damaged] | | |
| [damaged] | Dagger, sheaf of arrows, axe | Jack, sallet |
| [damaged] | | |
| [damaged] | | |
| [damaged] | | |
| John Wryght | Bow, 23 arrows, dagger | Jack, sallet |
| William Lehe | Jack, sallet, bow, 13 arrows, poleaxe, breastplate, dagger | |
| John Salmon | | Bow, pavise, lead mace |
| John Elys | Bow, sword, sallet | Sheaf of arrows |
| Thomas Stockfyshe | 2 jacks, 2 sallets, 2 bows, sheaf of arrows, 2 daggers, 2 swords | |
| Pithus Fletcher | Bow, sheaf of arrows, dagger | |
| Elia Payer | Sword, glaive | Pavise |
| John Dene | Bow, sheaf of arrows, sword, dagger | Pavise |
| John Elys | | |
| John Foster | | |
| John Pryckpillte | Jack, sword, buckler, 2 bows, sheaf of arrows, | Sallet |

|  |  |  |
|---|---|---|
|  | dagger |  |
| John Deny |  |  |
| William de la Fint | Bow |  |
| John Smith | Cleaver, bow, 2 sheaves of arrows, poleaxe, dagger | Pavise |
| William [damaged] | Bow, 12 arrows, mail shirt | Pavise |
| [damaged] | Sheaf of arrows, sword, dagger |  |
| [damaged] | 2 sallets, 2 bows, 2 [sheaves of?] arrows, poleaxe |  |
| [damaged] |  |  |
| [damaged] | Pavise, 3 sallets, 3 bows, 3 sheaves of arrows |  |
| [damaged] | Arrows, sword, dagge |  |
| [damaged] | Bow, 22 arrows, sword, buckler, poleaxe, dagger | Jack, sallet |
| John Hille | Jack, sallet, 2 bows, 2 sheaves of arrows, 2 swords, 2 axes | Jack, sallet |
| William Polly | Axe, sword | Bow, sheaf of arrows, sallet, dagger |
| John Atteller | Bow, 12 arrows, sword | Jack, sallet |
| Thomas Ermond | 2 bows, 2 sheaves of arrows, sallet, pair of gauntlets | Jack, sword, dagger |
| Robert |  |  |
| John Hille | Jack, sallet, bow, 13 arrows, sword | dagger |
| John Lehe |  |  |
| John Dabytayle | Glaive, dagger | Pavise |

153

| | | |
|---|---|---|
| John Edmunde | | |
| John King | Jack, sallet, bow, sheaf of arrows | |
| John Hewys | Jack, sallet | |
| William Irvinge | Bow, 12 arrows, sword, buckler | 12 arrows |
| Robert Shepherd | Spear, dagger | Bow, 2 sheaves of arrows |
| John Bryggod | Staff, dagger | Bow, sheaf of arrows |
| [damaged] Furbyr | | |
| [damaged] | Staff | Bow, sheaf of arrows, sword, axe, bill, sallet |
| [damaged] Falles | | |
| John Gillrude | | |
| William Gibbs | Jack, sallet, bow, sheaf of arrows, buckler | Pavise |
| John Wymote | | |
| Peter Goore | Jack, sallet, bow, sheaf of arrows, sword, buckler, dagger | |
| Roger Franklynd | Jack, sallet, bow, sheaf of arrows, buckler, dagger | |
| John Hille Smith | | |
| Nigel Batt | Sword, buckler | Jack, salet, bow, sheaf of arrows |
| John Stockfyshe | | |
| John But | | |
| Andrew Weler | | Bow, sheaf of arrows |
| Florens Oorded | | |
| William Sallandr | | |
| Alice Hamell | Jack, sword, buckler, 10 arrows, bow | Sallet, sheaf of arrows |
| Arthur Gregory | Jack, sallet, bow, sheaf | |

| | | |
|---|---|---|
| | of arrows, sword, buckler | |
| William Montagu | | |
| Robert Davies | | |
| John Bane | | |
| Peter Saxayn | | |
| Thomas Denys | | |
| Robert But | Jack, sallet, sword, buckler, axe, dagger | Bow, sheaf of arrows |
| Richard Quintrell | | |
| John Wewell | Bow, 3 arrows, dagger | 21 arrows |
| John Denys | Bow | Pavise, lead mace |
| Laurence Taylor | | |
| John Geoge | Axe, sword | Pavise |
| John Dolband | | |
| John Stand | | |
| John Stollker | | |
| Robert Watts | | |
| John Arundell | | |
| William Edmunde | Bow, sheaf of arrows, sword, dagger | Jack, sallet |
| John Rendall | Jack, sallet, bow, sheaf of arrows, sword, dagger | |
| John Welle | | |
| Frenshe | | |
| John Chast | | |
| John Strayne | Bow, sheaf of arrows, sword, dagger, poleaxe | |
| Reginald Baker | | |
| Robert Curer | | |
| John Mayolle | Bow, sheaf of arrows, dagger | Pavise |
| John de Blee | Jack, sallet, spear, sword, dagger | Bow, sheaf of arrows |

| | | |
|---|---|---|
| John Blasford | | |
| Margaret Atheyn | | |
| John Blupayn | | Bow, sheaf of arrows, staff, sallet |
| Thomas Ashe | | |
| Thomas Wey | Jack, sallet, bow, sheaf of arrows | |
| John Williams | Jack, bill, sword, buckler | |
| John Dom | Jack, sallet, sword, buckler, bow, sheaf of arrows | |
| Robert Hillary | | |
| John Symys | | |
| Richard Tayler | | |
| Thomas Parker | | Bow, sheaf of arrows |
| Thomas Barn | Bow, 1/2 sheaf of arrows, sword | Jack, sallet, dagger, 1/2 sheaf of arrows |
| John Crips | Jack, sallet, bow, sheaf of arrows, sword, dagger | Jack, sallet, bow, sheaf of arrows |
| William Poett | | |
| John Palmer | Jack, bow, sheaf of arrows, sword | Sallet |
| John Fugge | Bow, sheaf of arrows, sword | Sallet |
| John Algar | Sallet, 2 bows, sheaf of arrows, sword | 2 jacks, 2 sheaves of arrows, sallet, 2 daggers |
| William Pens | | |
| William Sheter | Jack, sallet, bow, sheaf of arrows, sword, buckler, dagger | |
| Robert Tolker | Bow, sheaf of arrows | Jack, sallet |
| John Bremytt | Bow, sheaf of arrows, sword, dagger | Jack, sallet |

| | | |
|---|---|---|
| Sally Pens | | |
| William Duny | | |
| William Jane | | |
| Edward Grey | Jack, sallet, bow, sheaf of arrows, sword, mail shirt, 'palet'[?] | |
| John Harrys | Jack, sallet, sword, buckler, 2 bows, 2 sheaves of arrows, pair of gauntlets | |
| Richard Pens | | |
| David Hanholt | Jack, sallet, bow, sheaf of arrows, sword, buckler, spear, pavise | |
| John Saget | Jack, sallet, bow, sheaf of arrows, sword, buckler, dagger, glaive | |
| John Pens | | |
| John Tengmouth | Jack, sallet, bow, sheaf of arrows, sword, buckler, dagger | |
| John Fozsey | Jack, sallet, bow, sheaf of arrows, sword | Pair of gauntlets |
| William Bowley | | |
| John Baasgate | Jack, sallet, sword, buckler, dagger, glaive | Bow, sheaf of arrows |
| John Bennet | Jack, sallet, sword, dagger | Bow, sheaf of arrows |
| William Brollus | Jack, sallet, sword, buckler, glaive, bow, sheaf of arrows | |
| Thomas Bones | | |
| [damaged] | | |
| Condefer wife | Bow, arrows, sword, buckler | |
| John Clemens | | |

| | | |
|---|---|---|
| Thomas Fulbrike | Jack, sallet, bow, sheaf of arrows, sword, buckler | |
| William Dinnygood | | |
| Thomas Chester | | |
| William Baasgate | | |
| Robert Byrche | A white harness with a bascinet | |
| Thomas Halle | | |
| Henry Rychybrike | Bow, 12 arrows | Lead mace, pavise |
| William F[indecipherable]tt | | |
| Robert Tyley | Bow, sheaf of arrows, dagger | Axe, pavise |
| Richard Glober | Bow, sheaf of arrows, sword, dagger | |
| John Skrybent | Spear, dagger | Pavise |
| John Brende | | |
| John Daley | | |
| John Pyther | Bow, sheaf of arrows, dagger | |

## 42. An Indenture to Serve in France, 1474[140]

*Numerous indentures made between knights or gentlemen and the king have survived from the medieval period, but this example, made between Edward IV and Sir Richard Tunstall[141] is among the most detailed. It lays out not only the wages received by Tunstall's archers, but also the regularity of their payment, the necessity of regular mustering, and the division of spoils of war between Tunstall's retinue and the king.*

This Indenture,

Made betwene the Kyng oure Soverayne Lord Edward the Fourth of the one Part, and his Trusty and Welbeloved Richard Tunstall Knight on that other Party,

Witnesseth that the same Richard is Retain'd and Beleft towards the same our Soverayne Lord, to doe him Service of Werre in his Duchie of Normandy, and in his Reame of France, for one hole Yere, with Ten Speres himself accompted, and one Hundred Archers well and sufficiently Abiled, Armed, and Arraied, taking Wages for Hymself of ij s. by the Day, for everiche of the said Speres xii d. by the Day, and Rewardes of vi d. by the Day for everich of the said other Speres, and for everich of the said Archers vi d. by the Day,

Of which Wages and Rewardes, as well for him as for everich of his Retinue, the said Richard shall be Paid, for the first Quarter of the seid whole Yere, at Westminster, the last day of January next comyng, by the handes of the Tresorer of England for the tyme being,

At which last day he shall have knowleche, on the King's behalfe, When and at what Place he shall make the hole Mustrez of Himselfe and his hole Retinue abovesaid,

At which Day of Mustrez the said Yere shall beginne,

---

[140] Rymer, *Foedera*, vol. 11
[141] Tunstall was a committed Lancastrian during the early part of the Wars of the Roses, but submitted to Edward IV after the battle of Tewkesbury. He was raised to the Order of the Garter by Richard III but deserted him and is believed to have served Henry VII at Bosworth.

And, for the Second Quarter of the said Yere, the said Richard shall be Paid of the Wages and Rewardes of Him and iche of his seid Retinue, of making of Mustres of him and the same his Retinue afore such Commissarys as shall be deputed thereto by the King our said Soverayne Lord, by the hands of the said Tresorer of England,

And for the Remenant of the said Yere, the said Richard shall be payed, of the Wages and Rewardes of Himselfe and iche of his said Retinue, on the yonder syde of the See, Monthly in English Money, or othre Money having Course and Rennyng there, to the Value of English Money, by the handes of the Tresorer of the Kynges Werres for the tyme being,

Soo always that the same Wages and Rewardes, at the ferthest, be payed within viij Dayes aftre the end of everich of the said Monthes, or elles the said Richard to be Quited and Discharged ayenst our sayd Soverayne Lord of any Covenant specyfyed in thees INDENTURES, the same INDENTURES notwithstanding:

And the said Richard shall make Watche and Warde, and also Mustres of himselfe and of his seid Retenue, from tyme to tyme, when and as ost, during the said terme abovesaid, as he thereto shall duely be warned and required on the behalfe of our said Soveraigne Lord the King:

And the same our Soverayne Lord shall find sufficient Shipping and Reshipping for the said Richard and his said Retinue, their Horse, Harneis and Vitailles:

And if it happen or fortune the said Richard, within the Terme abovesaid, in the Kinges presence or otherwise, for any resonable cause, by the Kings Licence to dispose him to Returne into England, and afterwards be Countermanded by the King, or be under Sale, than the same Richard, with such Retinue as he then hath, shall Serve the King to the end of the sayd Terme, taking Wages and Rewardes for him and the same his Retinue in manere and forme abovesaid:

And, in cas that, at any Moustres to be made beyond the See by the said Richard of his said Retenue, there lak any of his said Nombre of the same, otherwyse than by Deth or Sekeness proved, than the Wages and

Rewardes of them that so faile shall be Rebated, upon Payment to be made by the said Richard, from tyme to tyme as the case shall require:

Alsoe our said Soverayne Lord the King shall have the Thred part of Wynnynngs of Werre as wel of the seid Richard, as the Third of Thirds whereof his Retinue answering unto him of their Wynnyngs of Werre, duryng the tyme aforesaid, beit Prisoners, Prayes,[142] or other Goods or Cattels whatsoever it be; of which Third and Third of Thirdz the said Richard shall answer unto our said Soveraigne Lord, in his Exchequer in England, by his Othe, or by the Othe of his Deputy or Deputys accompting for him in this Party:

And, as touching the Prisoners and Praiez, that, during the said terme, shall be taken by the said Richard or any of his said Retinue, the said Richard, or he or thay that soe shall take such Prisoners or Prayes, shall within viii. Dayes after the taking thereof, or assone as thay resonably shal mowe, Certifye unto the Constable, or Marshall, or one of them, aswell the names of the said Prisoners as thaire Estate, Degree, and Condition, and alsoe the Nature, Quantity, and Value their said Getings by estimation, upon Payn of Forfeiture of the Prisoners and Wynnyngs abovesaid:

Also the said Richard shall have all maner of Prisoners, that shall happe to be taken by him or by any of his said Retinue, during the Terme abovesaid, except the King his Adversarie, and all Kings and Kings Sons his Adversarys of France, and also all the Lieutennants and Cheftains having the said Adversarys Power, which shall be and abide Prisoners unto the King our said Soveraign Lord; for the which he shall make resonable agrement with the Takers of them:

And our said Soveraign Lord Wol and Graunteth that in cas any Lands or Tenements fall unto the said Richard by Descent or otherwise in England, during the tyme that he shall be in the King's Service, such Lands and Tenements, for Defaute of Homage, Fealtee, or any other Service, shall not be reteigned in the King's Hands by his Eschetour or other Minstres, but the same Homages Fealtees and Services shall be respited unto the comyng of the said Richard into England, and by Processe in Chauncery they shall

---

[142] prize

be delivered unto the Attounaye of the said Richard, without contradiction or impechement of any Persone or Persones:

And also the King Willeth and Graunteth that, during the said Terme, noon Assise generall ne especial shall be granted ayenst any Persone of the said Retinue, ner noon Entre shall be made unto thair Livelods, but that the said Richard and every Persone of his seid Retenue shall have, during the said Terme, Lettres of Protection undre the Kings Privy Seal and Grete Seal, as many as shall be necessary unto them, by the Testification and Certificat of the said Richard undre the Seal of his Armes, to be brought unto the Keeper of the King's Prive Seal for the tyme being.

In Witnesse where of the Partie of this present ENDENTURE, remaigning towards our said Soveraigne Lord the King, the seid Richard hath doo bee put his Seel.

Geven at Westm. the xx Day of August, the Yere of the Raigne of our Soveraign Lord abovesaid.

## 43. Lord Howard's retinue, 1481[143]

*Like the militia muster rolls this document is not specifically about archery but sheds interesting light both on how archers were supplied in the field and on how the deficiencies of the militia's equipment was rectified. It helps to answer a number of long-standing assumptions about medieval military archers.*

*Sir John Howard was a staunch supporter of the Yorkist cause during the Wars of the Roses. He was knighted after the battle of Towton in 1461 and by 1470 had been raised to the peerage. One of the most prominent nobles of the era, he was admitted to the Order of the Garter in 1472, enjoyed numerous public offices, and was made Duke of Norfolk in 1483.*

*In 1481 he was given command of the fleet which campaigned that year against France and Scotland. Maritime combat had yet to evolve into the long-range artillery duel of later centuries and a warship's main strength was its complement of soldiers who could either fight boarding actions at sea or, as they did at Flodden for example, form landing parties in support of campaigns on land. The accounts show payments for both mariners and 'lande men,' and there is no reason to suppose that the soldiers attached to Howard's fleet were in any way different to the soldiers employed on land.*

*The accounts here cover payments and equipment for a total of 388 men, only a small part of the whole fleet, but the part that was personally recruited and financed by the Admiral. The first point to note is that while the cash payments for wages and suchlike were fairly extensive, the supply of military equipment was relatively minimal. Howard provided his retinue with only 35 brigandines, 6 mail shirts ('gestrons'), 36 helmets, 51 pairs of splints (arm defences), one corselet (back and breastplates), 1 unidentified 'harneys', and 45 pieces of mail - either collars (standards) or sleeves (gussets). The most commonly-provided piece of equipment were jackets of white cloth, of which 305 were supplied. There is a clear implication that the majority of the men brought their own equipment as they were required to do by the Statute of Winchester,[144] and*

---

[143] J. Payne Collier (ed.) *The Household Books of John, Duke of Norfolk, and Thomas Earl of Surrey, 1481-1490* (London, 1844) pp. 246-272
[144] See **Doc. 1**

*that for the most part they lacked only the white coat that marked them as an English soldier.*

*Of particular interest here is the provision of archery equipment, which has been highlighted in* **bold** *for ease of reference. Only 60 bows were provided, in four batches of 15 bows each, each batch accompanied by a chest of arrows. We know that there was more than 60 archers in the retinue, however, because 22 individuals were also provided with a sheaf of arrows. None of the men provided with a sheaf of arrows were provided with a bow at this time, suggesting very strongly that they provided their own bows for the campaign and were not issued bows from a central stock. No other offensive weapons were supplied to the men of Howard's retinue. Since some men were able to provide their own bows but not arrows it is probable that other men were also able to provide both bow and arrows for themselves.*

### Lord Howard's Retinue, 1481

Buriff of Brykesley
The xxiij. day of April, my Lord toke him xij. jaketes clothes

William Wyngfelde, hymselff and vj. men with him,
The xxviij day of April, my Lord toke him be Dalamar[145] handes iij li. x s
The xiij day of July, my Lord paid Master Wyngfele for a moneth wages xxx.s
M$^d$. That Thomas Dalamar hath paid Willm Wingfele for xl night[146] wages xv.s

Edmond Daniel, him selff and iiij men
Item, he hath received his jaketes, **a cheef of arowes,** a peir splentes.
The xxvij day of Marche, he rec. x. s
Also he received of Thomson for goonepoder xliij. s.

---

[145] Thomas Dalamar was a factor or servant of Sir John Howard and appears regularly in the accounts making disbursements of money.
[146] It is probable that 'xl night' here and throughout this document is the book-keeper's shorthand for 'fortnight' rather than a literal description of forty nights.

M^d. That Maister Daniel is al paid for xiiij wekes for his men, and Sampson men ar paid for xiiij vekes   xviij. s a man

Erdiswik
Item, he hath a peire brigandines, **a cheef of arowes**, a salate with a viser, a peir splentys, and his jakete
And he received of my Lord at London vj.s viij.d.
And he receive of my Lord at Orwel xx.d
The xvij. day of August he received x.s.

Richard Knyvet hath received
A peire brigandines, a standart, **a chef of arowes,** a peire splentes, and a salate, and a jakkett, a standart.
The xiij. day of August he rec. iij.s iiij.d

Edmond Gorge,[147] and iij. men.
Item he hath a perie brigandines, and jaket cloth for him and his men

Howyth him self, his childe, and viij. men.
The xxi. yere of the king, and in Marche he received of my Lord xlvj.s viij.d.
The xxij day of April he rec. xxxiij.s iiij.d. And he is served of all his jaketes.
He hath a salade with a viser
And Kunst is al paid be Buriff handes v.li viij.s viij.d
So he is al paid for xvij. men.
The xxth day May, my Lord deliverd him **xv. bowes and a cofer with arowes**.
The xiij. day of July, My Lord paid Edward Gauge for viij land men xl.s
My Lord hath paid to eche of them for xl night wages iij.s
The xvij. day of August Howith rec. xiij.s iiij.d

Edmond Yns, xix. men and him selff.
The x. day of April, he rec. for prest[148] of xix. men and him self x.li

---

[147] Anne Howard (1446-1474), Sir John Howard's second daughter, had been married to Sir Edmund Gorges
[148] Imprest money: a recruitment bounty or advance paid to cover expenses

And cloth for xj. jaketes.

The x. day of May, my Lord toke Ins opon rekeyng, for to bey vitels xij.li

Also my Lord toke him afore Yarmowth x. mrks.

The xxvj. day of June, my Lord toke him wages for his men amoneth wages v.li

The last day of July, my Lord toke Yns xxvi.s viij.d

*Steven Howyth, John Barker of Colchester, John Bocher, Willm Crosby, John Bayly, John Mendham, Steven Hawkyn, Robt Hawkyn, Watyr Bryan, Willm Hutoff, Hans Vanbrusel, Beck, Stannart, John Stronde, Steven Roydon, Robt Stronde, Nicolas Walsale, Willm Dalby, Robt. Basset, John Neve, Nich. Bateman, Robt Brown, Thomas Chandeler, Ric. Gilberd, Ric. Drawes, John Whygttop, John Brown, Robt. Strange, John Wyelde, Alen Crombye, Willm Gawdynell, John Browne, Rober Mercer, Willm Hyns childe.*[149]

Sir Willm Pirton, xxxix men and him self.

The x.day of March, my Lord toke him x.li

The xxiij.day of April my Lord toke him x.li

My Lord sent him be[150] Harry Rippes clothe for xl jaketes, and my Lord delivered hym for ij. jaketes more.

The xxiij.day of July, my Lord paid him for a moneth wages for xl men x.li

Also my Lord paid him for al his men for a xl night wages l.s

Thomas Sampson, xix men and him self.

The xxj.day of April, my Lord toke him for the wages x.li

He is served of his jakettes, the xxvij.day of April, be Watkyn Fowche his man.

The xiiij.day July, my Lord paid him for a moneth wages v.li

The x.day of August, Dalamar paid him for xl night wages xlvij.s vj.d

Sampson of Hempstyd, him self and iiij men

---

[149] These men are named alongside the entries relating to Howyth's, Gauge's, and Yns' retinues, but with the exception of Howyth himself and Willm Hyns (presumably a kinsman of Edmond Yns) it is impossible to tell which men served which master.

[150] by

The xx.day of March, my Lord toke him xxxiij.siiij.d
He hath cloth for jaketes
The vij.day of August, my Lord paid his men xxij.s

Seynclow, ix men and him self
*John Luter, John Bayly, Willm Colyn, Ric. Harris, Thomas Haschman, Redmayn, Watir Howsse, John Wellys, Tomas Balle*
The xv day of March, my Lord toke him xl.s
He hath Jaketes cloth for them al
And the xxviij.day of April he received xl.s
The xxiij.day of July he received xl.s
The xvj.day of August, he rec. for xl night

Sir Tomas Moys
He hath a peir brigandes keuvred with blak satin, a peir splentis, and a jakete, and **a cheff of arowes**, a salate be Manewaryng, a standart, a gusset be Manewarying.
The first day of Juyn, my Lord toke him iij.s iiij.d

Robard Mortemer,[151] xvij men and hym self.
The xxj. day of Marche, my lord toke hym ix.li
My Lord sente him be Harry Rippes for xviij. jakets, and a jaket my Lord sent him more be Maister Daniel.
The xx.day May, my Lord deliverd him **xv. bowes, and a cofer with arowes**.
The xxiij.day of July, my Lord tok him iiij.li x.s

Thomas Thorpe.
The xxj.day of March, xxj.year of the reigne of the king, he received for prest xv. lande men vij.li x.s
And for prest of xiiij maryners xxviij.s
He had cloth for xxviij jaketes
My Lord toke hym, the vij.day of May, for the wages of xxiiij. men   iij.li ij.s vj.d

---

[151] Isobel (or Elizabeth) Howard, Sir John Howard's eldest daughter, was married to Robert Mortimer

My Lord hath deliverd him **xv. bowes, and a cofer with arowes**.

Simond Reed and his sonne recd. of my Lord the xx.day May xiij.s iiij.d

And iiij.s they had before, and theyr jaketes.

The xvj.day July, my Lord paid Torpe for xxxvj persones in the *Paker* for a moneth ix.li

The viij. Day of August, my Lord toke Stasse[152] for xj men xlix.s iij.d

*Mortemer, Willm Baker, John Germain, John Page, Willm Smyth, John Kyler, Willm Haley, Willm Crowche, Tomas of Brykelsey, Harry Rippes, John Leveron, Willm Wryte, Willm Englysh, Pitre Alleyn, John Rippes, Thomas Qwyke, John Crowche, Tomas Benete, Stasse, Norwich, Willm Tapton, Ric. Larens, Thomas Grone, Roger Snodon, Roger Water, Willm Witer, Ric. Hey, Crakbon, Cobdoke, Willm Savige, Kyrkby, John Porser, Ric Haryson, John Blower, John Kerkby, Andrew Pelam, Ric. Mych, Willm Culpak.*[153]

Necolas Whitfelde, iij men.

The xxj. yer of the king, and in March, my Lord tok him prest xl.s

My Lord asigned him to take of George Bocher x.s

The xvj.day of April he rec. x.s; so he hath iij.li

Also my Lord toke him that day we cam to the see from Harwich x.s

Wisseman hath a peir brigandines keuvred with blak velwet.

He hath a salate, a standart, a peir splentes, and a jakete.

The xiij.day of August, my Lorde toke him iij.s iiij.d

Thomas Henyngham, Edmond Henyngham, vj men with them.

The ix.day of April, my Lord toke Sir John Henyngham for prest iiij.li

And theyr jaketes also.

The xiij. Day July, my Lord paid him for a moneths wages for vij men xxxv.s

And at his departing he rec. for xl night xvj.s

Harry Manewarying

---

[152] Elsewhere in Howard's accounts payment of 3s 4d is recorded to purchase Stasse a bow. See **Doc. 44**

[153] The retinues of Mortimer and Thorpe

Item, he hath a peire brigandines keuvred with purpil velvet, a salate, a standart, **a cheef of arowes**, a peir splentys, and his jakete, and a gusset.
The xiiij.day of August, my Lord toke him at Stoke vj.s viij.d

Corson hym self

Fastolff him self.

Becham.
Item, he hath his jaket, a peir splentis, a standart.
The xvij. day of August, my Lord toke him x.s.

Richard Boloke.[154]
Item, he hath a peire brigandines, a salate, **a cheff of arowes**, a peir splentys, and his jakete, a standart, a gusset.
The xvij. day of August, he received x.s.

John Bliant, him self and v. men.
He is served of his jaketes, and a peir splentes for hym selff, and anoder peire splentes.
The xxviij. day off April, he received l.s.
He hath a peire brigandines.
Also he hath anoder peir splentes.
The xvij. day of July, my Lord paid him for v. men for a moneth wages xxv.s.
The xiij. day of August, he rec. xv.s,

Jamis Atsel, of Kolcester.
He hath **a cheff of arowes**, a jakete, and anoder for Goorge Porter.
My Lord asigned to receive v. mrks.

John Barker, of Kolcester,
The xij. day of March, received prest ij.s.

---

[154] Don't laugh, this is serious history.

John Broone, of Kolcester.
The ij.day of May, my Lord toke him x.s.
And he hath his jakete, and for his man anoder.
The xiij. day of August, he rec. viij.s.

Bronning, of Ardeley.
The xvj. day of March, he received yj.s. viij.d.
The XXV. day of April, he rec. vj.s. viij.d.
He hath his jakete.
The xiij. day of August, my Lord toke him iiij.s. viij.d.

John Boone, of Harwich.
The XX. day of March, he received at Harwich of my Lord vj.s. viij.d.

Thomas Bornett.
Hath a peir brigandines, a peir splentis, and his jakete, a salate.

Raff Barlescolis.
Hath of my Lord **a cheef of arowes**, his jaket be Wolman, and my Lord toke him vj.s. viij.d.

John Baker, of Kolcester.
The xxiiij. day of April, my Lord toke him xv.s.
And a peyre of splentys, and **a cheff of arowes**.
And my Lord gaf him xx.d.

Willm Baker, of Kolcester.

John Boonfilde.
The xxj. yere of the king, and in April, he rec. xv.s.
He hath his jakete.
The xvij. day of August, my Lord toke him x.s.

Jamys Baker.
The xxiij. day of April, my Lord toke him x.s.

He hath his jaket, and a peir splentis.
The xxvij. day of August, he rec. viij.s.

Benam.
Item, he hath a peir brigandines, a peir splentes, a salate, and his jaket, a gusset.
And my Lord tok him at London vj.s. viij.d.
The xiij. day of August, my Lord toke him iij.s. iiij.d.
And at London vj.s. viij.d.

Arnolde Brouwam.
Item, he hath a peir brigandines, a salate, **a chef of arowes**, a peir splentes, and his jaket, a standarde, a gussete.
The xvij. day of August, he rec. x.s.

John Baker.
He hath a peir brigandines, a salate, a peir splentes, and a standart of meyle, and his jaket and a gussete x.s.
And he hath of my Lord the viij. day of May iij.s. iiij.d.

Richard Berebrewer.
Item, he hath his jaket, a peir brigandines, a peir splentes, a standart, a salate.
And at his departing my Lord gaf him iij.s. iiij.d.

Roger Bronfelde.
Item, he hath a peire brigandines, a salade, a standart, **a cheffe of arowes**, a peir splentes, and a gussete, his jakete, and he rec. at Stoke iij.s. iiij.d.
He received of my Lord at Harwich iij.s. iiij.d.
The xvij. day of August, he rec. x.s.

Baudwyn.
Received of my Lord xx.s.
His jaket and ...

John Calle.
He hath a peyre brigandines, a salade, a standarte, a gussete, a peir splentes, **a chef of arowes**, and his jaket, and he rec. iij.s. iiij.d.
He rec. of Dalamar xx.d.

John Cokke, of Harwich.
The xxiij. day of Marche, my Lord tok him ij.s.

Richard Koke, bocher.
The xiij. day of August, my Lord gaf him viij.s.

Richard Corteman, of Chelmesford.
The xxviij. day of March, my Lord toke him prest x.s.
He hath his jakete.
My Lord toke him the xiij. day of August viij.s.

John Carter, of Kolcester.

Robard Catelein, of Cromer.
He hath received of Maister Wyndham

Xpofer Cresford.
Hath received of my Lord upon his wages xxj.s viij.d
The xxj. day of May, he rec. xx.d

Thomas Cooke.
Item, he hath a peire brigandines, a standart of the best, a salate, **a cheff of arowes**, a peir splentes, his jaket, a gusset.
The xvij. day of August, he rec. x.s.

Robard Coke.
Item, he hath a peire brigandines, a standart, a salate, **a chef arowes**, a peir splentys, and his jakete, a gusset.
The xiij. day of August, he rec. v.s.

Robard Clerke, of Neylond, xiij. and him self.

*Robt. Clerke, Willm Hoore, Gefray Broone, Nicolas Rowte, John Newtone, Willm Fyte, Richard Toncliff, Robt. Harsson, Walyngton, John Roote, Robt. Stoone, Richard Hogson, John Sperling, Willm Ysbel.*

The X. day of March, my Lord toke him iij.li. x.s.

He hath jaketes cloth for them al.

And **a chef of arowes** for him self.

The xxv. day of April, my Lord toke Robt. Clerke iij. li. x.s.

So he is paid for viij. wekkes, him and xiij. men.

And my Lord hath taken him a peir splentes.

The xvij. day of July, he received for xij. men iij. li.

The xiij. day of August, my Lord toke him xl night wages xxxiij.s.

Richard Daniel.

The XXV. day of March, he rec. of my Lord x.s.

Afore Yarmouth iij.s. iiij.d.

And he hath his jaket.

The xiij. day of August, he rec. v.s.

Daniel, of Barfolde, his broder.

The XXV. day of March, he rec. x.s.

And he hath his jakete.

Dyago.

He hath a peir brigandines, a peir splentes, a salate, a standart, and his jaket.

And he had for prest ij.s.

The vij. day of April, he rec. iij.s. iiij.d.

And a shert.

John Davy, of Turton Strete.

He hath **a cheff of arowes**, a peir brigandines keuvred with russet velvet, a standart, a salate, a peir splentes, and a jaket.

Davy, of Neylond.[155]
The XX. day of April, he rec. x.s.
And his jakete be Willm Hore.
The xvij. day of July, he rec. be Robt. Clerk v.s.
And my Lord toke him iij.s.

Dalemare. x.s.
Hath received of my Lord his jaket.

John Eltherton, of Chelmesford.
Item, he hath a peir brigandines.
The xxvij. day of March, my Lord toke him x.s.
He hath his jaket.
He received of Dalamar at Harwich xx.d.
The xiij. day of August, he rec. jx. S

John Fyeryng, of Chelmesford.
The XXV. day of March, my Lord toke him x.s.
He hath his jakete.
The xiij. day August, he rec. ix.s.

Fynsche, of Dedham.
The xxvj. day of April, he rec. xiij.s. iiij.d.
And a peir splentes.
The xiij. day of August, he rec. v.s.

Edmond Frente, tronpete.
Hath his baner.
He hath received at ij. tymes xij.s.
The XX. day of May, he rec. xx.d.
At his departing my Lord gaf him vj.s. viij.d.

Willm Gilys.

---

[155] Possibly Morys Davy, who was given 3s 4d to purchase a bow. See **Doc. 44**

John Hobbes.
The xxiij. day of March, my Lord toke him prest at Harwich iij.s. iiij.d.
The xxij. day of April, he had of Dalamar at ij. tymes x.s.
He hath his jakete, and my Lord toke him v.s.

Willm Hil, tronpete.
My Lord toke Pinchebek to tak him prest x.s.
The xxij. day of April, he rec. x.s.
And his baner : the xx. day of May, he rec. xx.d.
The xiij. day of August, at his departing vj.s. viij.d.

Harbronde.
Item, he hath a peir brigandines, a salate, (be Johnson) a standart, a gusset, a peir splentis, his jaket.
He received of Dalamar in the schip xx.d.
The xvij. day of August, he rec. x.s.

John Hoonte.
The iiij. day of April, my Lord toke him x.s.
He hath a peir splentes, and a jakete, and a salate, a peir corsettes.[156]
The xiij. day of August, my Lord toke him iiij.s.

Edward Johnson.[157]
Hath a peir brigandines, a peir splentes, a salate, **a cheff of arowes**, and a jaket, and a standart, a gusset.

Davy John.
The xiiij. day of April, he rec. at London x.s.
He hath a gestron keuvred with blake velvet, **a chef of arowes**, a salate, a standart, a peir splentes, and his jaket.
The xiij. day of August, he rec. at Stoke iij.s. iiij.d.

---

[156] Corselet - back and breast plate.
[157] Possibly the Johnson who was given 8d to buy a bow. See **Doc. 44**

Palmer Jamis.
Item, he hath received of my Lord ix.s. iiij.d.
The XX. day of May, my Lord toke him iij.s. iiij.d.
And his jaket.
The xiij. day of August, he rec. iiij.s.

Kunste, of Wisnowe, ix. and him self.
*Kunste, John Mors, John Pache, John Jacobe, John Hawkyn, Harry Smyth, Robt. Kunste, John Crouche, John Lopham, Robt. Crabtree, Sander Lovel, John Bryksam, Richard Ensent, John Welde, John Barker, John Schore, John Tynby, Thomas Chamberlain, John Venavale, Edward Gauge, Coteler, Katby, Benton*
The xv. day of March, he rec. xx.s.
Howyth hath for jaketes xvj. yerdes white, that is for xiij., and besede Kunste jaket.
M$^d$. That Buriff hath deliverd to Kunst, and to his feleschip xl.s. iiij.d.
And my Lord rekened with Kunste for xvij. men.
The vij."" day of May, my Lord toke to Buriff to Kunste and xxj. men with him v.li. viij.s. viij.d.
And Buriff toke them before xl.s. iiij.d.
And thei had of my Lord xx.s.
So thei ar al paid for xvij. men.
And my Lord toke Buriff for Barker and Shore xvj.s.
My Lord gaf them that werketh opon the *Barbara* vj.s, viij.d.
My Lord gaf Kunste to drynke ij.s. vj.d.
My Lord gaf the feleschip for ther parte of an ankyr v.s.
The purser, Gauge, rec. for xix. maryners for a moneth iiij.li. xv.s.
M$^d$. That at ther departing my Lord gaf eche of the maryners for xl. night iij.s. iiij.d. a man.

Katby, of Harwich, and his sonne.
The XV. day of March he rec. vj.s.
He hath jaketes ij.
And my Lord toke him at Harwich v.s.

John Kenton, of Harwich.
Hath had prest of Katby ij.s.
That day we made seile, I, Dalamar, toke him v.s.

Lulay, of Harwich.
The X. day of March, he rec. prest iij.s, iiij.d.

Thomas Lalford.
Hath his jaket be Wolman.

John Larke, gooner.[158]
The xx. day of March, he rec. vj.s. viij.d.
The xvij. day of April, he received iij.s. iiij.d.
The xiij. day of August, he rec. vij.s,

Renolde Morgan.
The vij. day of April, my Lord toke him x.s.
He hath his jaket of my Lord, and he rec. iij.s. iiij.d.
The xiij. day of August, he rec. iiij.s. viij.d.

John Newton.
M$^d$. That my Lord hath taken him at London, in Lenten, the xxj. yere of the king, and in April, at ij. times xiiij.s. iiij.d.
He hath his jakete.
The xiij. day of August, he rec. iiij.s.

Oliver.
He hath a pair brigandines, a salate, a standart, a peir splentes, **a cheff of arowes**, and his jaket.
The xvij. day of August, he rec. viij.s.

Willm Palgrave.
He hath a peir brigandines, a salate, a standart, a jakete.

---
[158] gunner

Parker, of Harwich, and x. men.
The X. day of March, my Lord toke him vj.s. viij.d.
And to prest x. men xx.s.

George Porter.

John Croos.
Barlescolis broght him : had prest xx.d.
He hath a peir brigandines, a salate, a standart, a peir splentes, and his jaket.

Piper, of Brykelsey, and v. men.
My Lord toke him prest xij.s.

Robard Petman, iiij. men.
My Lord toke him prest, and iiij. x.s.

John Partrigge, the yonger.
The xiij. day of Marche, my Lord toke him prest vj.s, viij.d.

John Partrige, the elder.
The xiij. day of Marche, my Lord toke him vj.s. viij.d.

Personne, of Manetry.
The XXV. day of Marche, he rec. prest vj.s. viij.d.
The xxiiij. day of April, I, Dalamar, toke him iij.s. iiij.d.
He hath his jaket.
The xiij. day of August, he rec. ix.s.

Pierson, of Croomer.
My Lord toke him prest ij.s
Maister Windham hath taken him…

Pynchebek, tronpete.

Hath his baner.
And he hath received of my Lord at ij. tymes xx.s.
The xx. day of May, he rec. xx.d.
At his departing he rec. vj.s viii.d.

John Porter, tronpete.
Hath his baner.
And he hath received of my Lord at ij. tymes xx.s.
The xx. day of May, he rec. xx.d.
At his departing he rec. vj.s. viij.d.

Peverel, of Barfolde.
The xxiiij. day of April, my Lord toke him prest x.s.
He hath his jakket.
The xiij. day July, my Lord toke him v.s.
My Lord sent him by Robt Coyke iij.s.

Harry Pigote.
Hath a gestron of my Lordes, keuvred with damask, a peir splentis, and a jaket, a salate, a standart, a gusset.
The xxix. day of April, he rec. v.s.
The xiij. day of August, he rec. xx.d.

Robard Rys, tronpete.
Hath his baner.
And he hath rec. of my Lord at ij. tymes xx.s.
The xx. day of May, he rec. xx.d.

Willm Scheele.[159]
Item, he hath a gestron, a salate, a standart, a peir splentes, **a cheff of arowes**, and his jakete, a gusset.
The XX. day of May, my Lord toke him x.s.
The xiij. day of August, he rec. iiij.s.

---

[159] Scheele was given 6d to buy a bow on another occasion. See **Doc. 44**

Jamis Stoll.
Hath a peir brygandines.
The xxiij. day of April, he rec. of Dalamar x.s.
He hath his jaket.

Giles Senclowe.
Hath a peir brigandines, a peir splentes, and his jaket.

Richard Skynner, of Higham.
The xxiij. day of March, he rec. x.s.
He hath his jaket, and a peir splentes.
The xvij. day of July, he rec. v.s
The xiij. day of August, he rec. iij.s

John Schore, of Kolcester.
He hath received prest be Barker handes ij.s.

John Schipman.
He received of my Lord, the xxiiij. day of Marche x.s.
He hath his jakete.
The xvij. day of July, he rec. of my Lord v.s.
The xiij. day of August, he rec. iij.s.

Robard Strong, of Cromer.
He hath received of Maister Wyndham ...

Sebryth.
Hath a peir brigandines, his jaket, a peir splentes, and a salate, a standart.
The xiij. day of August, he rec. v.s.

John Taylor, of Stoke.
Received x.s.
And the xiij. day of August he rec. viij.s. iiij.d.

Thomas Thyrfilon.
A peir brigandines, a salate, a standart, a gussete, a peir splentes, and his jaket.
The xx. day of May, my Lord toke him iij.s. iiij.d.
The xiij. day of August, he rec. v.s.

Thomas Tenche, and i. man.
The xx. day of April, he rec. xx.s.
He hath his jaket, and his man.

He hath harneys[160] of my Lord and a moneth wages x.s.
And at his departing xl. night wages iij.s.

Whitchirch, of Barfolde.
The xxj. day of April, he received of my Lord x.s.
And a peir of splentis.
The xvij. day July, he rec. v.s.
The xiij. day of August, he rec. iij.s,

Robard Worsseley, and iij. men.
Harry Worseley, John Scharpe, William Taylor.
He had of my Lord xxx.s.
The xvij. day July, he rec. xv.s.
The xiij. day of August, he rec. x.s.

John Wady.
The xix. day of April, he received of my Lord x.s.
He hath a peir brygandines, a standart, a salate, (per Ediswik) a peir splentes, **a cheff of arowes**, and his jaket.
The xiiij. day of August, he rec. iij.s. iiij.d.

William Witby.

John Porser, of Stoke.
The xviij. day of April, he received x.s.
A peir splentys, and a jakete.
The xiij. day of August, he rec. viij.s.

Klegge.
He hath a peir brigandines, **a cheff of arowes**, a peir splentis, and a jaket, a salate be Erdiswik. Klegges standart. He rec. xiij. Aug. x.s.

Laurens of the Hal.

---

[160] armour

He hath a gestron of mayle,[161] a peir splentes, and a jakete, and a salate, a standart.
The xiij. day of August, he rec. iij.s. iiij.d.

Roger, of Stabul.[162]
Hath a gestron, a peir splentis, and a jaket, and a salate, a standarte.
The xiij. day of August, he rec. iij.s. iiij.d.

John Fryere, that was with Maister Craen.
He hath a peir brigandines, a salate, **a cheff of arowes**, a peir splentes, and jaket, and xx.d.
The xiij. day of August, he rec. xij.d.

Garard Franchmen.
He hath a peir brigandines, a salate, a standart, a peir splentes, and a jaket.
He rec. of my Lord iii.s. iiij.d.

Willm Dacy, baker.
He hath his jaket, and a gestron, and a salate, a peire splentis; and my Lord gaf him ij.s.

Willm White, of Stepney, himself and xv. men.
The xxj. yere of the king, and xv. day of April, my Lord toke White the ful of v.li. vj.s viij.d. to take xiiij. men, and himself and Borges.
And they had before for prest xxviij.s.
vj.li xij.s. viij.d.
The vij. day of May, my Lord toke White for the ful wages of xiiij. men vij.s. iiij.d.
They have theyr jaketes.
Torp is paid for a moneth wages for xxij. persones, lande men and maryners ix.li.

---

[161] mail shirt
[162] It may be coincidence that in 1517 Robert Stabuls of Nottingham was described as a 'gestronmaker': *Records of the Borough of Nottingham* (London, 1885) v. 3, p. 140

The xiij. day of August, my Lord toke eche of them that ar merked with an *. iij.s. iiij.d.

And to Robt. Sergeant xx.d. to drynk.

*Willm Barbor, Willm White, John Hobbes, Davy Yong, John Bartram, John Dowe, Robt. Fawcon, John Aschman, Edmond Johnson, John Instisse, Edward Johnson, Willm Schepard, Ric. Goodryge\*, John Browne, John Xpofer, Thomas Armorer\*, Robt. Sargeant\*, John Adam, John Pak\*, Harry Pak\*, Willm Greges, John Dewe, Willm Rede\**

Hans Vanbrusel, gooner.
The xij. day of April, my Lord toke Howith, to by him gere withal vj.s. viij.d.
The XV. day of April, my Lord tok him xij.d.
The xxiiij. day of April, he received xvij.d.
He hath his jaket.
The xvj. day July, he rec. of my Lord iij.s. iiij.d.

Perrin, crosbowe maker.
The XXV. day of February, my Lord toke hym pres tiij.s. iiij.d.
The xvj. day of April, my Lord toke him vj.s. iiij.d
Also my Lord toke him, to by gere withal iij.s. iiij.d
He hath his jaket.
The xxvij. day of August, my Lord toke hym vj.s. viij.d

John Vandelf, gooner.
The xvj. day of April, he received pres tiij.s. iiij.d
The xxiij. day of April, he received xx.d
He hath his jakete, ij. yerdes.
The xiij. day of August, he rec. vj.s. viij.d

Xpofer, taboret.
Valentin, taboret.
Item, eche of them had a goon[163] coste my Lord v.s. x.d. ob.

---

[163] gown

Item, eche of them had xvj.d. to make ther gons ij.s. viij.d.
And to by them self hosen thei had v.s.
Also they received of Dalamar ther prest iiij.s.
Item, Valentyn had to go to Southampton ij.s. ij.d.
Item, the xj, day of Marche, eche of them had viij.d. that is xvj.d.
The xxij. day of April, thei had ij.s.   to by bonetes.
Also thei have had schertes, and other gere.
The xiij. day of August, thei rec. at Harwich iij.s. iiij.d.

Royngton, of Hadley.
He hath his jakete, and a peir splentes, and he received of my Lord x.s.
The xiij. day of August, he rec. viij.s.

Kolwyn, bocher.
The XXV. day of April, my Lord toke him x.s.
And his jaket, and a peire splentes.
The xiij. day of August, he rec. iij.s. iiij.d.

Wolman.
The xxj. yer of the king, and viij. day of May, my Lord toke him x.s.

Andrew Partrigge.
Hath a peir brigandines, his jaket, and a peir splentes.
The xiij. day of August, he rec. xiij.s. iiij.d.

Maister Charles.
The xxiiij. day of April, my Lord toke him xx.s.
He hath his jaket.
The xiij. day of August, he rec. x.s.

Richard Wardel, Barlescolis is seurte[164]
The ij. day of May, he rec. x,s.
The xiij. day of August, he rec. viij.s.

---

[164] Wardel stood surety for Barscolis

Here foloweth the mennes namys that are with Edmond Daniel.

Robard Ferme.
Hath rec. of Edmond Daniel, gentilman x.s.

Willm Hyde.
He hath received of Edmond Daniel x.s.

John Wellys.
He hath rec. of Edmond Daniel x.s.

Nicolas Armurer, of Ermewe, gooner.
The iij. day of May, my Lord toke him vj.s. viij.d.
And ij, yerdes white.[165]

Harry Tomson, gooner.
Item, iij. day of May, my Lord toke him vj.s.

Lambe Tomson, of Seryksee.
The ij. day of May, my Lord toke him x.s.
And ij. yerdes of white.

Koteler, of Wysnowe.
The vj. day of May, he rec. prest x.s.
And his jakete.

Willm Barbor.
The vij. day of May, my Lord tok him x.s.
And his jaket.
The xiij. day of August, he rec, x.s.

Gauge.

---

[165] Presumably white cloth for a 'jakete'.

The xiij. day of May, my Lord toke him a peir brigandines x.s.
And he hath his jakete and xx.s.

Richard Coke.
The xx. day of May, my Lord toke him iij.s. iiij.d.
And his jakete.

Crepage, Maister of the *Trenete* of Seint Osis.[166]
The xx. day of May, he rec. prest x.s.
John Vinsent received prest x.s.
Willm Moher x.s.
Item, Laurens May x.s.
Thomas Crepage x.s.
John Frane x.s.
Willm Goldyng x.s.
Hansse, gooner x.s.
Richard Davy x.s.
Richard Barbor viij.s.
John Toley x.s.
My Lord delivered the maister for xj. jaketes.
Delivered Maister Mortemer **xv. bowes, a chast with arowes**.

*John Cobbe, Robard Smyth, Willm Palmer, Harry Godfray, Willm Allybryth.*
The xxj. day of May, my Lord toke to Harry Framyngham for v. men l.s.
The xviij. day July, Crepage received for a moneth wages iiij.li.

---

[166] The *Trinity* of St. Osyth

## 44. Howard Household Books, 1481-1490

*Miscellaneous entries from the Howard account books. The Howard household books are littered with entries recording a wide variety of payments for myriad sundry expenses. The entries below cover the entire period, 1481-90, and have been removed from their context for the purpose only of illustrating the prices of various items. In 1482 and again in 1487 the maximum price of a yew bow was established by statute as 3 shillings and 4 pence,[167] so it is interesting to find a payment of five shillings to William Aston for a bow. Possibly it was something other than a yew bow, perhaps a steel 'Turkey' bow or a crossbow (though crossbows are frequently mentioned as such in the Howard accounts), or possibly it was simply a matter of flouting the law for a particularly fine bow. Four men were given 3 shillings 4 pence for bows, suggesting that the maximum price for yew bows established by the statutes became* de facto *a standard price for good quality bows, but Johnson and Scheele were given 8 pence and 6 pence respectively for their bows, which might give us some indication of the cost of the cheapest 'mean' wood bows in the late medieval period. This also tells us that noblemen did not routinely provide their retainers with the best equipment available. Poynes was given 2 shillings and 6 pence for a bow, suggesting perhaps a poor-quality yes bow, or a good quality 'mean' bow. The cost of bow-cases, arrows, and girdles are also mentioned.*

> Item, I tok to the bower upon reckning for making of bowes xx.d.
>
> My Lord gaff Morys Davy for a bowe iij.s. iiij.d.
>
> The xvj. day of August, Dalamar toke to Peverel, of Barfold, that my Lord owght the bower of Barfold vij.s.
>
> Item, Johnson for a bowe viij.d.
>
> Item, to the bowyer of Berfolte for mendyng of my Lordes bowis viij.d.
>
> Item, to the bower vj.s.
>
> Item, to Benam for brekking of his bowe viij.d.
>
> Item, to Scheele to by a bowe vj.d.

---

[167] See **Docs 12** and **14**

Item, for a bowcase xij.d.

Item, for a gyrdell for your bow j.d.

Item, to hym that brout the bowes fro Mongomery ij.d.

This day, my Lord sent to Masons wiff, Xpofer Cresford standyng bye, vj. long bowes,

Item, the same day, paid to the caryere for bryngynge home bowes from London to Stoke viij.d.

My Lord cam aboorde, and broght with him, Item, xxvj. blak billes : item, ij. askes : item, his bowes that Tomson hath in the store hows : item, a dossar with arras, corsins, and a panyer with spises.

Item, my Lord gaff hym for his bowe iij.s. iiij.d.

Item, the xxx. day of Jenever, my Lord gaff to Poynes that dwellyd with my Lord of York, for to bye with a bowe ij.s. vj.d.

Item, payd to Willm Aston for a bow for Hawkyn v.s.

Item, for a bow to Stasse iij.s iiij.d.

Item, to Amolde for a bow iij.s. iiij.d.

Item, the same day, my Lord delyverd to Merbury to bey a schef arowes v.s.

## 45. The Guild of St. George, 1537[168]

*The Honourable Artillery Company claims, with some justification, to be the oldest regiment in the British army and traces its origin to 1537 when Henry VIII authorised the Guild of St. George to promote shooting with bows, crossbows, and guns. Members of the guild enjoyed certain privileges such as exemption from jury duty and, most remarkably, immunity from prosecution in the event of a fatal accident or wounding during archery practice. The so-called 'King's pardon,' excusing archers from charges of murder or manslaughter, has often been cited by historians and others, but the Royal patent makes clear that it only applied to members of the guild. Although the patent mentions members of the guild in all parts of the realm there is little evidence to suggest that its membership extended beyond London and its suburbs.*

THE PATENT OF King HENRY VIII. Concerning ARCHERIE.

HENRY the Eight by the Grace of God King of England and of France, Defendour of the Fayth, Lorde of Irelond, and in Erthe Supreme Hede of the Churche of Englond,

To all Judges, Justyces, Mayres, Sheryffys, Baylyffys, Counstables, and other our Offycers, Mynysters, and Subgyettys, aswell wythyn the Lybertyes as wythout thyes oure Letters herying or seyng, Gretyng,

We let yowe wyte, That of our Grace especyall, certeyn scyence, and mere mocyon, We have graunted and licencyd, and by thyes Presentys doo graunte and licence for us and our Heyres, asmoche as yn us ys, unto our trusty and welbeloued Servauntys and Subgyettys Sir Crystofer Morres Knyght, Mayster of oure Ordenauncys, Anthony Knevett and Peter Mewtes Gentlemen of oure prevy Chambre, Overseers of the Fraternytye or Guylde of Saynt George; And that they, and every of them, shalbe Overseers of the Scyence of Artyllary, that ys, to wyt, for Long-bowes, Cros-bowes and Hand-gonnes, &c. which Syr Crystofer Morres, Cornelys Johnson, Anthony Antony, and Henry Johnson, that they and every of them shalbe Maysters and Rulers of the saved Scyence of Artyllary, as afore ys rehercyd, for

---

[168] Printed in Sir William Wood, *The Bow-man's Glory, or Archery Revived* (London, 1682)

Long-bowes, Cros-bowes, & Hand-gonnes, which Syr Crystofer Cornelys, Anthony and Henry, we by thyes Presentys do ordeign, make, and conferme foure Maysters and Rulers of the sayed Fellyshyp of Artyllery for ever, duryng theyr lyves: And that the sayed Maysters and Rulers, and theyr Successours, Maysters and Rulers, alwayes beyng foure of oure Servauntes, Englyshemen or Denysens, maye begyn, founde, edefye, make, ordeygn, gadre, krytte and establysshe a certeyn perpetuall Fraternytye of Saynt George, and that they maye have full power and auctorytye to chose accept, take, and admytte unto theyr sayed Fraternytye or Guylde Almaner, honeste parsonnes whatsoever they be, aswell beyng oure Servaintys and Subjettys as Straungyers, Denysens or not Denysens, at theyr lybertyes. And that the sayed Maysters and Rulers, and suche Brethern as they shall electe, admytte, take and accepte to them, shall yn thyng and name be oon bodye and Commynaltye Corporate, havyng successyon perpetually by the name of Maysters and Rulers and Commynaltye of the Fraternitye or Guylde of Artyllary of Long-bowes, Cros-bowes, & Hand-gonnes: And thesame four Maysters, Rulers and Brethern, and theyr Successours, we yncorporate and make oon Bodye by theys Presentys; And that the sayed Maysters and Rulers and Commynaltye, and theyr Successours, shall ymplede and be ympleded by the name of Maysters and Rulers of the sayed Bretherhed or Guylde; And also shall have power and auctorytye to chose and elect among themselfys, wyth theyr assystence, foure undre Maysters and Rulers of the same Fraternytye or Guylde, to oversee and governe the same Fraternytye from tyme to tyme, and to have the governaunce and custodye of such Landes, Tenementys, Reutys, Possessions, Goodys and Catallys, as hereafter shall happen to be purchased, betwethed, gyven, graunted or assygned by any maner parson or parsons to sayed Fraternytye or Guylde: And they every yere as yt shall best pleas them, shall mowe, ordeygne, and chose successyvely foure undre Maysters and Rulers, Englysshmen, Straungyers, Denysens or not Denysens, of good name and fame; And they, or any of them, yf nede requyre, to amove, put out, and discharge, and an other yn hys or theyr name and place, as ofte as shall pleas them to name, put yn, electe and auctoryse by the counsayll of the four Maysters and Rulers, and theyr sayed Assystence. And furthermore, That the same Maysters and Rulers maye have and use a Common seale for all thynges and necessaryes belongyng to the sayed Fraternytye or Guylde. And that they may be of habylitye or capacitye yn the Law, to ymplede or be ympleded, answer and be aunswered before any Judge or Justice, spyrytuall or temporall, whatsoever they be, yn any Court or Courtes of thys our Realm; And yn all and syngular Accyons, Demaundes, Duarretys, Sutes reall or personall, lyke as all other oure Lygemen have habylytye and capacytye. And furthermore, the sayed Maysters and Rulers and Commynaltye of the sayed Fraternytye or Guylde, amongys themselfys, shall or may have full auctorytye and power to make, ordeygne and establyshe Lawes, Ordynauncys and Statutys for the good state, rule and governaunce of the sayed Fraternytye or Guylde, for thencrease and good contynuance of the same, and suche Lawes, Statutys and Ordenaunces so made from tyme to tyme, as ofte as by them shalbe thought necessary and convenient, to chaunce, and to transpose, or keap at theyr pleasure; And to put yn use and execution wythoute hurte, challenge, greve or perturbaunce of us, oure Heyres or Successours, Offycers, Mynisters or Subgiettys, or theyr Heyres or Successours, whatsoever they be. And furthermore, That the sayed Mayster and Rulers and theyr Successours for the tyme beyng, haue full power and auctorytye to purchase Landys & Tenementys, and other Hereditaments whatsoever they be, which be not holdyn of us in Capite, To have and to hold to the sayed Maysters, Rulers, and Commynaltye, and theyr Successours (the Statute of Mortmayn, or other Statute or Statutys, or any other thyng passed to the contrary notwithstandyng). And furthermore of oure habundaunce Grace, we have graunted, given and lycencyd, and by thyse Presentys do gyve, graunte, and lycence unto our foresayed welbeloved Servauntys, and to every of them, and to all and every theyr Successours, Maysters, Rulers, Commynaltye and Brethern of the sayed Fraternytye or Guylde that for the tyme shalbe, aswell beyng oure Servauntys and Subgyettys, as also Straungyers, beyng Denysens or not Denysens, beyng of and yn the sayed Fraternytye or Guylde, for the better yncrease of the defense of thys oure Realme, and mayntenaunce of the scyence or Feate of Shotyng yn Long-bowes, Cros-bowes and Hand-gonnes, that they, and every of theyr Successours, honest parsonnes of the sayed Fraternytye or Guylde, for theyr dysporte and pastyme from tyme to tyme for ever hereafter and perpepetually, may use and exercise the shotyng yn their Long-bowes, Cros-bowes and Hand-gonnes, at Almaner, Markys and Buttys, and at the Game of the Popyniaye, and other Game or Games, as at Fowle and Fowles, aswell yn oure Citye of London, the Suburbes of the same, as in all other places wheresoever yt be wythyn thys oure Realme of England, Ireland, Calyce,[169] and our Marches of Wayles, and ellyswhere wythyn any of our Domynyons (oure Forestys, Chacys and Parks, without oure specyall Warrant, and the Game of the Heyron and Feysaunt withyn two myles of any of oure Manners, Castellys, or other placys where we shall fortune to be or lye for the tyme onely excepted and reservyd) And also that the sayed Maysters, and Rulers, and Brethern, and their Successours, and every particuler parsonne of them may reteigne and keap theyr sayed Long-bowes, Cros-bowes and Hand-gonnes yn theyr Houses, Chambres, and other places, and theyr Servauntys to bere the same Cros-bowes and Hand-gonnes, when and as often as yt shall lyke them, at theyr lybertye for ever, without any damage, daungyer, penaltye, losse or forfaicture to ensue unto them, or any of them, for the same. But nevertheless the sayed Servauntes that so shall carry theyr Maysters Cros-bowes or Hand-gonnes, shall not by vertue of thys oure Lycence, shote yn the sayed Cros-bowes and Hand-gonnes at no manner of Fowle: And yf case be that any suche Servaunt be takyn shotyng at any Fowle with any Cros-bowe or Hand-gonne, the sayed Offender so takyn to forfacte the penaltie according to the Acte (thys Fraternitye or Lycense notwithstanding:) And also that none other then the Fraternytye or Guylde aforesayed, shall wythyn any part of thys oure Realme or Domynyon, keap any other Bretherhed or Guylde, oneles it be by lycence of the foresayed Maysters and Rulers of the sayed Fraternytye or Guylde. And furthermore of oure more ample Grace by theys Presentys we do lycence the foresayed Maysters and Rulers, and Commynaltye of the sayed Fraternytye or Guilde, or any pertyculer parsonne or parsonnes, and every of them, to use and weare any maner ynbrowdery, or any cognysaunce of sylver at hys or theyr lybertye, in theyr Gownes, Jackettys, Cootys, and Dublettys, and any maner of Silkys, as Velvet, Satten, and Damaske, (the

---

[169] Calais

Colours of Purple and Scarlet oonly excepted) yn theyr Gownes and Jackettys, and all and synguler Furres yn theyr Gownes or elswhere, not aboue Furres of Martirnes without renuying unto any maner daungyer, forfeyture, loss or penaltye; Any Acte of Apparell, or any other Acte, Proclamacyon, thyng or matyer yn any wyse had, made, or gyven, or to be had, made, or gyven to the contrary notwithstondyng. And furthermore of our further Grace especyall, we have lycencyd, and by theys Presentys doo lycence the foresayed Maysters and Rulers, and theyr sayed Successours, for the tyme beyng, that they, nor any of them, shall from hensforth be enpanelled, or compelled to be upon any maner of Queste or Jurye, upon what matyer soever yt be withyn our Cytye of London, or other place withyn thys oure Realme. And overthis, we wott and graunte for us, oure Heyres and Successours, to the sayed Maysters and Rulers and Commynaltye by thyes Presentys, that when and as often as the sayed Maysters and Rulers and Commynaltye, and theyr Successours, or any of them, shall use, pronounce, and openly speke thys usuall worde commonly used to be spoken before he or they shote, that is, to say this worde Faste. And after this worde spoken, yf yt shall happyn any parson or parsons, by the oversight of any parson or parsons, ronnyng, passyng or goyng betweene any suche shoter, and the marke or place whereto any such Maysters and Rulers and Comynaltye, or any of them shall hereafter shoote, to be kylled or otherwyse hurt, so the same be a usuall and a knowne marke set yn an open place, accustomed to be shote at, that then any such Mayster, Ruler, and Brother whatsoever, shall happyn not by that occasion be attached, arrested, ympryysoned, sued, vexed, troubled, or otherwyse ynonpetted,[170] nor shall not be ympeched nor otherwyse molessed or troubled for the same, nor shall not suffer death, nor lose any membre, or forfeicte any maner, good, landys, tenementys or herediramentys, or any goodys, catellys, or other proffyttys for the same; Any Acte, Statute, Proclamacyon, Prouysyon, or any other matyer or thynge yn any wyse had, made, given, proclamed or provyded, or hereafter to be had, given, made, proclamed or provyded at any tyme to the contrary notwithstanding. And furthermore, we wott and graunte that thyes oure Letters Patentys shall

---

[170] Impeded?

passe under oure Great Seale wythout Fyne or Fee, great or small, in oure Chauncery, to oure use, or to thuse of oure Heyres, or ye the hanaper of oure sayed Chauncerye to be contented or payed for the same. That expresse mencyon of the true yerely value, or of any other value or certentye of the Premysses, or of any of them, or of any other Guiftes or Grauntes by us, or by any of our Progenitours or Predecessours to the aforesayed Crystofer, Antony, and Peter, or any of them before thyes tymes made in thyes Presents ys not made, Or any Statute, Acte, Ordynaunce, Provysyon or Restraynt thereof to the contrary before thyes times made, ordeyned, or provyded, or any other thynge, cause, or matter whatsoever yn any wyse notwythstanding. In wytnes whereof we have caused thyes oure Letters to be made Patentys, Wytnes oure self at Westminster the xxv daye of August, the xxix yere of oure Reigne.

## 46. Bridport Muster Roll, 1539[171]

*Tudor muster rolls have survived in much greater numbers than medieval muster rolls and afford an excellent opporunity to examine the prevalence of bows in the twilight years of English military archery. The Bridport roll of 1539 has been selected here in order to facilitate direct comparison with the earlier roll from the borough of 1457.[172] Despite the oft-cited decline in archery by and during the reign of Henry VIII the Bridport musters show a fairly close level of continuity in bow-ownership at least: in 1457 bows were available for 45% of adult males in Bridport, in 1539 the figure had only dropped to 42% (40 bows for 95 men). Fifteenth-century muster rolls have not survived in sufficient quantity to determine how typical the 1457 muster roll was in a more general sense, but the 1539 roll is broadly typical of militia muster rolls in the second quarter of the sixteenth century.*

*Tudor muster rolls also offer us more information about the quality of archers available, by categorising men as 'able archers,' or mere 'archers,' and not all men who owned bows were even classed as archers at all (see below, for example, Robert Haserd who mustered with a bow and arrows but was classed as a billman). This differentiation between good archers and the merely adequate is found in various documents from the Tudor period, though the terms used sometimes differ: able archers or archers; archers or mean archers; best archers or mean archers, etc. There is ample evidence too that the selection of archers for military campaigns was not limited only to the best archers. For example, when the Earl of Arundel sent troops to join Henry VIII's invasion of France in 1544 they consisted of 'able men 1,272, whereof archers principals 300, mean archers 200, principal billmen 500, mean billmen 200, household servants 106.'[173] Unfortunately, no record survives of what criteria were used to judge a man as an 'able' or 'mean' archer, but a number of contemporaries spoke of many archers being incapable of 'strong shooting' so it seem likely that 'able' archers were those capable of shooting the most powerful bows.*

---

[171] T.L. Stoate (ed.), *Dorset Tudor Muster Rolls, 1539, 1542, 1569* (Bristol, 1978), pp. 10-11
[172] See **Doc. 41**
[173] *Letters and Papers of Henry VIII*, vol. 19, item. 273

| Name | | Equipment |
|---|---|---|
| Nicholas Lamseham | | harness, bow, ½ sheaf of arrows |
| John Cowper | | harness, bow, sheaf of arrows |
| William Charde sen. | | harness, bow, sheaf of arrows |
| Robert Haserd | billman | harness, bow, sheaf of arrows |
| Richard Sadler | | bill |
| Richard Furlock | | bow, sheaf of arrows |
| Thomasmas Charde | able billman | |
| Thomasmas Brownyng | | harness, bill |
| Richard Mone | | harness, bow, sheaf of arrows |
| John Catell | able billman | harness, bow, sheaf of arrows |
| Henry Harman | | harness, bill |
| John Tylly sen. | | Sallet, bill |
| Jon Isacke | | bow, ½ sheaf of arrows |
| William Showre | | Pr. Brigandines, bow, ½ sheaf of arrows |
| Giles More | able billman | harness, bow, sheaf of arrows |
| Richard Davenage | | harness, bill |
| John Hoges | able archer | |
| John Hudson | able archer | bow, ½ sheaf of arrows |
| Richard Vycary | able archer | bow, ½ sheaf of arrows |
| Richard Webber | archer | |
| Hugh Jonys | able billman | bill |
| John Smythe | billman | |
| William Davege | billman | |
| John Gralagg | | bow, ½ sheaf of arrows |

| | | |
|---|---|---|
| William Folyatt | | Sallet, bill, pr. brigandines |
| John Haserd | archer | bow, sheaf of arrows |
| John Tucker | billman | bow, ½ sheaf of arrows |
| William Downe | able billman | |
| John Geffrey | able billman | |
| William Colyns | | bow, ½ sheaf of arrows |
| William Preston | | harness, |
| Stephen Showre | billman | |
| John Downe | able billman | |
| John OStler | able billman | |
| Robert Score | archer | bow, ½ sheaf of arrows |
| Thomas Buckerell | | bow, sheaf of arrows |
| Thomas Norrys sen. | | bow, sheaf of arrows, bill |
| Thomas Norrys jun. | able billman | |
| Thomas Mynson | billman | |
| John Tuchyn | billman | |
| Thomas Barne | able billman | |
| William Jamys | archer | bow, ½ sheaf of arrows |
| Robert Locke | archer | bow, ½ sheaf of arrows |
| Robert Catell | archer | bow, ½ sheaf of arrows |
| John Seyle | able billman | |
| Thomas Balstone | able archer | bow, ½ sheaf of arrows |
| William Ekerdon | able archer | bow, ½ sheaf of arrows |
| John Gybbys | able billman | bow, ½ sheaf of arrows |
| Thomas Syngleman | able billman | |
| William Edmonds | able billman | |

| | | |
|---|---|---|
| John Elewurthe | able archer | bow, ½ sheaf of arrows |
| Thomas Robyns | able billman | bill |
| Christopher Downe | able billman | |
| John Downe | able archer | |
| Edward Pere | able archer | bow, ½ sheaf of arrows |
| John Furley | able billman | |
| Robert Parker | archer | |
| William Furlock | able billman | |
| Thomas Furlock | able billman | |
| William Buckerell | able billman | |
| Henry Ley | | bow, ½ sheaf of arrows |
| William Chyke | able archer | Jack, bow, sheaf of arrows |
| Christopher Bettyscombe | able billman | |
| Richard Byllyng | able archer | |
| John Alford | able archer | bow, sheaf of arrows |
| William Gollope | able billman | |
| Thomas Chauntrell | able billman | |
| Henry Pratte | able billman | |
| John West | billman | |
| Robert Bettyscombe | able billman | |
| John Daly | able billman | |
| Walt Glover | able archer | |
| John Mylward | able billman | |

**Frenchmen**

| | | |
|---|---|---|
| Richard Harvest | | bow, sheaf of arrows |
| William Curteys | | bow, sheaf of arrows, bill, dagger |

| | |
|---|---|
| James Barger | bow, ½ sheaf of arrows |
| John Canyngton | bill |
| Nowell Neveyr | bow, sheaf of arrows |
| Nicholas Overy | sword |
| John Pynnar | |
| Richard Halyar | bow, sheaf of arrows |
| Francis Helyer | bill |
| Vincent Pepyn | bow, ½ sheaf of arrows |
| William Taylor | |
| Martin Fusshe | bill |
| Stephen Herby (or Hervy) | bow, ½ sheaf of arrows |
| George Davy | bill |
| William Choyse | |
| **'Dutchmen'** | |
| William Douche | bow, ½ sheaf of arrows |
| Henry Harmon | bow, ½ sheaf of arrows |
| James Johnson | |
| Fred Arnold | |
| John Harrys | bow, ½ sheaf of arrows |
| Arnold Gerard | |
| Vytys Turlandye | |

## 47. The Decline of Archery, 1549[174]

*The Sixth sermon preached before King Edward, 12 April 1549. (Extract)*

*Hugh Latimer, Bishop of Worcester and Chaplain to Edward VI, was raised in a farming family in Leicestershire in the late fifteenth century and, like many or most rural boys, learned to shoot at a young age. Despite entering holy orders he retained his affection for the bow and mourned its demise in the sixteenth century. Just a few months after Latimer delivered this sermon the Western rebellion and Kett's rebellion broke out simultaneously in Devon and Norfolk respectively, and the battles of these two rebellions were the last major confrontations in which archery played a major part. Latimer was burned at the stake in Oxford in 1555 and did not live to see the bow finally cast aside as a weapon of war.*

There be such dicing houses also, they say, as hath not been wont to be, where young gentlemen dice away their thrift; and where dicing is, there are other follies also. For the love of God let remedy be had, let us wrestle and strive against sin. Men of England, in times past, when they would exercise themselves, (for we must needs have some recreation, our bodies cannot endure without some exercise,) they were wont to go abroad in the fields a shooting; but now it is turned into glossing, gulling, and whoring within the house. The art of shooting hath been in times past much esteemed in this realm: it is a gift of God that he hath given us to excel all other nations withal: it hath been God's instrument, whereby he hath given us many victories against our enemies: but now we have taken up whoring in towns, instead of shooting in the fields. A wondrous thing, that so excellent a gift of God should be so little esteemed! I desire you, my lords, even as ye love the honour and glory of God, and intend to remove his indignation, let there be sent forth some proclamation, some sharp proclamation to the justices of peace, for they do not their duty: justices now be no justices. There be many good acts made for this matter already. Charge them upon their allegiance, that this singular benefit of God may be

---

[174] George Elwes Corrie (ed.), *The Works of Hugh Latimer, Sometime Bishop of Worcester* (Cambridge, 1844), i. p. 197

practised, and that it be not turned into bowling, glossing, and whoring within the towns; for they be negligent in executing these laws of shooting. In my time my poor father was as diligent to, teach me to shoot, as to learn me any other thing; and so I think other men did their children, he taught me how to draw, how to lay my body in my bow, and not to draw with strength of arms, as other nations do, but with strength of the body: I had my bows bought me, according to my age and strength; as I increased in them, so my bows were made bigger and bigger, for men shall never shoot well, except they be brought up in it: it is a goodly art, a wholesome kind of exercise, and much commended in physic.

# Part 3

## L'Art d'Archerie

## 48. L'Art D'Archerie

In 1874 Dr. Desbarreaux-Bernard drew attention to a previously unknown pamphlet, of which only a damaged and partial copy survived, entitled L'Art D'Archerie and published around 1515 by Michel le Noir, a Parisian printer and bookseller active from the 1490s until his death c.1520. In the early years of printing the concept of copyright was fluid, and le Noir was frequently accused of publishing and selling books without their author's permission. L'Art D'Archerie falls into this category, and although we know that it was printed by le Noir the author remains anonymous. Linguistic evidence suggests the author was a native of Picardy in North-Eastern France.

In the last years of the nineteenth century Henri Gallice purchased a late fifteenth-century untitled manuscript which, by comparing it with the remaining printed fragments, he was able to identify as the complete text of L'Art D'Archerie. Gallice published a transcript of his manuscript in 1901, and an English translation by H. Walrond was published in 1903. Walrond's translation, with slight corrections and annotations by the present editor, is printed below.

Despite its relative brevity L'Art D'Archerie should not be dismissed easily, for it is the earliest known book specifically about archery, predating Roger Ascham's better-known and much fuller Toxophilus by at least thirty years. It is impossible to date the authorship of L'Art D'Archerie precisely, but references to the hunting book Les Livres du roi Modus et de la Reine Ratio, published in the second half of the fourteenth century, suggest that L'Art D'Archerie cannot have been written much earlier than the 1370s at the earliest. This date is supported by further reference in the text to Pietro de Crescenzi's Ruralia Commoda which, although it was written c.1309, was translated into French on the orders of Charles V of France in 1373. Probably L'Art D'Archerie was written sometime later than the 1370s, and the survival of a late fifteenth-century manuscript copy, together with the first printing and more widespread reading of Crescenzi's book in 1471, may suggest that the first book on archery was written c. 1470-1510.

# L'Art D'Archerie

Here follows a small and good treatise teaching how to shoot with the long bow, written and composed by one who does not give his name, at the request of many who wish to learn.

That many young men, noble as well as others, willingly spend time shooting with the bow, I am not astonished.

We learn from the first book of the Bible that the bow has been in use since the beginning of the world, for in it we are told that Lamech slew beasts with it.[175] Further on, David took a sign from it from Jonathan, as appears in the first book of Kings.[176] Again, as appears from his history, Hercules, the most mighty archer of his time, killed with it, while he was crossing the river, the giant who had robbed him of his wife. Also it was used by the archers who lived in the time of the Trojans. Similarly the book called *The Art of War*,[177] says that the ancients taught their children to shoot with the bow, hold it in the left hand, and draw it with the right, of which more hereafter.

Vegetius says that constant and persistent use of the bow is necessary even by skilled shots. Cato in his book speaks of how useful good archers are in battle. Claudius testifies that by his archers he several times overcame his enemies in battle, though they were few in number, and similar testimony is born by the gallant Scipio Africanus. Yet in no book which I have ever read, have I ever found anything about archery, except in the book of Modus and Ratio, which states that Sexmodus instructed his son, Tarquin,

---

[175] *Genesis* makes no mention of Lamech hunting with a bow, but in the early-medieval period a popular legend expanded on the brief life of Lamech laid out in the Bible to include him killing his ancestor, Cain, in a hunting accident. The legend, although not canonical, was popular throughout the medieval and early modern period, as numerous artworks from the period depicting the event attest.

[176] The author of *L'Art D'Archerie* was clearly more familiar with the bow than tha Bible. This incident is not in 1 Kings, but in 1 Samuel c.20, v.20: 'And I shall shoot three arrows beside that stone, and I shall cast as exercising, either playing me at a sign.'

[177] I have been unable to identify this work. The famous book of that title by Sun Tzu was not translated into any European language until the eighteenth century, and appears to have been unknown in Europe in the medieval period; Machiavelli's *Art of War* was not published until 1520, by which time *L'Art D'Archerie* was certainly in print.

to shoot with a bow; the said Tarquin being such a skilful archer that he never failed to hit, at thirty dextres,[178] an apple stuck on the top of a stake.

Inasmuch as owing to illness I have been obliged to abandon the said exercise, it is my fixed determination, as a pastime, to write down all I have learnt, so as to stir up those who are willing to learn. And, as the Philosopher says, the better the things known are, the more worthy are they to he loved and held dear.

True it is that archers have many times, during wars, prevented countries and kingdoms from being pillaged, and this not only in their own country. On the other hand, they have been the cause of other countries being conquered, as many great battles, both in this Kingdom and others, have been won by the archers.

There is therefore good and sufficient reason that these things should clearly be brought to the knowledge of men, and they will be divided into five principal parts, of which the first will speak of the bow, the second of the horns, the third of the string, the fourth of the arrows, and the fifth and last, of how to shoot. And as I know that many take a pleasure in archery, I have resolved for my amusement, to write some things down. Not that I am not fully aware that there are many who know more about it than I do, and that it is unnecessary that I should speak Latin before monks, but solely because I wish that every one should become a good archer, begging that if there are faults they may be corrected, and that whatever may be found useful, may be taken in good part.

## Concerning the Nature of Wood for Making Bows

As the first part of this treatise deals with the bow, you must know that there are three things in a bow, the wood, the shape, and the horns. First of all, bows can be made of any wood, but the best are of yew. Respecting this, Petrus de Crescens[179] says, that yew is only useful for making bows and crossbows, and that there are two sorts of it, the white and the red.

---

[178] Yards or paces.
[179] Pietro de Crescenzi, whose book *Ruralia Commodia* was written c. 1309 and first printed in 1471.

The white is called Portuguese yew, and it is usually soft and of open grain. And the more open the grain of a wood is, the softer it naturally is. On the other hand the redder yew is called Italian yew. This is found of straighter grain than any other, and has a sharper cast, and there is no comparison in the time it retains its strength. However, it is harder to work, and to string at first, and breaks more easily than the white Portuguese yew. Now if you want to know the best points of a bow, look at its sides and see if the grain is close and long, and if you find it so, you may be certain that that wood is very good and fitted for long distance shooting, which I shall hereafter, at the proper time and place, explain to you. Nevertheless, I have formerly seen very long shots made with bows of whitethorn and also of seshus,[180] but only for one shot, notwithstanding that whitethorn and seshus are of entirely different natures. But after one or two shots have been made they become more and more sluggish. The other bows, made of yew, are very good for butt shooting, as I shall show and explain at greater length in the next and following chapter.

**Of the Make of Hand Bows**

Bows are made of two patterns, that is to say, square and round, which are used for three kinds of shooting. The square are best for butt shooting for three reasons: first, because they have more back and therefore last longer; secondly, because the arrow lies better against their side, and thirdly, because they shoot straighter and keep their cast longer. A bow should be the same shape for the butt and target shooting. Round bows are also made of two patterns for target and flight shooting.

Those made for target shooting have a broader back than the others, as more arrows are shot at it, for if they had too narrow a back, they would not last. Those made for flight shooting have narrower backs and are the better for it, as the back only makes them slower and more sluggish. Sexmodus speaking to his son Tarquin says- 'If you wish your bow to last,

---

[180] Unknown wood. Possibly a vine: cissus, from the Greek *kissos*, meaning 'ivy.'

its length should be that of two arrows and two small fists.'[181] But Sexmodus does not mean this to apply to bows used for flight shooting, as they should only be one hand's breadth, by which one holds them, longer than the said two arrows' lengths, and at the most only two or three arrows a day should be shot from them.[182] And every bow should be stronger in the upper limb than in the lower for three reasons- the first is that one has two fingers under the arrow, and the hand by which it is held should properly be opposite the centre of the bow. The second reason is that all bows, which by their make bend, always shoot in the direction of their weakest limb, so that when the lower limb is the strongest (the arrow), jumps and shoots high, and farther. The third reason is that all men

---

[181] Sexmodus, in the medieval hunting text *Roi Modus*, says that arrows should be 10 *poignees* in length, and the bow two arrow-lengths and two *poignees* in length. 'Poignee' means, literally, a fist width, but at times was used to refer to a fixed measure of 3-3.5", and it is impossible to know which definition of 'poignee' the author of *Roi Modus* intended.
[182] Clearly the author is not describing bows intended for military use here.

who wish to shoot far, must, to do so with the greatest advantage, shoot with the wind and high ; but all the same, every one does not know this, and you must know that when a bow is strongest in the lower limb, it corrects this fault of itself. And a good bow should be very gradually reduced to within a palms-breadth of the ends, and then reduced to small size. For though the principal spring comes from the ends, it could not be good if it was not strengthened towards the centre. And every good and well made bow should be reduced as much as can safely be done near the horns. For the more tapered and gradually reduced a bow is from the centre to the top and bottom, the greater and sharper spring will it have, and in this there is no harm.

**Of the Horns for Bows**

Since I have spoken of the wood and make of bows, it is reasonable that I should say something about the horns. Generally, the horns of bows are made of cows' horn, the reason being that it is softer and less elastic than other horns are, and it is well suited for the square and round bows used for target shooting, as it is not too springy. But for flight shooting they are best when made from the tips of stags' horns, for the harder the horn, the greater spring it will give to the bow. And you must know that all horns should be fairly large where they fit on the bow, so as to keep the string away from the wood, and the shorter they are the better, as long as the bow can be strung. Some people have silver horns put on their bows, but I have found this neither useful or profitable, and I have tried both.

**Of Bow Strings**

In the second part of this book, which will treat of bow strings, you will be told of the number of ways in which strings should be made, and of what the best are made. Bow strings are made of raw green silk and of hemp. Strings made of silk are good for flight shooting for three reasons, as Sexmodus tells us. The first is, that silk is so strong that it lasts longer without breaking than any other material. The second is, that the string can be made as thin as may be desired. The third is, that when properly made the string is so springy that it propels the arrow further and with greater force than when made of any other material The silk should be naturally green, and not burnt by dyeing, for it is spun green by silkworms. The other material of which strings are made is hemp, and this is of two kinds, male and female. The male is thick and coarse, and consequently is worthless for bow strings. The female sort is good, but it must be carefully picked and very well chosen. A good string should be gummed and not glued. The loop should be as small as possible, and well stretched with a stone weight. And if you wish to know if a string is good, untwist the middle of it, and if the three strands are separate and distinct, it is a good one, provided always that when the string is twisted up again, it is hard and firm, for the harder it is, the better it will be.

**Of the Shaft Used With the Bow**

In order to do my work properly it is necessary that in this third part I should speak of the arrow, as in the first and second I have spoken of bows and strings.

You must know that there are only two sorts of shafts, the glued and the waxed.[183] Waxed arrows are of two kinds, of which one is feathered with the front wing feather, and is only good for butt shooting, and the other which is feathered with the hinder wing feathers, and is both good and favourable for target shooting. And understand that a good round waxed arrow should be feathered from the wing of a swan, except those for flight shooting, of which I will speak later. Many arrows are made and feathered from the wing of the goose, but they are not so good, and are only fit for war arrows. Waxed arrows are also feathered with gyrfalcon's feathers, these are better, and fit and proper for flight shooting, but for no other purpose. But these should have very light iron heads, and they should be scarcely thicker than a flight arrow, and of the lightest and stiffest wood, as I shall explain hereafter.

---

[183] 'Waxed' here seems to describe fletchings pressed into a waxy compound and whipped.

If the head of the arrow is light, the feathers should be cut low and short, if it is heavy the feathers should be higher and longer. Arrows for butt and target shooting should have the barbs in the same direction as the nock, but for flight arrows there is no danger, as the heads of these should be round like horn ones.

The harder the silk is on the wax, the better the arrow will fly and the stiffer it will be. The wood of which arrows are made should not be much baked, especially for flight arrows, as if it is, the jar on hitting the ground breaks them. Every good arrow for butt or target shooting should be made of aspen, seasoned by being kept a year or two, and without artificial heat. Flight arrows may be made of stiffer wood, such as birch or cherry.

Many arrows are made of ash, but they are only fit for proving armour. They should be large at the point and reduced at the feathers so as to stand the jar on impact.

Arrows are likewise made hollow, like ballista arrows, and with a long head, but they are only used for holding a flight arrow to win bets, and are varnished above and below; this is enough as regards waxed arrows.

In order to embarrass an adversary's choice, flight arrows are also made which look alike, though some are for shooting against the wind, and borne with it, so that the chooser is not in fault if he loses when on the shooting ground.

**Of the Glued Arrow**

There are two sorts of glued arrows, sheaf and flight. The sheaf arrows are usually thick, with high swan feathers, cut large, in the same shape as those of flight arrows, and have round iron heads. They are the regular arrows which the English use for butt and target shooting, for they find them, as they are, truer than any waxed arrow.

And if you would know what is a sheaf arrow, according to the English, every glued and iron-headed shaft, whether big or little, is called sheaf arrow.

**Of Flight Arrows**

Every flight arrow should be made of light and stiff wood.

The flight arrows made in this country are not so good as those made in England, because in this country we have not got the same wood as the English use for making good flight arrows, and for this reason there is no flight arrow so good as the English, for their wood is lighter and stiffer than any we have.

Every flight arrow should he feathered with pigeon or duck's feathers, and there is only one quill in each wing fit for the purpose, namely, the first. Properly speaking, a flight arrow is a slight arrow which flies further than any other small feathered arrow, and its head may be of horn or iron; some have three feathers, some six, and others nine. Those with six feathers have the ordinary feathers, like those with three or more, and between them and the horn nocking have three lower feathers, and their heads must be light. Those with nine feathers have them between the higher feathers and the horn nocking, and the more feathers they have, the heavier must the heads be. And in truth they are only for show, as they are worth very little to shoot with. For the best are those with three feathers, and of these there are two sorts; that is to say, the hollow and the solid. The hollow are bored from the head to within three finger's breadth of the feathers; some fill them with lead, others with quicksilver, and these are the most advantageous. The others are solid, and are the most honest to shoot.

For the hollow are deemed dishonourable, owing to the advantage which they give, which is undiscoverable.

These flight arrows have three small fingers' width of feathers close to the nock.

**Of Putting a String on a Bow**

I have told you of the make of the bow, of strings and arrows, but this neither could or would help you much if I did not tell you how to put a string on a bow. You must put the loop of the string in the nook of the upper horn, then stretch the string by pulling it along the bow, and at three fingers from the lower horn, make a running loop without a knot, taking as few turns as possible, as the fewer there are the better it will Cast. To shoot properly a bow should be strung up a little less than half a foot. If it is reflexed or follows the string it must be adjusted accordingly, for if reflexed it requires more, and if it follows the string less, stringing up.

**Of the Way of Shooting With the Bow**

As a book called "The Art of War" tells us, an archer who wishes to shoot in good style must attend to several points, both as respects his body and his feet. First of all his arrows must be on his right side, as his sword is on his left. He should poise his bow on the thumb of the hand with which he holds it when he shoots, and for butt shooting balance it exactly. If the bow is well made the upper limb will be the longest. While doing this, he should draw an arrow from his quiver in two motions, the reason being that unless he had a very long arm, the arrows would remain jammed in the quiver, from which the feathers would suffer. Then, holding the arrow by the middle, he must put it in the bow, and there hold it between two fingers, and you must know that these two fingers are the first and second. And every good archer should, as I have said before, draw his bow with three fingers and to his right breast, as by doing so he can pull a longer arrow. The foot of the side on which he holds the bow should be in front of the other, the toe only touching the ground, so that when the heel is brought down (without moving the foot), the side may turn towards the butt, and give a good impetus to the arrow. As to drawing, it can be done in two ways; some draw with the bow hand raised, and some with it low down, and both are good in different ways. Drawing with the bow hand low is good for butt and target shooting, and is a more natural way of shooting than with the bow hand high, besides which it assists the loose, and also because the arm, not being raised so high, is, in case of necessity, less exposed.

You must know also that there are several ways of loosing, but all depending on two things - on the drawing hand, for one must have and hold the string on the second joint of the first finger, and on the first joint of the third, and on the step, of which there are three kinds, that is to say, with one, two, or three steps, the one step loose is done in two ways; one is stepping forward with the foot of the bow hand side, and the other by bringing back the arm, pushing out the bow and arrow, and at the same time stepping back with the other foot; this step straightens the arm, but it must be a long and sharp step back. The two other ways are by taking two steps and three steps. To shoot with two steps, a backward step must be taken with the hindermost foot, so that on bringing the front foot down, sufficient impetus is given to effect the loose. For the three step, the front foot is moved forward, then the bow is thrust forward as explained above, and the hinder foot is brought back in such a way that when the arrow is loosed one can step forward with the front foot.

According to custom a good archer should draw ten palms' breadths of arrow.[184] There are many who draw more, but of those who draw more, there are many who shoot a weaker arrow by doing so. There are many good archers who don't draw so much, yet do not fail to make long shots and shoot as strong as the others, but if their reach is sufficient, they should pull the above-named length, for they would be finer archers by doing so. I venture to say that it is impossible to shoot a long arrow in an ungraceful way, if the bow is pushed forward.

If you wish to become a good archer you must practice in two ways, namely, at the butts under the screen, and at a target. For it is easier to learn to shoot by shooting under the screen, than in any other way, and in order that you should know how the screen is fixed, I will tell you. The screen should be placed across the range, half way between the butts, the bottom edge being one foot above the ground for every ten paces there is between the butts. Thus if the butts are one hundred paces apart, the

---

[184] As the following paragraph makes clear, this was not a standard which was always adhered to.

screen would be ten feet high, and the bottom edge should have bells on it, so that even if the feather of the arrow should touch it, one may know it by hearing the bells ring. And the said screen should be at least half an aune[185] in depth, so that no mistake may be made.

For target shooting, as I have already said, round bows should be used. For good archers the range should be three hundred paces. Nevertheless I have formerly seen shooting at four hundred paces, but it must be admitted that the archers were first-class ones.

### The Conclusion of This Treatise

As I have written of the four points named in the prologue of this treatise, I may well stop. For when I began it, I did not intend to say all that there is to say concerning this pastime, but only what I have seen and known from good archers, and also the result of my own experience.

I beg all who read or hear read this treatise that they will kindly correct the mistakes, if there are any, and of their courtesy supplement my ignorance.

---

[185] Another tricky measurement, the *aune* was used to measure cloth but in medieval France varied in length depending on what kind of cloth was being measured and in which town. At its longest the aune was a little under 6'6", but might be as short as 2' or a little less.

# Part 4

# BOWS AND GUNS

## 49. In Support of the Bow, 1589[186]

*In 1589, perhaps as a result of the mishandling of archers at the Tilbury muster in 1588, bows were dropped from the Trained Band arsenals, and began their descent into military obsolescence. Many old soldiers disapproved of the move but none was more vocal than Sir John Smythe, who immediately put pen to paper in defence of the bow. Smythe entered military service c.1550, certainly before 1553, and served in various positions for most of the next two decades, including the defence of English possessions in France, against the Spanish in the Netherlands, and against the Turkish Ottomans in Hungary and the Mediterranean, before returning to England in 1572 at the age of about 38.*

*Throughout his writings, and in his actions at home, Smythe comes across as an intelligent and humane man who opposed unnecessary wars and cared deeply for the plight of the common soldier. He was critical of officers who failed to look after their men properly, and even more critical of commanders and politicians who sent men to war without sufficiently good cause. He opposed conscription of soldiers except in defence of their home country, and publically questioned the legality of conscripting soldiers to fight in foreign wars. His* Certain Discourses, *from which the following extract is taken, is best-known as a defence of the bow as a weapon of war, but was also a scathing attack on the English military leadership of the 1580s. Two weeks after the book's publication in May 1590 it was banned by the authorities, and was later used as evidence in Smythe's trial for sedition which saw him confined to the Tower of London for two years. Despite the ban it is said that 1,200 copies of* Certain Discourses *were sold.*

The imperfections of the Long bowe, doo consist onlie in the breaking of the Bowe or bowstring, for the which in times past[187] (when there was great accompt made of Archerie) there was speciall care had, that all

---

[186] Sir John Smythe, *Certain Discourses Written by Sir John Smythe* (London, 1590), ff. 20-29
[187] It is unclear whether Smythe was referring here to the early-mid sixteenth century, or to earlier periods still. Throughout his book Smythe mentioned soldiers of his acquaintance who had served in the rebellions of 1549 and other sixteenth-century campaigns when archers had made good account of themselves, and the final sentence of this paragraph suggests that it was to them he was referring when writing of 'times past.'

Liveray, or warre Bowes[188] being of the wood of Yewgh, were longer than now they use them, and so verie well backed and nocked, that they seldome or never brake: Besides that, the Archers did use to temper with fire a convenient quantitie of waxe, rosen, and fine tallowe together, in such sort that rubbing their Bowes with a verie little thereof laid upon a wollen cloath, it did conserve them in all perfection against all weather of heate, frost, and wet; and the strings beeing made of verie good hempe, with a kinde of waterglewe to resist wet and moysture; and the same strings beeing by the Archers themselves with fine threed well whipt, did also verie seldome breake; but if anie such strings in time of service did happen to breake, the soldiers Archers had alwaies in readines a couple of strings more readie whipt, and fitted to their Bowes, to clappe on in an instant. And this I have heard of divers Yeomen, that have served as soldiers Archers in the field.

And now having before in this discourse declared all the greatest and most perfect effects of Harquebuziers and Mosquettiers for services in the field, and but a part of the imperfections of them, and their weapons of fire; because there are many more, which for brevities sake I have omitted, and that I have last of all declared that the imperfections of the Bowe do consist onelie in the breaking of the Bowe and bowstring; because that Archers, if they bee well chosen, and sound of limbes, their weapons doo not permit anie such accidentall imperfections and failings in them, as the forenamed weapons of fire doo in the soldiers that doo handle and use them; which hath alreadie appeared, and shall after in this discourse bee made more manifest. I will now therefore proceed to the consideration and examining of three most important things, in the which al effects of Mosquettiers, Harquebuziers and Archers, and their weapons do consist; and that is, whether Mosquettiers or Harquebuziers with their weapons of fire, or Archers with their Bowes and sheafes of arrowes, upon all occasions in the field, bee most readie with all dexteritie and celeritie to execute the effects of their weapons, by discharging and giving volees at their Enemies. The second is, whether the Archers with their weapons, or the other soldiers with their weapons of fire, doo faile least to shoote, discharge, and

---

[188] This is the earliest reference I have discovered to a 'war bow.'

give their volees. And the third is, whether by reason and common experience the bullets of weapons of fire in the field, or the arrowes of Archers doo annoye the Enemies most, bee they horsemen or footmen.

To the first I think, that there is no man of any experience in the aforenamed weapons, that will denie, but that Archers are able to discharge foure or five arrowes apeece, before the Harquebuziers shall bee readie to discharge one bullet;[189] I meane the Harquebuziers beginning to charge when the Archers doo begin to take their arrowes to shoote. The reason is this, because good Harquebuziers are first to charge their peeces with powder by one of three waies: the first (which is best) is out of the mouthes and charges of their flaskes: the second is by certeine charges filled with powder, which Harquebuziers doo weare, or carrie divers waies: and the third is by cartages, with the which they doo charge their peeces both with powder and bullet all at one time, and yet by which of all these waies soever, or anie other they do charge them, they must (if they bee good Harquebuziers) use with their scouring sticks to thrust a quantitie of paper or felt, or something els both before, but chieflie after their bullets, to keepe them close to the powder; to the intent that their bullets upon no accidents may fall out, or at least lie loose unrestrained from the powder, as also that their peeces may carrie the further poynt and blancke, and their bullets give the greater blowes; which done, they must presentlie put touchpowder into their pans, and their matches into their cocks or serpentines; al which to performe requireth a good time. Whereas the Archers in the field continuallie having their Bowes bent, have no more to doo but to drawe their arrowes out of their cases and sheafes, to nocke them in their Bowes, to drawe them to the heads and shoote; all which is performed almost in an instant.

Now to the second; Archers have no accidents nor impediments to hinder them from the performance and execution of their dischargings and volees, whereby they should anie waies faile to discharge the same, unles their Bowes or bowstrings should breake: whereas Harquebuziers have not onlie

---

[189] This estimate from such a pro-bow partisan as Smythe, even writing after the heyday of military archery had passed, should lay to rest any idea that archers were *required* to shoot ten or twelve arrows per minute.

the same let, in case their peeces by overcharging, or overheating, or crackes, or rifts, doo breake, but also if that through the negligence of the Harquebuziers, the powder with the which they charge their peeces, by anie accident have received anie wet, or moysture, or that through the lacke of the closenes of their flaskes, the ayre of some moyst weather hath penetrated and entered into the flaskes, and caused the powder to give and danke, by meanes whereof the Harquebuziers giving fire with their matches and serpentines to the touchpowder, oftentimes their peeces doo not discharge, or sometimes lieth fissing in the touchhole or peece, untill the Harquebuziers have lost their poynt and blanke, and then peradventure in vaine doo goe off. The touchpowder in the touch-boxes also, if either by the negligence of the Harquebuziers (as aforesaid) or by the fault of the touch-boxes, through the moystnes of the weather, the powder hath given, and become dancke, then oftentimes the powder will take no fire; whereby the Harquebuziers doo not onlie faile of their dischargeings, but also become unprofitable, till they have dried or chaunged the same. Harquebuziers and Mosquettiers also in powring touchpowder into their pannes, the winde (if it bee great) will blowe and disperse the same, in such sort, that they shall verie often faile to discharge their peeces; and so likewise if Harquebuziers in putting their matches into their serpentines do faile to set them of a convenient length, that therby they may strike just in the powder and pannes, but that they doo set the same too long, whereby the matches, if they be anie thing too lythe, do hang downeward, and with the comming downe and stroke of the cockes they fall double and short of the pannes and powder; or if the same matches by anie accident have received outwardlie anie wett or moisture, then the coales doo burne inward, leaving a beard outward, so as thereby although the endes thereof doo light in the middest of the pannes and powder, yet the same doo give no fire to the towchpowder. By all which aforesaid meanes and accidentes, with divers others both Mosquettiers and Harquebuziers, do faile to discharge their peeces: of all which imperfections and other accidentes, Archers with their Bowes are voyde. So as by all reason and experience, it is most manifest that Archers are foure tymes more readie to give their volees of arrowes, than Harquebuziers, or Mosquettiers their volees of bulletts. Besides all which unreadynesses, and failings before mentioned, if in the tyme of anie battle, great encountre, or skirmish, the weather doth happen to raine, haile, or snow, the aforenamed weapons of fire can worke no effect, because the same doth not onelie wett the powder in their pannes and touch holes, but also doth wet the match, put out, or at least dampe the fire, and doth marre the powder in their flaskes and towchboxes; unlesse the souldiours have very good provision, and besides be wonderfull carefull with their faltenbergs or mandillions to encover and preserve the same. Whereas contrariwise, neither haile, raine, nor snowe, can let or hinder the Archers from shooting, and working great effects with their arrowes. All which argueth and proveth a singular advantage and excellencie of Archers and their weapons, above al Harquebuziers and Mosquettiers with their weapons of fire. Now, peradventure some not skilled in the perfections and imperfections of Harquebuziers and Mosquettiers, will say that they have seene the soldiers of those weapons of fire, charge and discharge with a great deale more celeritie than I have before mentioned; whereunto I answer, that although it be verie commendable for all Harquebuziers and Mosquettiers to knowe how to charge and discharge apace, with all other particularities belonging to weapons of fire, yet such Harquebuziers or Mosquettiers as do use to charge and discharge so fast, are the worst of all others. For by often experience, such soldiers for hast do commonly charge their peeces with uncertaine charges of powder, and do neither use with their scouring sticks to thrust paper nor anie thing els betwixt their powder and bullets, nor yet after their bullets to restraine and keepe close the same, whereby their dischargings against the enemie might be the more effectuall: besides that, in their dischargeings, they take no kind of sight at poinct and blank, nor yet at the ends of their peeces, but doo discharge at a venture; wherby it commeth to passe, that such quick and hastie Harquebuziers, doo worke no other effect but spend powder, match and shot, and heate their peeces oftentimes to their owne mischiefes; and therefore (in troth) are more meete to scarre Crowes in a corne field (unles they reforme themselves) than with anie weapons of fire to be employed against the Enemie.

And now to the third, and last; which is, whether by reason and common experience, the bullets of weapons of fire in the field, or the arrowes of

Archers doo annoye the Enemies most, be they horsemen or footmen. I thinke it superfluous againe to reiterate, and set downe the different advauntages and chiefe effects of Harquebuziers, Mosquettiers, and Archers; because I have alreadie made them so manifest, as also that the Reader hereafter shall see in manie parts of this discourse divers reasons, and manie notable examples and experiences, that Archers in the field doo farre exceed and excell all Mosquettiers and Harquebuziers in terrifying, wounding, and killing both horses and men. And therefore wil onlie in this place answere one objection, which I have divers times heard alleaged in commendation of the effects of weapons of fire, and the dishabling of the effects of Archers, and that is; there are manie that have reported that the blowes of the bullets of Mosquets and Harquebuziers, are no lesse than death to such as they light upon; whereas contrariwise the blowes of arrowes doo but onelie gall, or lightlie wound: which in troth is greatlie mistaken by all such as doo hold that opinion. For that by common experience it hath been seene in all skirmishes and great encounters, that for everie one that hath been slaine dead in the field by the shot of Mosquet or Harquebuze, there have been foure that have not died by the hurts of such weapons of fire, although some of them have remained ever after maimed, and some not. Whereas by true experience, Archers with their arrowes doo not onlie greatlie wound, but also sometimes kill both horses and men, in such sort as they never depart out of the field alive, as it shall hereafter appeare by divers aunccient as also moderne examples. Besides that, I, and divers other Gentlemen of our Nation yet living, that were in France in King Edward the sixts time,[190] and also divers times since, have manie times heard French Captaines and Gentlemen, attribute al the former victories of the English against themselves and their ancestors the French, more to the effect of our Archers, than to anie extraordinarie valiancie of our Nation; and therewithall further report and say, that they did thinke that the English Archers did use to poyson their arrowe heads; because that of great numbers of the French Nation that many times had been wounded or hurt with arrowes, verie fewe had escaped with their lives; by reason that their wounds did so impostume, that they could not

---

[190] Presumably defending Boulogne and the Pale of Calais. Boulogne was surrendered to the French in May 1550, while Calais and its surrounding fortifications held out until 1558.

be cured. In which their conceipts they did greatlie erre; because in troth those impostumations proceeded of nothing els but of the verie rust of the arrowe heads that remained ranckling within their wounds; and therefore by the common experience of our aunceint Enemies, (that we have so often vanquished) not onlie the great, but also the small wounds of our arrowes have been alwaies found to bee more daungerous and hard to be cured, than the fire of anie shot unpoysoned.

Besides all which, it is to bee noted, that horses in the field being wounded, or but lightlie hurt with arrowes, they through the great paine that uppon everie motion they doo feele in their flesh, vaines, and sinewes by the shaking of the Arrowes with their barbed heads hanging in them, do presentlie fall a yerking, flinging and leaping as if they were mad, in such sort, as be it in squardron, or in troupe they do disorder one an other,[191] and never leave untill they have throwne, and cast their masters. Whereas contrariwise, horses that are in their vitall partes hurt with bulletts, or that the bones of their legges, shoulders, or backs be broken, they do presently fall down, or otherwise, although they be striken cleane through, or that the bulletts do still remaine in them, they after the first shrinck at the entring of the bullett doo passe their Carrire, as though they had verie litle or no hurt: And this of the hurting of horses with bulletts, both I my selfe, and all others do know, that have seene any actions performed in the field. And the other of the great disordering of horses with the hurts of our English arrowes I have read in divers histories, and also heard reported by divers Gentlemen of our nation that have seene the same. But now because I have divers times heard manie vaine obiections obiected by some of our Captaines of the Low Countries against Archers, to the disgracing, and dishabling of them, and their weapons in comparison of Mosquettiers and Harquebuziers and their weapons of fire: I will (with the helpe of almightie God) answere as manie of them as shall fall into my memorie; and therefore will begin with one of their litle fancies that they doo alledge against the Longbow, and so proceed to their greater, and greatest obiections.

---

[191] See **Doc. 36**

Among manie other their fancies they do alledge, that the Archers bowes, being by them used against the Enemie in the heate of sommer, will grow so weake, that thereby they will leese their force and effects. Whereunto I answere, that this objection is a new fancie, and a verie dreame contrary to all ancient and moderne experience of English Archers, whose Bowes being made of that excellent wood of Yewgh, doo never so decay in strength, neither by hotte nor wett weather, nor yet by often shooting in them, but that they will with arrowes wound, and sometymes kill both men and horses a greater distance off, then the shott and bullets of Harquebuziers and Calivers being employed and used in the open fields, by skilfull Conductours and Leaders; by reason of the wonderfull failings and uncertainties of those and all other weapons of fire maniable: divers of the particularities wherof: I have before in this dicourse made manifest.

Also they do further alledge, that upon an invasion of foraine dominions beyond the seas, the weapons, and furniture of Archers, as of Bowes, sheafes of arrowes and bowstrings, can not be found and provided where Archerie is not used; whereas contrariwise, all kinds of munition belonging to the weapons of fire, are easie to be found and provided in all foraine dominions. Which is as much, as if they should say, that if an Armie of five and twentie, or thirtie thousand of our English nation under some sufficient Generall were sent to invade France, and disembarking in Normandie, and winning Newhaven and Roan, should straight march to Paris: (which is no more than divers Kings of England and their Generalls have done) where after some encountres and skirmishes the Armie comming to lack powder and shott, they should with facilitie for money provide the same in the hart of the Enemies Countrie, where all the Townes in which that provision is to bee had are fortified, which is a verie mockerie and dreame to bee thought on. But some of our such men of warre peradventure will further alledge, that they might have the same provision by the way of convoy, either from Newhaven or Roan, in case they were possessed of those Townes: whereunto it is to bee answered, that first the convoy had need to bee verie strong; besides that, there is no man of anie consideration and judgement, but that doth verie well knowe, that Mosquets, Harquebuzes, powder, match and lead, are as heavie, and a great deale more heavie to bee carried, than Bowes, sheafes of arrowes and bowstrings are. Besides that, by such their ignorant objections, they doo evidentlie shew that they have not read, nor heard, or els for lacke of reason not beleeved, the proceedings of the notable Kings of England in their invasions of France, and other Dominions; for if they had, they would not then doubt, but that a King of England, or his Lieutenant generall invading forraine dominions, would upon such an enterprise carrie all sorts of munition, belonging to Archers, to serve them for many battailes and great encounters, as well as King Edward the third, and Henrie the fift, and their Lieutenants generall did, whose Armies did sometimes consist of nine, or ten thousand al Archers, and not above foure or five thousand armed men on horsebacke and on foote; which Princes, and their Lieutenants did never omit (according to their milicia) to carrie great plentie of sheafes of Arrowes, Bowes, and all other things requisite aswell for their Archers, as for their armed men, and all other effects. Besides that, by that their simple and fond objection, they do discover that they have very seldome or never seene an Armie royall march in the field; for if they had, they then would verie well know, that there is no puissant Armie formed either to invade or defend, that doth consist of a well ordered milicia, that doth not in the publique carriages of the Camp, ordinarylie carrie all kindes of munitions of weapons and armours offensive and defensive, with all other munitions and necessaries requisite for all purposes, for the publique employments and use of Camp, Towne, and field.

Now, whereas some of our aforesaid men of warre do further alledge, rather upon fancie than upon anie souldiourlyke reasons and experience, manie vaine and frivolous objections, partlie against the Bowes (as aforesaid) but chieflie against the Archers that do use them, how good soever they be, saying that Archers when they have lyen some long tyme in Camp in the field, will become so decayd in strength either by sicknes, or otherwise, that they will not be able to draw their Bowes, and worke that effect that Archers should do; whereas contrarywise, Mosquettiers and Harquebuziers will give as great blowes with their bulletts out of their peeces being decayd in strength by long lying in Camp, or sickenes, as if they were whole. Thereunto I answere, that true it is, that the small love that such men of warre as they are, have borne to their souldiours in the Low Countries, allowing them nothing but provand, and lodging them in Churches, upon the bare stones and pavements, aswell in winter as in sommer, with manie other their abuses and disorders, contrarie to all discipline militarie, have made most of their souldiours unfit and unable to use any sort of weapons, as soldiers should do in the field: howbeit in favour of Archers, to convince their simple and ignorant opinions, I say, that if Harquebuziers happen to be decayd in strength by sicknes, or that by long lying in Camp in the field, they shall happen to have anie ache, or aches in their necks, shoulders, armes, backs, thighs, leggs, or feet, although that they be otherwise hart whole enough, shalbe as litle, or rather lesse able in services in the field to perform the effect of Harquebuziers, than Archers the effect of Archers; for Harquebuziers in such services must be lythe in all their joints and sinewes, that they may stoupe to their peeces, and traverse their grounds, now retiring having discharged, giving place to their fellowes, and then advancing againe, giving their fellowes retiring tyme againe to charge, with such agilitie, and dexteritie, that they may be readie upon every opportunitie, to stoupe, and take every litle advantage of hillocks, bancks, vines, trenches, shrubbes, or anie such like; besides that, they must have their armes and shoulders verie sound to carrie their peeces firme in their dischargings at the Enemie, as also to use their scouring sticks, and charge againe; which effects they are no wayes able to performe if they be grown weak by lying in the field, or if they have achs, or cricks in anie part of their limbes, as aforesaid.

Mosquettiers also, it doth behove to be strong and puissant of body without sicknes, achs, or other impediments, and everie way sound of wind and limbe: for if they be decayd in strength of body by lying in the field, or that they have anie impediments of cricks, or aches in their necks, shoulders, armes, backs, thighs, or leggs, it is not possible that they should be able to use their Mosquets in the field to the annoyance of their Enemies, their peeces being so wonderfull heavie, and they troubled with the carrying and use of their rests, and loden with their other ordinarie and heavie furniture, if they be anie wayes decayd, as aforesaid, and therefore are become unprofitable for services in the field: whereas Archers that are not troubled with so heavie weapons and furniture as the Mosquettiers, nor bound by the effects of their weapons to any such nimblenes, stoupings and agilities, as Harquebuziers are, may very well draw their Bowes, if they be sound without aches from the girdle upward, what aches soever they have from that part downward, so long as they are able to march as fast as armed men Piquers, because that according to the ancient and true use of that weapon, they are to be used rather for battles and great encountres, than for light skirmishes.

Armed men also Piquers and Halbarders, will bee verie unable to march in the field armed, and with their weapons, if they bee decaied in strength of bodie by long lying in the Campe, or by sicknes, or that they have any aches, or cricks in their limmes, besides that, upon such diseases they will be a great deale lesse able to encounter with their enemies in the field upon anie occasion of battaile or great encounter, and to use their piques and other weapons, as armed men should doo in such actions. All which rightlie considered, their unconsiderate speaches, and enablings of Mosquettiers and Harquebuziers, and disabling of Archers upon the accidents and occasions aforesaid, doth argue their insufficiencies in matters militarie; because such as pretend to bee men of warre, or old soldiers, should not speake rashlie, and (as the Frenchman saith) a la volee, but with consideration, reason and judgement; for otherwise, how long soever they have served in warres, it may bee rightlie deemed that they have spent their times, and employed themselves more to some other base and vile occupations, than to the consideration and exercises of matters Militarie. Moreover, they object against Archers, that men in this age are not so mightie and strong of bodie, as they have been in former ages, and therefore cannot shoote so strong, and work so good effects with their arrowes, as their forefathers have done in times past; which is as frivolous an obiection as all the rest: and the reason is this, that they may see by experience, (if they list) throughout England, as also amongst other Nations, as manie sonnes, as tall or taller than their fathers, or bigger and stronger, as they shall see lower, slenderer, and weaker. Now, peradventure with more troth some may say, that the subiects of England within these thirtie or fortie yeares, have not had so much exercise in Archerie, as their forefathers in times past were wont to have, whereby it commeth to passe, that Archers in number are greatlie decaied, which I confesse to bee verie true: howbeit, that hath chieflie proceeded through the great fault and negligence of sorts of Magistrates, who having excellent statute and penall lawes established in other kings times for the increase and maintenance of Archerie, and that boyes from their young yeares should bee taught the exercise and use of the Bowe, that being come to mans state, they might bee the better able to serve their Prince and Countrie with that kinde of weapon, have so neglected, or rather contemned the due performance and execution of those lawes, that a great deale more through their owne fault, than through the fault of the people, it is now come to passe, that the Realme hath so fewe good Archers: which their negligence, or contempt, whether it hath proceeded of that they have been carried into the fancies of liking the aforesaid weapons of fire, because they fill mens eares and eyes with such terrible fire, smoake and noyse, or els that they have been perswaded thereunto by some old newfangled men of warre, that do neither understand the true effects of Mosquetterie, Harquebuzerie, nor Archerie, I wot not. But this I knowe, that if that weapon hereafter shall come to be forgotten and extinguished, through the negligence and lacke of good execution of such good lawes, that whereas in times past we were wont to give battaile, and fight with our Enemies with a weapon so terrible unto them, that they never had anie use or skill of, but onelie to their mischiefe, and therefore of great advauntage for us, and wherein our people and Nation of a singular gift of God, and as it were by a naturall inclination with good execution of lawes, came to be so perfect and excellent, without anie publique cost and charges either to King or Realme, we shall then upon anie occasion of warre offensive or defensive, bee driven to fight with them with their owne weapons, to our great disadvantage, that is, with the Harquebuze and Mosquet, in the which they had and have continual practise and exercise, by reason that they are in the continent, where everie kingdome and state doth joyne one to another without anie partition of sea, and therefore driven to keepe continuall garrisons and exercises of warre, whereas wee contrariwise living in long peace without anie such exercises Militarie, upon the occasion of a warre (as aforesaid) must leavie and enroll new soldiers, and goe about to traine and exercise them with those weapons that they never handled before, when wee should goe to fight and give battaile to the Enemies Armie, that is, of old soldiers of long time trained and exercised in those weapons.

Now, these weapons the Long Bowes (which our such men of warre have so much condemned) being in the hands of such soldiers Archers as can well use them, are weapons of singular advantage and effect for battailes and great encounters, both against horsemen and footmen, and chieflie being so evill armed, as all Nations in these our daies both on horsebacke and on foot are, because that the Bowe is a weapon wonderfull readie in all seasons, both of faire and foule weather (which Mosquets and Harquebuzes are not) and doth wound, gall and kill both horses and men, if the arrowes doo light upon anie disarmed parts of them; besides that, the Archers being good, they doo direct their arrowes in the shooting of them out of their Bowes with a great deale more certaintie, being within eight, nine, tenne, or eleven scores, than anie Harquebuziers or Mosquettiers (how good soever they bee) can doo in a much neerer distance, by reason that Mosquettiers and Harquebuziers failing in their points and blancke, doo neither kill nor hurt (unlesse it happen as the blind man shooting at the Crowe;) besides that, in their points and blancke, through the imperfections before declared, they doo verie seldome hit, whereas contrariwise the arrowes doo not onelie wound, and sometimes kill in their points and blank, but also in their discents and fall; for if in their discents they light not upon the Enemies faces, yet in their lower discents they light either upon their breasts, bellies, codpeeces, thighes, knees or legges, and in their lowest discent, and fall even to the verie nailing of their feete to the ground, which with the terrible comming of the arrowes in the eyes and sight both of horsemen and footmen, causeth in them a wonderful feare and terror. Whereas contrarywise, Harquebuziers and Mosquettiers with their weapons of fire do no wayes terrifie neither horses, nor men that are but foure, or five tymes used to their crackes, smoke and noyse, unlesse by great chaunce they happen to be striken with bullets; and the reason is this, that the bullets being discharged are invisible, and therefore doo no wayes terrifie the sight; whereof it commeth to passe that when horses and men that have been in three or foure skirmishes do see that they receive no hurt neither by the fire, smoke, nor noise, nor that in manie thousands of Harquebuze and Mosquet shot, there are not twentie men slaine nor hurt, they grow after to be farre lesse in doubt of those weapons of fire, than of Piques, Halbards, Launces and swords: Howbeit the volees of Archers arrowes flying together in the ayre as thick as haile do not onely terrifie and amaze in most terrible sort the eares, eyes and harts both of horses and men with the noyse and sight of their comming, but they also in their discents doo not leave in a whole squadron of horsemen, nor footemen (although they be in motion) somuch as one man nor horse, unstriken and wounded with divers arrowes, if the number of the Archers be answerable to the number of the squadron. And therfore for the experience that both I and manie others, both Noblemen, Gentlemen and great Captaines of many nations, that I have served amongst, have had of the small effect of weapons of fire in the field, with the reasons and differences before alledged; for my part I will never doubt to adventure my life, or many lives (if I had them) amongst eight thousand Archers complet, well chosen and appointed, and there withall provided and furnished with great store of sheafes of arrowes, as also with a good overplus of Bowes and Bowstrings, against twentie thousand of the best Harquebuziers and Mosquettiers, that are in Christendome. For this I know (as it is before declared) that Harquebuziers, if they be led by skilfull Conductours, are not to give anie volees of shot above three, or foure scores, and that at the most, nor Mosquettiers any volees of bullets above eight, ten or twelve scores, at anie squadrons of horsemen or footmen in motion; and yet that too farre, unlesse their leaders doo thinck rather to terrifie their Enemies with smoke and noyse, than with anie hurt of the bullets. Whereas Archers reduced into their convenient formes, being in so great numbers (as aforesaid) doo dimme the light of the sunne, darken the ayre and cover the earth with their volees of arrowes, eight, nine, ten and eleven scores distant from them; in such sort, as no numbers of Mosquettiers, Harquebuziers, or Argolettiers, nor yet squadrons of Launces nor of footemen, being so ill armed as in these dayes they are, shalbe found able to abide the incredible terrour of the shot of such infinite numbers of arrowes. For there is no doubt but that Archers with their volees of arrowes, will wound, kill, or hurt above an hundred men and horses, for everie one that shalbe slaine or hurt by the volees of so great numbers of Harquebuziers and Mosquettiers, as are before mentioned.

## 50. The Case Against Archery (1), 1590[192]

*Sir Roger Williams never rose to great prominence as a military commander, but he was one of the most experienced and active professional soldiers of the late sixteenth century. His military career probably began in 1557 under the Earl of Pembroke, and he was certainly in military service fighting alongside the Dutch rebels against the Spanish in 1572-3. Following his Dutch service he attempted to join a Protestant army being raised in the Palatinate, but on his way home was captured by the Spanish in the Netherlands. He was offered, and accepted, a chance to join the Spanish fighting against the Dutch, and served in the Spanish army until 1577. Between 1578 and 1587 Williams was again in the Netherlands and earned fame by capturing Balthasar Gerard, the assassin of William of Orange. 1588 saw Williams as second in command of the cavalry assembled to oppose any landing by the Spanish Armada, and from 1589 to 1593 he fought in Spain and France.*

*To some extent Williams' comments on the failings of archery in his* A Brief Discourse of Warre *feel like a response to Smythe's writings,[193] but Williams had been preparing his manuscript for some time before its publication so if he decided to insert the passage extracted below in response to Smythe it must have been a hasty last-minute insertion. Williams and Smythe must certainly have known one another, if only by reputation, and Williams was one of the kind of men that Smythe sought to excoriate. The war of words over the value of the bow in 1590-92 was well known to the general public and it has been argued that Shakespeare's Fluellen was a deliberate pastiche of Smythe and Williams, a combination of Smythe's views on warfare and Williams' personality.*

**To proove Bow men the worst shot used in these days.**

Touching Bow men, I persuade my selfe five hundred musketers are more serviceable than fifteene hundred bow-men; from that rate to the greater numbers in all manner of services: my reasons are thus, among 5000. Bowmen, you shall not finde 1000 good Archers, I meane to shoot strong shoots; let them be in the field 3. or 4. months, hardly find of 5000. scarce

---
[192] Sir Roger Williams, *A Brief Discourse of Warre* (London, 1590), pp. 41-44
[193] See **Doc. 49**

500. able to make any strong shootes. In defending or assayling any trenches, lightly they must discover themselves to make faire shoots; where the others shot spoile them, by reason they discover nothing of themselves unlesse it be a litle through small holes. Few or none do any great hurt 12. or 14. score off; they are not to be compared unto the other shoots to line battels, or to march, either in the wings of any battailes, or before, as we terme them from the Almaine phrase *forlorne hope*. Divers wil say, they are good to spoile the horsmen; I do confesse it, if the horsemen come within their shootes, and can not charge them by reason of their trenches or guards of pikes. Lightly when the horsemen approach within twelve score, the trumpets sound the charge; if it be on shot, that lies where they cannot charge, they are ill conducted that leade any great troup of horsmen to charge trenches. Commonly the Cornets or Guydons charge one another if there be any of both sides: if not, few horsemen well conducted, will charge either trenches, or battailes of footmen, unlesse they see a faire entrie, or the footmen begin to shake, as good Captains wil soone perceive. If they do charge, they will be sure to be well accompanied with small shot, which soone terrifieth bowmen, especially the musketters: besides the horsemen are all well armed, in such sort that Bowmen cannot hurt the men; let them say what they list, when the men are sure the arrowes will not pierce them, they wil be the valianter: although the horses be killed, and the Masters service lost for that day, notwithstanding they thinke it better to be taken prisoner sixe times, than killed once, beside the munition that belongs unto Bowmen, are not so commonly found in al places, especially arrowes: as powder is unto the other shot. Also time and ill weather weakneth the bowes as well as the men. In our ancient wars, our enemies used Crossebows, and such shoots; few, or any at all had the use of long bowes as we had; wherefore none could compare with us for shot: but GOD forbid we should trie our bowes with their Muskets and Calivers, without the like shot to answere them. I do not doubt but al, honorable and others, which have served in the Low Countries will say as I doo: notwithstanding some will contrarie it, although they never sawe the true triall of any of those weapons belonging eyther to horse or foote, alledging antiquitie without other reasons, saying, we carried armes before they were borne. Little do they think how Caesar ended all his great actions

in lesse than twelve yeeres, by their reckoning none could proove great Captaines that followed him, which began and ended in that time, as Duke D'Alva said, the longer experted, the more perfect. True it is, long experience requires age, age without experience requires small Discipline. Therfore we are deceived, to judge men expert because they carried armes fortie yeeres, and never in action three yeeres, during their lives counting all together. Some wil say, what discipline could there be seen in the actions of the Netherlanders and France, counting them civil wars: touching the Netherlanders, the worlde doth know their warres dured 23. yeeres, without anie peace, putting all together not 15. months. The wars of France dured 30. yeres: true it is they had often peace, and a long time together: wherefore it cannot be compared unto the other; notwithstanding, in these actions were imployed all the bravest Nations of Europe, their greatest Captaines, engeners, and counsellors for warre.

## 51. The Case Against Archery (2), 1592[194]

*Humfrey Barwick was a soldier and sometime mercenary who fought in the French army against Spain and the Spanish army against France and appears, from internal evidence, to have been aquainted with a number of the leading English soldiers of the second half of the sixteenth century. He was, apparently, present at Tilbury in 1588 when an English army mustered there to oppose any landing by the Spanish Armada, and he must have been a fairly mature old soldier by that time since he claims to have first entered military service in 1549 at the age of 18. Barwick began his military career as an infantryman but rose through the ranks until, when he wrote his Discourse in 1592 he could describe himself as a 'gentleman, souldier, [and] Captaine'. He dedicated his work to Henry Carey, Lord Hunsdon, who saw action against rebel archers in 1549, the same year Barwick took up arms.*

*Barwick's preference for firearms over bows needs no explanation: some people[195] think that guns are better than bows. What is more curious and more difficult to explain is the very defensive attitude evident in his writing. For example, although he acknowledged elsewhere in his work that an archer could shoot six times in the time it took a musketeer to shoot once, he was a great pains in his ninth discourse (below) to argue that that did not mean an archer had a higher rate of fire than a musketeer because the musketeer could load multiple balls at once. While it is technically possible for a musketeer to shoot as many projectiles as an archer by this method it rather feels like Barwick was clutching at a rather ridiculous straw in order to disprove the main undisputed advantage that the bow had over early firearms. Other authors were able to acknowledge the bow's superior rate of fire and still conclude that the musket was the better weapon overall. For Barwick, it seems, it was vital to prove that the bow was inferior to the gun in every respect, and the more one reads the more childish Barwick appears.*

---

[194] Humfrey Barwick, *A breefe discourse, concerning the force and effect of all manuall weapons of fire and the disability of the long bowe or archery* (London, 1592), ff. 16-20
[195] People who are wrong.

**The 9. Discourse.**

And now to answere unto the first parte of Sir John Smithes argumentes, which is in the 20. Page, the 15. line.[196] I will now saith he proceede, to the consideration and examination of three most important things, in the which all the effectes of Muskettiers, Harquebuziers, and Archers and their wepons doo consist.

And that is whether Musketiers and Harquebuziers be most readiest to give vollies, etc.

The second is, whether the weapons of fire, or the bowe doo faile, in discharging and shooting, etc.

The third is, whether by reason and common experience, the Bullets or the arrowes doo annoy the enemies most, be they horsemen or footmen.

To the first I answer thus, I will not follow sir John Smith, in his answere unto the same, but rather the true observation, which by all good Souldiers is not forgotten to be perfourmed upon any occasion of seruice. The Harquebuzier dooth firste charge his peece in good order, as to a Souldier it needs no rehearsall, and to other not knowing how to doo it, it is but folly without exercise: But thus, having charged his peece, he goeth towards his enemies, as dooth the Archer with his Bowe bent, and one arrow in his hand: the Harquebuzier hath also for his first shot, all thinges in more readines then any Archer can have: for wheras the Harquebuzier against the time that his officer shall commaund him to shoote, his match of a yarde in length is fired at both the ends, and ready set in his serpentine: that doon, he hath nothing to doo, but lay his peece close to his shoulder, and marke his enemy just. The Bowman though he have his arrowe readye nocked, yet must he drawe the same to the head, the which I have seen oftentimes very slenderly perfourmed: and the drawing of that to the head, dooth require more time then the fiery weapon doth, being in the readines as is aforesaide.

But this is the effect of the matter. If it must be as Sir John Smith dooth say, that a Harquebuze may not discharge but within 8. 10. or 12. yardes: I think

---

[196] See **Doc. 49**

that if that be allowed, that the Harquebuzier may discharge the first, before the Archer, being ready as afore is said. And if it be at horsemen and the horsemen be so neer as within 10. or 12. yards: then is it too late to charge again, or to shoot, for the horsmen being so neer as aforsaid, wil either enter or els immediatly retire, with yt[197] they have already received: for it is a thing most certain, that horsemen in their charge if they be Souldiers, when they are within danger of the shot, will either not charge at all, or else being neer, will with all possible speed perfourme their charge: for otherwaies, they should be counted but simple Souldiers, for even so was one of the Tresmains (in hovering in the charging of footmen) slaine at Newhaven: and as for shooting 4. for one, there is no Archer that can shoote 2. for one, if the Harquebuzier be perfect and well trained.[198]

The Harquebuzier that dooth perfectlye knowe how to use himselfe and his weapon: will discharge more Bullets, then any Archer can doo Arrowes: and by this way and meane. If it be a Musket, so much the better for my purpose, and this is to be doone in great incounters, whereas armies cannot marche but easilye, for that the numbers are great, and being a Musket, I would firste deliver a single Bullet, at 24. score off or there abouts, by that time they had marched fourescore neerer, I would deliver another Bullet, and at 12 score two, and at eight score three, at forescore 6. Pistoll Bullets, with lesse pouder than at the first by the third part, for alwaies the more lead the lesse pouder, and yet shall the force be never the lesse.

Now consider, that betwixt eight score and the joyning of the battell, how many arrows can a bow well deliuer? for within that distance, both the battailes dooth come on with great speede, or else not at all. But no man can tell how to fight, but as the time, the ground, and the number shall either give leaue or suffer.

Now even as I have declared for the Musket, so dooth it stand with the Harquebuze, but not to begin so farre off with the Harquebuze, as with the

---

[197] that

[198] Elsewhere in his work Barwick himself admitted that an archer could shoot six arrows in the time it took to load and fire a musket, so his assertion that a musketter could shoot more bullets by loading his weapon with up to six bullets at a time looks rather like sour grapes.

Musket: and take this for most certain, that a Musketiere or a good Harquebuzier, will deliver more bullets, and of greater force than any archer can do arrowes, be it in short time or long time: for as before is declared, if the enemy be so neere that the Archer can shoot but one, then maye the Harquebuzier let fall another Bullet into his peece, and shoot two for the archers one. And if the enemy be far of, then may it be perfourmed as afore is said.

And touching the second point, that is, whether the Archers with their weapons, or the other Souldiers with their weapons of fire, doo faile least, to shoot, discharge and give their vollies.

As touching this second point and question, I answer thus, that touching the certainty of neere shooting, or failing to hit the enemies, the Bow cannot be able to come neer the Harquebuze or the musket, for the firie weapons dooth shoot with a certain Levell, as it were by rule, and the Bowe but by gesse, as I have sayde before sufficiently touchinge that pointe. And for fayling, as in respect of dankishnes of powder or matche: with a good souldier it is never to be founde but that he wyll bee as carefull thereof as of his lyfe, and for the rest that maye happen in fayling, it is nothing to bee compared to the fainte drawing that the archer dooth use, in not drawinge his arrowe to the heade, when he is neere his enemies, as by many yet living, that can witnesse the same, as well as my selfe, and how lewdlie they will at the halfe Arrowe flirte them into the ayre and withall stoope, as though everye shoote of Harquebuze that went off, were shot at them.

And where as it is set downe in the same place, that there can nothing hinder the archer, but ye breaking of his Bowe or bow-string, yet I take it that there are divers other lettes, the which I have seen dyvers archers complaine of.

Fyrst, for that he coulde get no warme meate, nor his three meales every daie, as his custome was to have at home, neyther his body to lye warme at night, whereby his joyntes were not in temper, so that being sodainely called upon, as the service doth often fal out: he is lyke a man that hath the

Palsie, and so benommed,[199] that before he get eyther to the fire, or to a warme bedde, he can drawe no bowe at all.

And it is further set downe in the saide booke, that neyther Raine, Hayle nor Snowe, can hinder the Archers from shootinge, but I am not of that minde, for that the archer lyinge in Campe, where as hee maye not lye foorth of his appointed place, and having not to cover his Bowe nor scantlie his heade, then, I thinke his bowe to be in danger to dissolve the Glewe in the hornes of the bowe, and something hinder his stringe and sheffe of arrowes, whereof he dooth make his pillowe: but to conclude in this pointe, howe shall a man make a stronge argument or aunswer, unto a matter of no substance? except he have helpe by Logike the which for my part, these fewe lines may witnesse, that it is not my profession.

Nowe to aunswere the thyrd question, which is whether the Bullets of weapons of fyre, or the arrowes of archers, doo annoy the enemie most, which question is frivolous, for by the propounding of the question, and aunswered by the authour him selfe, it dooth carrie a showe in wordes, to be taken as a thinge most certaine, with such especallye, as dooth not understand to the contrarie.

But with all souldiers, Captaines and skilfull Conductors of the warres, it is evidently and manifestlie knowen, that where as there hath beene one slaine with arrowes, there hath been a huundred slaine with manual wepons of fire, since the use of the same hath beene practised and rightlie knowen. Wherefore if death be annoyaunce to eyther Horse-man or foote-man, let this suffise: for it is not woundes or small hurtes, that daunteth the souldiers where as death is not greatly to be feared, as before is declared.

And where as Sir John Smith dooth saye himselfe, that the archers doo hurte and wounde, as in the face and places unarmed[200] yet dooth hee confesse, that the same dooth but sometimes kill, whereby it may well be understoode to be a thing of small force, in respect of the weapons of fire.

---

[199] numbed
[200] ie. unarmoured

Againe, whereas it is sette downe in the same place, that the arrowe heades beeinge rustie, is the cause that woundes given by the same will not heale, whereby some will imagine, that it is for the best to have their arrow heades rustie.

But truelie I never did see any archer in the warres, that had any other then such rustie arrowe heades: and besides I did not at any time see, anie of those archers goe about to mende them, and to make them cleane and smooth, that thereby the same might the better enter through the doubletes, or garmentes of theyr enemies: for by common reason and dailie proofe, any thinge that is rustie, be it Bodkin or Dagger, or arrowe heade, it will not with great force enter through any meane thing if it were but a meanely bumbasted doblet.

And I am of that opinion, that the doubletes used in these dayes, are as good a defence against a rustie arrowe, as a Target of the best proofe: and as touching the heades of the archers arrowes beinge barbed, and broade before, by reason whereof, it can not enter as a smooth sharpe heade would doo therefore it must of necessitie bee that the same heades, was devised for galling of naked horses. And doubtlesse the same being of so small force, and entring so little waie into the horse, should immediatelie fall foorth againe, whereas by reason of the barbe it was supposed to stay, and trouble the horses the more. All which annoyaunces are but meane stuffe towardes the defence or invadinge of a kingdome, as by some other argumentes hereafter shall by Gods helpe be showed and prooved.[201]

But first to conclude with these our archers and of their disabillitie, in respect of the service of these dayes: true it is, that before the weapons of fire, were invented, and unknowen, as also untryed, to be weapons of great force and effect, in all service on horse-backe as one foote, as before is declared: and yet but of late dayes that the same have beene made publicke in armes, and not as yet throughlie and generallie knowen unto this our Nation, as unto some of the greater calling, and to the most of the meaner sorte, as the Long-bowe or archer is, by reason that we are brought up therewith, even as a parcell of our cheefe pleasure.

---

[201] In fact, the galling of horses could have a significant effect on a battle. See **Doc. 36**

But yet there is good hope, that by reason of suche good provisions as are made, within this realme, that in some convenient time the same may be more used and practised then it is, and speciallye the Musket, the Harquebuze and the Pistoll: the which without exercise can not bee commodious or profitable in any good sorte to be answerable against the usurping enemies the Spaniards, who are wholy and fully practised therewith, and specially with ye Musket and Harquebuze: And would it pleased God, our Prince and Majestrates, to have our able men in England, to be used and trained in the same weapons of fire: it would not onely incourage them, but also be a great delight to theyr Captaines and leaders, the rather to incounter with those wicked enemies or any other.

And also it wold be a terror to al our enemies, that should chance to offer any injurie to this realme of England or Ireland: for wee may assure our selves that it is our want of skill, that maketh these forreine enemies the more bolde to invade upon us.

For if wee were practysed in our weapons as they are, they would never seeke us in England nor else where: For in respecte of this nation, the Spanyardes in deede are but peevishe weedes. For by experience I doo know, that in al the time of the wars, continued betwixt the Emperor Charles and Henry the 2. French king: the Spaniards were the least accounted off in the field, of any other nation whatsoever: they will doo wel in skirmishes with their shot, or in defending of a hold, or assaulting of any breach: but for any other great incounters, you shall heare little of their dooings to any great purpose. For the overthrowes that were at Saint-quintins[202] and at Graveling[203], was not doon by them (though King Phillip bare the name) but by the Duke of Savoy and the Counte Egmond, with his Wallons,[204] and by the Duke of Brunswick and those Almaigns,[205] all which was doone with horsemen, insomuch that without exercise of our weapons, we shalbe a great deale woorse able to encounter with them, but to our great greefe and losse.

---

[202] Battle of St. Quentin, 1557
[203] Battle of Gravelines, 1558
[204] Walloons: Flemish troops
[205] Germans

# Epitaph

Let Gunners gunne it as they may I will not lose my roome,
There is a blacke and dismall day, where bowmen seem to come,
Eor one shot three sheffe arrows we can ripely seeme to spare,
The barded horse and horsemen too, we gall both neare and farre.
(Anon, 1588)

Lightning Source UK Ltd.
Milton Keynes UK
UKHW020927081221
395216UK00003B/81